Criticism and Public Rationality

A volume in the Routledge Geography and
Environment Series

Edited by Michael Bradford

Criticism and Public Rationality

Professional Rigidity and the Search for Caring Government

Harry Smart

London and New York

First published in 1991
by Routledge
11 New Fetter Lane, London EC4P 4EE

Simultaneously published in the USA and Canada
by Routledge
a division of Routledge, Chapman and Hall, Inc.
29 West 35th Street, New York, NY 10001

Typeset by
NWL Editorial Services, Langport, Somerset, England

Printed in Great Britain

British Library Cataloguing in Publication Data
Smart, Harry, *1956–*
    Criticism and public rationality: professional rigidity and
    the search for caring government. – (Routledge
    geography and environment series)
    1. Great Britain. Local government. Policies. Formulation
    I. Title
    352.000470941

    ISBN 0–415–03072–2

Library of Congress Cataloging-in-Publication Data
Smart, Harry, 1956–
    Criticism and public rationality : professional rigidity and
    the search for caring government / Harry Smart.
        p.   cm. — (Routledge geography and environment series)
    Includes index.
    ISBN 0–415–03072–2
    1. Strathclyde (Scotland).   Regional Council.   2. Local
government—Scotland—Strathclyde—Decision making.   3.
Urban policy—Scotland—Strathclyde.   I. Title.   II. Series.
JS4206.S76S62   1991   90–46920
352'.0004725'094141—dc20   CIP

JAN PALACH

GEOFF SHAW

ALAN WOOD

WILLIAM STILL

Contents

Acknowledgements

I would like to thank the following people in particular: Nick Williams, of Aberdeen University, for his supervision of the original research and for his encouragement throughout the project; Brian Robson and Michael Bradford for their help during the long haul towards publication, and Jon Chaplin, for his support during the later stages of the preparation of the book. My wife, Catriona, has persistently stimulated me throughout the course of the books development. Above all, the project would have been impossible without the support of officers and members of Strathclyde Regional Council, who showed remarkable generosity in allowing access to documents and to the process of decision-making, and in the way that they gave time to help with general investigation and to record interviews.

Thanks are due to the following for permission to quote from copyright materials: Cambridge University Press, for *The Reorganisation of British Local Government: Old Orthodoxies and a Political Perspective*; Oxford University Press, for *Objective Knowledge*; Harper & Row Ltd, for *Urban Deprivation and Government Initiative*; Heinemann Group, for *The Positivist Dispute in German Sociology*; The Controller of Her Majesty's Stationery Office, for *The New Scottish Local Authorities: Organisation and Management Structures*; The Home Office Voluntary Service Unit, for *CDP: Objectives and Strategy* and *Gilding the Ghetto*.

The original research on which this book is based was carried out with the help of a grant from the Social Science Research Council, a body which has since changed its name.

Thanks are due to the following for assistance: Appropriate Technology (Aptec) Ltd, for provision of a 'Genius' A4 monitor and of Bitstream Fontware; Fujitsu UK Ltd, for the loan of an RX7100PS laser printer; Xerox UK Ltd for Ventura Publisher v.2.0 with Professional Extension; WordPerfect UK Ltd for WordPerfect 4.2. The Dedication and the figure in chapter five were produced with Corel Draw, provided by Software Forward Ltd.

Introduction: rationality and power

This book is about the way that political institutions take decisions; more specifically, it is about the way that Strathclyde Regional Council, one of Britain's biggest public authorities, tackled decision-making from the mid-1970s up to 1980. Although the book looks at local government, the principles it puts forward apply equally to national government and to less formal sorts of public debate, from the media to the parish council. It is about political culture; about the way we *think* about political argument, and about the principles which control any relatively organised political argument. In particular, it is about principles which control the way we conduct *criticism*, since criticism is at the heart of any political discussion, and at the heart of any attempt to change things.

The book tries to get inside Strathclyde by merging anecdotal accounts of local government with more theoretical material. The essence of the method is an attempt to sift out of the language of practical politics the philosophical assumptions which – even in the most unphilosophical Glasgow patter – can be found shaping arguments and criticisms. In doing this the book does not force a 'system' on to anecdote; it assumes simply that people think coherently, and that philosophical ideas which enter popular culture can survive. As people pick up these ideas (during their education, or by whatever means, often without being aware of the process) and as they try to think coherently about real problems, a sort of reconstruction of theories of knowledge takes place, which is parallel to the academic construction of theories, and which may, in some respects, be better. It is this anecdotal philosophy which we aim to uncover, or, more precisely, we aim to uncover the conflicts between different *sorts* of philosophies as those conflicts are played out in the arena of practical politics.

To express it more formally, the book proposes a way of looking at public institutions in which rationality, or conflict between different conceptions of rationality, provides a degree of explanation of the decision-making process. At the same time the decision-making process sheds light on conceptions of rationality which surface in practical life. The book examines the policy-making process not primarily as an arena within which different groups or individuals compete to exercise power, but rather as an arena within which critical debate takes place. Inevitably such critical debate involves institutions in self-examination, reviewing policies, structures and traditions; it is while this is happening that philosophical ideas flavour the arguments which are offered. Language is peppered with philosophically derived vocabulary, and it is this which provides a point of access into the way that people think.

This gives us our method, then, for the analysis of Strathclyde Regional Council. The book considers Strathclyde's attempt to conduct an analysis of its own policies. This self-analysis was begun when, shortly after its formation, the Council set about tackling Clydeside's problems of urban deprivation, recognising that past and present government policies had done a great deal of harm.

The book focuses on obstacles to decision-making (or to critical analysis). It is often pointed out, usually with wry humour, that 'the decision-making process' is a misnomer; we should really try to understand government as a *non*-decision-making process. There is more to the observation than humour, however, and the book takes the underlying point seriously, making one particular instance of non-decision-making the central focus.

In spite of this specific empirical focus we are dealing with philosophical issues, and for this reason the book refuses to let questions of rationality become mere background material, as if considering philosophy were simply preparation for the real business of empirical analysis. So while this book is an exercise in empirical analysis, it is equally an exercise in critical theory, and it is unashamedly philosophical. It raises issues of 'public administration', calling into question some details of social legislation, for example, where it safeguards the privilege of 'professional judgment' enjoyed by senior officers in local government. It also questions, in particular, the privileged position in British intellectual life of empiricist philosophy, and thus the book raises directly philosophical questions. In doing so, however, it tries to avoid that evasion which consists in engaging simply with professionally organised and articulated empiricism, the empiricism of professional philosophers. Professional empiricist philosophy is important primarily because of the legitimating or validating role it performs for the empiricism of practising administrators, just as legislation ensures their privilege of professional judgment.

To ground these issues in the day-to-day affairs of local government, we can listen to a senior elected member voicing his frustration over the sort of problem which the book tackles. The following is an extract from an interview with Councillor R. G. Young, Secretary of the Labour Group in Strathclyde. He was a member of one of the smaller local authorities which disappeared in the reorganisation of local government in the mid-1970s (when Strathclyde Regional Council came into being) and here he compares that experience with his experience in Strathclyde. The interview was conducted in 1979:

> **Young** I think that there are interesting generalisations you can make in relation to the size of an authority. I think what characterises the smaller authorities is parochialism. They think it's possible to control, and I think they fall into myths. In the larger authorities it's obvious we don't control. So I don't think we fall into the same trap.
>
> **Smart** By 'control' you mean control your professional staff?
>
> **Young** Yes, and actually take policy decisions. Yes, it's patently obvious in Education, for example, that we don't.[1]

Already issues of power and of rationality are bound up together in a way which challenges a fundamental democratic ideal – that of political authority resting with elected representatives. Taking decisions implies rationality, analysis, the evaluation of alternatives, perhaps; but if these decisions cannot actually be carried through they are worthless, and so Councillor Young speaks of 'decision-making' and 'control' as synonymous. A great deal of the vocabulary of both rationality and power has this ambiguous character, either as it is generally understood, or as it is typically used by politicians and officials. One item of vocabulary in particular has this character and appears frequently throughout the book; it is the word 'judgment'. The judge both considers and controls.

These remarks point not to one neatly parcelled problem but to a network of interconnected ones, and it will be necessary to return to the job of disentangling them later on. For the moment it is sufficient to state that the book works by giving primacy to issues of rationality, and in this way it tries to break with what has become a tradition in social theory, that is, giving primacy to issues of power.

This is not to say that the analysis of power relations is unimportant, but it does raise problems. The more important ones as far as this analysis is concerned relate to the danger of circular argument. A process is explained in terms of power; the differences in the power of the parties to the process (a process of participation or consultation, for example) are taken to account for the outcome of the process. Yet the power of the parties is defined primarily in relation to the process itself, and their ability to determine the outcome. This leads to another problem, one that might be called the 'black box' approach. A system is identified, for example a system under which development plans are assessed, and the relevant components are distinguished: developers, residents, and the key institutional elements such as committees, their chairmen and members, and the officers of particular departments. The interests of the relevant actors can be identified and regarded as the initial state of the system, and the decision which the committee reaches can be regarded as the outcome. The disappointing aspect of these studies is the tendency to 'explain' the outcome of the system primarily, if not wholly, in terms of the initial state of the system. That is, to regard the process itself as an unknown and almost, by implication, an irrelevant part of the system. If the black box is to be understood, it must be solely in terms of its ability to produce a particular output given certain inputs. What seems a natural curiosity in the process itself goes unsatisfied.

An excellent example of this is Simmie's work on decision-making in Oxford.[2] A great deal of valuable data is collected on both the initial state of the system (the interests of councillors, for example) and the output. Yet little light is shed on what actually happens in committees or in staff discussions. This does not invalidate Simmie's research, but the feeling is unavoidable of a significant incompleteness. The corporatist perspective which Simmie adopts seems, at the end of the work, to be only loosely tied to the valuable empirical material which is presented. Davies' *Evangelistic Bureaucrat* hinted at the relationship between rationality and power, but was also unable to explore it significantly:

> The exercise of power precludes discussion. It restricts the partners to the debate to fellow officials and colleagues; and in so doing immunises the official or councillor to the clarity of thought and logic or argument that characterises policies that have to be justified in the face of scepticism.[3]

Similarly, managerialism, while it has generated a substantial body of work, seems to have returned too quickly to the analysis of total structures in society, and hence to looking almost exclusively at the social context of managerial decision-taking.[4] The box itself remains unexplored. Thus, without prejudicing the validity of studies of power relations, this book aims primarily at an understanding of what goes on inside the box itself. This can perfectly well be rationalised as an interest in the mechanisms of the exercise of power, undoubtedly a neglected area.

We assume, therefore, that there is a process going on within local government whereby statements are made and attempts are made to justify them; conclusions are reached (to some degree) on the basis of the statements. The process itself (of report writing, committee discussion, proposing and choosing between competing options) is, at least in principle, capable of being understood as a process of argument, debate, dialogue, discussion or discourse. Time and again it involves groups of people meeting, face to face, to argue and, significantly, to generate texts. In all these situations, it is suggested, the conduct of criticism is inescapable, change is proposed and opposed, and any rational intention to change must at least imply criticism of past or of present circumstances.

The book's aim is to examine the process of criticism which takes place within the local authority. It looks 'inside the box', at a process of rationality and, specifically, at a process of criticism. It sees the criticism of ideas, statements, proposals or policies as central to rational discourse and at the same time sees this criticism as the point in the policy-making process where discourse is most prone to break down; hence 'criticism and public rationality'.

It may be useful, however, to note the significance of looking at Strathclyde Regional Council. The authority, created in the mid-1970s, is one of the largest local authorities in Europe. It certainly dwarfs any other local government institution in Britain. It has responsibility for a population of approximately 2.5 million people, roughly half of Scotland's population, centred on Scotland's real capital, Glasgow. Other local authorities may have responsibility for larger populations, but Strathclyde's range of service responsibility is unmatched in British local government (except, for much smaller populations, by the other Scottish Regional and Islands authorities). The Regional Council is responsible for all the major local government services, with the exception of housing (where it has only an advisory and coordinating role) and local planning.

To gain some 'feel' for such an authority one might, for example, consider a composite authority created by lumping together the Inner London Education Authority, the Social Work functions of the Inner London Boroughs, the Metropolitan Police, and those activities of the now-defunct Greater London Council which related to Inner London. Such an authority would have most of the functions of Strathclyde, would require a comparable staff and budget, but would have far less clout in relation to the rest of English local government than Strathclyde has in relation to Scottish local government. The composite London authority would also have a far weaker position in relation to Whitehall than Strathclyde has in relation to St Andrews House (the Scottish

Office). Put simply, Strathclyde Regional Council is one of the biggest institutions in Britain. Few institutions can match it in terms of budget, staffing, or political significance. That this importance is not reflected in national awareness of it is a testimony, perhaps, to the skill with which it has been governed since 1975.

However, the size of the authority is significant for other reasons as far as this book is concerned. One is that few other institutions (if any) in British public life, in the course of their management decision-making, come up against the vested interests of the professions as comprehensively as does Strathclyde, and the role of the professions – or the defence of professional interest – is central to the book. No established discipline considers professional ethics in a comprehensive fashion. Jurisprudence raises philosophical issues for the legal profession, and within education or medicine, for example, there are established traditions which consider philosophical or ethical issues, but there is almost no overview. Looking at Strathclyde's struggle with professionalism is one way of moving towards a comprehensive consideration of the issue.[5]

Secondly, when the 1971 census data were examined, the Department of the Environment carried out a range of studies of the incidence of deprivation in Britain. One study ranked Britain's enumeration districts (each includes roughly 160 households) according to their 'performance' against a range of indicators of deprivation. Different combinations of indicators (overcrowding, for example, or access to basic amenities) gave different rankings, although a general pattern was relatively stable. One table in such a study identified where the 'worst' 1 per cent of these enumeration districts were located. Of these, 98 per cent were in Clydeside.[6]

This gives an indication of the scale of the problems which Strathclyde faced in 1975. The authority has hardly solved them all but, since its institution, it has consistently been a source of innovative and challenging ideas and practice. Within local government in Britain many of these achievements are common knowledge: the Officer–Member Groups in Social Work, for example, or, more recently, the institution of a department to coordinate policy for under-fives.

Thus, in considering issues of public rationality, which are necessarily raised in connection with any public institution, there could hardly be a more appropriate empirical focus than the early years of Strathclyde Regional Council and its struggle to produce a coordinated policy for the regeneration of Clydeside's areas of deprivation.

THE ORGANISATION OF THE BOOK

Since the book's agenda makes for an occasionally disorienting text, it may help the reader if we indicate briefly the way in which the book works. The fundamental point to grasp is that the book deals primarily with texts and with the consideration of the more overt messages of those texts – their ostensible content – as well as their language or rhetoric. The rather disparate nature of the texts means that readers may well find some of them difficult. Central to the book is the assertion that the philosophy of knowledge and the analysis of social policy have a great deal to learn from each other, but we would hardly suggest that, as things stand, the two worlds talk each other's language.

Nevertheless, the coincidences of language are often surprising, and the opening chapter, 'A rational response to deprivation', looks at some of these coincidences. It looks at texts from both worlds which highlight problems of understanding, language, and perception. The chapter introduces two key questions, one from each world, and simply notes their similarity. From the world of social policy comes the question, 'How are we to understand deprivation?' From the world of social theory and the philosophy of knowledge comes the question, 'What sort of knowledge is appropriate for understanding society?' These two questions are raised in terms which often overlap, and we maintain that this is because the two questions are fundamentally inseparable.

Sadly, the two worlds (of policy analysis and philosophy) remain largely ignorant of the ways in which they share language and preoccupations. The only way to overcome this problem is for each group to be exposed to the language of the other. In a sense, this is what this book attempts; it confronts texts from one tradition with texts from the other.

So a little preparatory language-learning is necessary. A large part of the book is, effectively, a preparation for the main examination of Strathclyde texts in chapters six and seven. In chapters two and three we look at the language and preoccupations of social policy – these are (overtly) managerial and institutional in character. In chapter four we look at the language and preoccupations of philosophy, particularly the philosophy of knowledge. In all three of these chapters we look at texts primarily on their own terms, taking seriously the questions which they raise and the language in which they raise them. It is at this point that readers from one background or the other will most need to exercise patience; in fact, readers from a social policy background may feel that they can skip chapters two and three, while readers with a background in philosophy or social theory may wish to skip chapter four. I hope that they will not, since these three chapters also refer across the divide and introduce important background material which is particularly relevant to Strathclyde. For example, Strathclyde policy documents which are examined in chapter six are first introduced in chapter three, while sketching in the background of national and local deprivation policy initiatives.

This introduces another characteristic of the book which some may find a little disorienting, namely that there is no sharp distinction between 'background' and 'data'. Several documents appear more than once, and it may help to think of them as background material in the first instance, and as data in the second, although the distinction is sometimes artificial. It may help, as an alternative, to think of the whole book as an attempt to immerse the reader in a series of texts, with texts being re-examined in the light of further reading. Seen in this light, the book attempts to encapsulate a process which is open ended. It would be a pity to overstress this process, however, as if it were not important to reach conclusions. It is as important to reach conclusions as it is to be wary of them.

If chapters two to four are preparatory, while chapters six and seven contain the empirical analysis, chapter five is the hinge between the two sections of the book. Chapter five, 'The Positivist Dispute', tackles the philosophy of knowledge by looking at the debate between Karl Popper on the one hand, and the Frankfurt School on the other. This is a debate about the theory of knowledge, but both sides show a concern for the practical and political implications of philosophy, although the debate remains at the theoretical level. Chapter five of this book examines that theoretical debate, attempting to resolve some of the important philosophical questions which it raises, but it goes on from a purely philosophical analysis to attempt a translation of philosophical theories of knowledge into practical or policy-related language. It is in the light of this characterisation of philosophical positions that the policy-related texts of chapters six and seven are examined. These texts are drawn from two main sources, formal policy documents, and informal interviews with officers and members of Strathclyde Regional Council. Readers who (quite sensibly) have little patience with academic philosophy or with the newspeak of policy documents will find that much of the interview material is unmistakeably from Glasgow; it is direct, and the lessons it contains can be widely applied. I hope that the interviews will add to the book's appeal, quite apart from the surrounding theoretical arguments.

1 A rational response to deprivation

During the 1970s a string of government initiatives linked attempts to tackle deprivation with attempts to promote coordinated, unified, or corporate management. Within local government these initiatives were often seen as attempts at 'area management' introducing coordinated policies for particular urban areas. These initiatives repeatedly encountered the problem of departmentalism, entrenched in both central and local government.

In 1976, following the reports of the Inner Area Studies, the Labour Government introduced a white paper, *Policy for the Inner Cities*. It proposed 'partnerships' between central government and selected local authorities. The white paper emphasised the importance of economic regeneration for the inner city, but there were few real economic proposals. The emphasis for partnership authorities was on coordinated central and local government action. This was described as 'the unified approach' and it appeared in the white paper as follows:

> The urban studies of recent years have shown that urban problems cannot be tackled effectively on a piecemeal basis. The problems interlock: education, for example, is affected by social conditions which in turn are affected by housing and by employment. The best results are likely to be achieved through a unified approach in which the different activities and services of government are brought together. Concerted action should have a greater impact. It should lead to a more efficient use of resources by avoiding duplication or conflicts of effort, and it ought to be more sensitive to the needs of the public who do not see problems in departmental or agency terms.
>
> The difficulties should not be underestimated. Central government and local authorities are organised on a functional basis. Government departments are responsible for specific fields of policy, and local authority departments with the provision of specific services.

This is sensible and efficient for the most part. Where, however, it is necessary to adopt an area-based approach to public sector activities, as it is in the inner city areas, it requires special efforts of coordination and joint working which cut across established practices. These efforts are needed within both central and local government, and in their relationships the one with the other.[1]

There were good grounds for not underestimating the difficulties. An earlier initiative within the Home Office, the Urban Deprivation Unit (UDU), had aimed to coordinate government action for deprived areas. It was established by the Conservative Government in 1973, but in 1974, with a change of government, responsibility for it fell to Alex Lyon. Later he commented on the experience:

When I went into the Home Office, therefore, I was delighted to think that we ... were charged with the duty of providing, for the first time in our history, an inner city policy or urban deprivation policy. I looked forward to it with eager anticipation. It never came. It is too painful to explain why that was not so ... All that I shall say is that three years were lost, not because there were not people in Government who desperately wanted to do something about it, but because there was departmental resistance to the necessary will to do something about it.[2]

The departmental resistance here is probably central governmental, but the problem is identical in local government. This was the conclusion of the Area Management Trials, whereby central government invited local authorities to participate in a monitoring exercise, comparing different operational forms of area management. *Tackling Urban Deprivation: the contribution of area-based management* was the title of the second interim report from INLOGOV (the Institute for Local Government Studies), who coordinated the initiative. It identified limits to the efficacy of area management:

it is the exception for area management to develop strongly in terms of policy making and resource allocation. These are very sensitive stages of the policy process and only where there is a strong political commitment to an area approach to problem-solving ... do they provide fertile ground for the growth of area management.[3]

The report concluded that:

the ease with which an effective area approach can be developed ... depends on whether or not it crosses traditional service boundaries. Although an area approach developed within a particular service challenges the centralised power of senior officers and committee chairmen it is, nonetheless, operating within the functionally differentiated structure of most local authorities. More general, co-ordinated approaches, on the other hand, challenge the autonomy of service departments and committees as well as corporate structures organised around programme areas and thus meet with considerable resistance. The essence of all the area management schemes is their interdepartmentalism, a feature which contributes particularly towards resistance to their development in the fields of policy making and resource allocation.[4]

This passage is one of the few frank statements of the problems of implementing a corporate approach to be found in the entire corporate planning literature. For this reason, although the report has not achieved the notoriety of some products of the deprivation industry, it deserves to be regarded as one of that industry's most important texts. Corporate planning, with its interdepartmentalism, challenges the autonomy of departments and elevates this challenge from a one-off piece of aberrant professional behaviour to the central task for the professional staff of an authority.

The sensitivity described here 'underlines the importance of political commitment for an area based strategy against urban deprivation'. The problems are even more acute when area management is considered as a vehicle for community involvement in the policy process. Here the question arises of how far this form of community involvement in local authority activities (i.e. the area approach used for the 'relaying of community perceptions of problems to the local authority') is likely to effect any real change in the position of the deprived.

In spite of the difficulties which the UDU faced, it continued to exist, and one of its most significant commissions was undertaken by INLO-GOV and published as *Local Government: Approaches to Urban Deprivation*. The report has two sections; the first outlines hindrances to effective action on deprivation (primarily departmentalism in central and local government), the second examines perceptions of deprivation held by local government employees. It looks at their understanding of the impact on deprivation of their own services and those of other departments or agencies.

On officers' perception of deprivation, the report concludes that there is 'no generally accepted definition', that many officers 'had not really considered the question previously'; however, 'most had some intuitive notion about "urban deprivation" although they may have been uncertain about its validity'.[5] The report goes on:

some officers did take a wider view of the nature of urban deprivation and tried to identify the underlying causes. Some even argued that the departmental approach was one of the major problems in dealing with deprivation. They thought that urban deprivation did not fall neatly within particular professional categories. The problem was one of getting the various professional interests within Local Government to focus on the problem. The number of officers taking such a broad view was small. However, the study shows that a not insignificant number of officers were simply not aware of the problems and their relationship to them. The interview itself had an impact on their views. There is clearly some scope for changing the perception of urban deprivation held by many officers.[6]

We can see this as identifying professional interests as the *real* problem, and along with this the power of the professions in defending those interests. What is particularly interesting here is the response to departmentalism: 'we need to change officers' perception' or 'we need to change attitudes'. The problem may be rooted in defence of interests, but it is equally rooted in thinking or rationality: 'understanding the world by imposing on it a set of fixed categories' functions as a rough summary both of the cognitive task of professional officers and, surprisingly, of Kantian philosophy. By contrast, trying to grasp elusive realities *intuitively* is a Platonic way of thought, and, until the decisive moment arrives, namely the achievement of a pure perception, the thinker is beset with uncertainties. For the local authority officer, professional categories struggle with intuitive perception, and he or she typically gives up. The response of the INLOGOV paper is inadequate in that it fails to recognise the rootedness of its own vocabulary in the problem of understanding. It has this in common with virtually all of the literature on corporate planning, area management and deprivation policy. However, in so far as that literature does address questions of learning, meaning, or comprehension, we need to consider it.

We can look at Hambleton's use of the word 'learning' in his *Policy Planning and Local Government*. He describes his book as 'intended to deepen understanding of these changes, which may yet herald the development of a "learning local government" and a revitalisation of local politics'. In his description of corporate planning he speaks of 'learning to learn', and makes the resulting conflict explicit: 'Corporate planning has not all been consensual. It has, in particular, involved conflict with traditional methods.'[7]

He describes how 'dynamic conservatism ... has employed a number of strategies to resist change'. He says, 'most of those who have worked in local and central government will know of promising initiatives which they feel never quite delivered the hoped-for goods. We need to ask why?' In answering his own question he says:

> part of the explanation will almost certainly be specific to the particular situation – one or two personalities may have been critical, the timing may have been wrong, an incident may have shifted the political focus and so on. But perhaps there are deeper reasons. Perhaps we have paid insufficient attention to dynamic conservatism and the realities of bringing about change.[8]

He goes on to quote Donald Schon as arguing for 'a complete change of gear in our ideas about public learning'. Schon's view is that:

> We must become able not only to transform our institutions, in response to changing situations and requirements, we must invent and develop institutions which are 'learning systems', that is to say, capable of bringing about their own continuing transformation.[9]

Texts which reviewed deprivation policies raised philosophical questions in another important area; they raised questions about the way deprivation itself should be studied, measured, understood, perceived, or *known*.

John Edwards criticised the use of 'indicators' of deprivation, constructed from census data or similar statistical data. The meaning of the data and how they relate to the human experience of deprivation is questionable to say the least: 'The application of precise and detailed statistical techniques to such an ambiguous area is about as meaningful as using a micrometer to measure a marshmallow.'[10] In a similar vein:

> The concentration on the statistical niceties and technical details of social indicators, especially as they are applied to the identification of areas of urban deprivation, has been misplaced and the concern for the 'arithmetic of woe' has diverted attention away from some of the more fundamental assumptions underlying their use.[11]

Joan Higgins adds her own comment to Edwards' remarks, making the link with ethics more obvious:

> The difficult qualitative question was transformed into a quantitative question which was very much easier to deal with. The social indicators strategy was a red herring which researchers pursued with great alacrity. It was, of course, simpler to handle the technical issue of how areas should be chosen than the moral issue of whether distinctions should be made between deprived areas.[12]

She quotes Mays on the 'collaboration' of 'the social researchers and academics' which allows that 'the bureaucratic machine goes on its way untroubled by radical questions'. Higgins sees this as 'yet another illustration of the well known *trahison des clercs*'.[13] This is very like Dearlove's attack on academic institutions which were involved in the corporate planning movement.

> It is one thing for management consultants and those in local government to concern themselves with solving this problem [of implementing corporate planning]; it is surely quite another matter when we find academics involving themselves in solving the problems of government and limply defining themselves as the servants of power. Those academics who know the most about corporate planning have an institutional and professional stake in its success, and so are more committed to solving and even minimising the problems than they are to subjecting them to serious study.[14]

This attack is directed particularly at John Stewart of INLOGOV, whose involvement in deprivation initiatives and the corporate planning movement has already been noted. Dearlove concludes:

> This practical and relevant orientation to those in power has meant that all these institutions have tended to engage in a special kind of research which, because of its starting brief and assumptions, is objectively deficient and ideological. In addition to 'policy analysis', 'policy studies' and studies of 'feasibility', these institutions have also been involved in selling systems of corporate planning through the provision of training courses designed to overcome the 'comprehension gap' and break down the last vestiges of old-fashioned and bigoted resistance to the kinds of rational change that these institutions have chosen to define as in the interests of the whole community.[15]

Dearlove's approach to his analysis of reorganisation is aimed at the criticism of 'old orthodoxies' in local government and the creation of a 'political perspective'. One of the basic assumptions he makes is this:

> we can really only understand anything by setting it within a context which gives it some sort of meaning and significance. If we are to avoid the danger of abstracted empiricism, then no matter what we are studying we have to set it within a wider societal context; we have to see how it fits into the historical trend of our times; and we have to assess its significance for the different groups and interests in society ... The necessity for this cannot be doubted when we are faced with something of such massive significance as local government.[16]

Dearlove makes explicit some of the assumptions which are implicit in the work of Higgins, Lawless, Edwards and others. He is one of the few critics of the corporate planning movement to show any awareness of the foundational nature of theories of knowledge. In the passage above, for example, he notes the danger of uncritical empiricism and, more astutely than other writers, he identifies not just 'muddle' but a consistent cognitive disability.

What is evident in a significant proportion of the criticism of deprivation initiatives is a concern over what might be called the cognitive base, the assumptions of methodology and philosophy which underlie action and research. Even from within a relatively naïve philosophical apparatus it is clear that issues are consciously raised which are ethical in character, or which question the construction of an autonomous technical realm, with the technician absolved from the responsibility of moral reflection. Here, perhaps, PPBS (the Planning, Programming, Budgeting System which inspired the corporate planning movement) is important.[17] PPBS works with a primarily financial and numeric framework of what we might call 'target setting cognition'. This framework is necessarily quite rigidly categorial and analytic, and it is hard to see how it could ever absorb a focus on something which is grasped 'intuitively'. It seems likely that in the development of corporate planning a conceptual or categorial apparatus derived from PPBS has been established at the core of the policy process, yet that this apparatus has never been subject to critical review from 'outside', at least not in Britain or America. To find a review of the sort which is required we have to turn to Europe, and in particular to the Frankfurt School. Habermas' *Legitimation Crisis*, for example, in examining Luhmann's apologia for systems theory, considers closely related issues, although without exploring the practical implementation of systems theory.[18]

If we are to sustain a focus on the practical problem of knowing deprivation, however, we still need to consider how the problem arose in Strathclyde, and this will also involve looking carefully at one particularly significant text from the deprivation industry, a document from the Community Development Project which was particularly influential in raising questions about how deprivation and the deprived were understood by policy makers.

STRATHCLYDE: CRITICISM WITHIN THE LOCAL AUTHORITY

Strathclyde Regional Council was established in 1974 and formally took power in 1975. It was required to produce, one year after institution, a Regional Report – a comprehensive review of the region's physical, social and economic fabric. The report came to serve as a corporate 'position statement', and led to the establishment of policy priorities for the whole authority. It identified two key issues: unemployment and deprivation.

The latter problem had already been identified in a series of reports as particularly acute in Clydeside. For example, the Department of the Environment identified, according to a series of 1971 census indicators, the 'worst' one per cent of all British enumeration districts (each has roughly 160 households); of these, 98 per cent were in Clydeside.[19]

The Regional Report contained a survey of the areas within Clydeside where deprivation was concentrated. It claimed that one of the major causes of the pattern of deprivation was a series of earlier policies, notably in housing and development, and began thereby what became a major theme in the Region's response. Past policies had been misguided, uncoordinated, designed often with inadequate community participation, and often implemented with little or no sensitivity by staff from a wide range of departments. Against this background the Region began to speak of 'putting our house in order'.[20]

The intention was that there should be a critical review of policy from mainstream departments; this was to lead to a policy of positive discrimination, directing more departmental resources into deprived areas. It meant a change of policy content and, perhaps more significantly, it meant a change of *style* of service delivery. Key ideas in this changed style were to be 'community development', an increased 'sensitivity' and 'commitment' on the part of professionals delivering services to people in deprived areas, and increased 'coordination' of services. At the same time the authority attempted to use the opportunity provided by reorganisation to adopt a corporate approach to policy making in general.

In November of 1979 Councillor Young, then Secretary of the Labour Group in Strathclyde, led the discussion at a meeting of the Labour Group to review progress on the deprivation strategy. He spoke to a paper from which the following paragraphs are taken.

The watchword we used in 1976 [when the document *Multiple Deprivation*, the central statement of the Region's deprivation strategy, was produced] was 'putting our own house in order'; this reflected our awareness that whilst local authority services on their own could clearly not tackle the deep-rooted forces at work here, there was a major problem of accessibility and relevance of statutory services to people in these areas [of deprivation] and until we took effective action in this respect, we would find it much more difficult to persuade other agencies to take appropriate action. We recognised the problem of accessibility was partly one relating to the physical location (and level) of facilities – but also one of the ways in which we delivered our services in these areas.[21]

Seven areas were chosen to be the subjects of initiatives, jointly with District Councils, in providing coordinated and accessible services. These would be 'a test-bed for new approaches which might tackle the problem of cynicism and improve coordination and accessibility'. Councillor Young's document of 1979 says:

> One of the biggest of the problems confronting the Area Initiatives seems to be the lack of support coming from several of the District Councils, and the way departmental practices seemed to continue to cut across these initiatives ... we have encountered so many cases of departmental ignorance or downright obstructiveness ... we have discovered such things as ... undermining of parts of the strategy not only by other agencies but in some cases, for the best of intentions, by our own departments.[22]

This view of the problem had already emerged in early reports from some of the individual projects. In January 1979 a first annual report was produced by the Priesthill Area Initiative. At a number of points in the document, Ian Kilbride, the Area Coordinator (the key official in the Area Initiative), described problems similar to those which Councillor Young later reported to the Labour Group. For example, from the introductory chapter which sets the report in a geographical and historical perspective, he states:

> Government – whether local or national – has evolved a system of individual services, based on a hierarchical model and controlled from the centre (with promotion based on your 'quality' as a professional) with staff encouraged to be Department men. Such loyalty is bound by its very nature to undermine commitment to the public. ... Unfortunately the existence of such feelings and pressures has appeared time and again within the first year of the initiative.[23]

Similarly, describing one particular organisational sub-unit of the initiative:

> It would be naive to assume that the group 'settled in' easily to being a Team ... the members of the team were subject to constraints which can be a reminder given to them by either middle or senior management that their loyalty or responsibility is to their 'line manager' or Department ... equally, if an individual member is being challenged by the Team, their 'line management', in seeking to support 'their

man', often interpret that challenge as criticism of their Department rather than the legitimate function of the group.[24]

Councillor Young's comments raise the question of officer–member relationships, and the degree to which staff are 'insulated' from member control. Given that Labour hold approximately 75 per cent of the seats of the authority, this would suggest a very effective means of insulation to be operative. Ian Kilbride's comments, on the other hand, are concerned primarily with the closedness of departments to constructive criticism by other officers. These officers are not acting obviously improperly in offering criticism, they are acting within the legitimate function of a properly constituted component of the authority.

Neither asserts an impropriety of motive on the part of professional staff in the insulated departments. Councillor Young speaks of policy being 'undermined', but 'with the best of intentions'. Ian Kilbride speaks of officers who 'understandably are unsure' that action suggested by staff of the initiative will benefit the people to whom the service is delivered. The problem, then, is to explain why officers and members are unable to *understand* a programme of corporate self-analysis and reform, even although many of them have an interest in seeing such a policy succeed. Clearly this raises questions of power, but the ability of a power relations perspective to explain what happened is limited. If there is something there which has the power to kill criticism, the question 'what is that something?' still arises.

As a vehicle for examining the problem (for short, 'why could Departments not be criticised constructively?'), the book focuses on one example in particular of the breakdown of criticism. This involved senior managers developing a confrontation out of a proposal made by an officer working in an interdepartmental officer–member group. The incident began, ostensibly, with a serious and reasonable policy proposal and ended with the officer concerned (a Depute Director, hereafter referred to as Stan Hughes) facing warnings 'concerning my future with the authority'. This confrontation resulted in the proposal being dropped without full examination by the officer–member group or by the mainstream department particularly concerned in the proposal. The value of the proposal itself is thus not at issue, only the method of presentation, and the criticism which it implicitly contained of a particular department's policy. The question outlined above for the book then becomes, for practical purposes, 'why was Stan Hughes' proposal rejected out of hand?'

The book proposes an answer to this question but, before it can be stated, we need to extend the narrative of non-learning in Strathclyde, and to introduce the philosophical dimension of the book's thesis more directly. To do this we consider a text about the rationalisation of deprivation (from the Coventry Community Development Project) and a text about the rationalisation of rationality (from the so-called 'Positivist Dispute'). These two texts help us towards an hypothesis for the book as a whole.

RATIONALISING DEPRIVATION: COVENTRY CDP

The final report of the Coventry Community Development Project included a typology of conceptualisations of urban problems. This explored the characteristic vocabularies and preoccupations of people whom the project team had encountered, including local government officers and members, and it related understandings of deprivation to broad ideological positions. The typology was widely read and was taken up by other writers, including Councillor Young in Strathclyde.[25] The typology is reproduced in the table on page 20.

The potential of such a range of understandings for producing organised chaos seems clear. Any specific policy proposal can be fitted into one or other of the theoretical models, leaving proponents of the other models to attack it, or to fail to understand it. More interestingly, the continuum of conceptualisations broadly corresponds to a continuum of political attitudes; people with right-wing views tend towards the 'culture of poverty' conceptualisation, while those with left-wing views lean towards the 'structural class conflict' model. The typology was understood in this way by a number of officers and members in Strathclyde.

It is a typology of *concept*ualisations and, in so far as it recognises ideology, it offers an indirect link with questions of epistemology, although this link is not explored by CDP writers. Material from CDP (including *Gilding the Ghetto*[26] and the Coventry Report) expresses *disillusion* (using that word in a precise sense) with policy initiatives aimed at alleviating deprivation, but it does not explicitly address questions of epistemology.

The concern with ideology is clearly expressed in the Coventry report. The authors themselves choose a structuralist model of urban problems and reject the other models. Their explanation of the problems of Hillfields (the area of Coventry where the project was situated) is in terms of class conflict. Thus the experience of Hillfields residents is typical of that of 'large sections of the working class in other parts of the city, or indeed the country as a whole' and these residents 'must be treated, therefore, as part of that class, not as a separate minority sub-group'. [27]

Conceptualisations of Deprivation: the Coventry CDP typology

Theoretical model	Explanation of problem	Location of problem	Key concept	Change aimed for	Method of change
Culture of Poverty	Problems arising from the internal pathology of deviant groups	In the internal dynamics of deviant groups	Poverty	Better adjusted and less deviant people	Social education and social work treatment of groups
Cycle of Deprivation	Problems arising from individual psychological handicaps and inadequacies transmitted from one generation to the next	In the relationships between individuals, families and groups	Deprivation	More integrated and self-supporting families	Compensatory social work, support and self-help
Institutional Malfunctioning	Problems arising from failures of planning, management or administration	In the relationship between the disadvantaged and the bureaucracy	Disadvantage	More total and co-ordinated approaches by the bureaucracy	Rational social planning
Maldistribution of resources and opportunities	Problems arising from an inequitable distribution of resources	Relationship between the underprivileged and the formal political machine	Underprivilege	Re-allocation of resources	Positive discrimination policies
Structural Class Conflict	Problems arising from the divisions necessary to maintain an economic system based on private profit	Relationship between the working class and the political and economic structure	Inequality	Redistribution of power and control	Changes in political consciousness and organisation

Source: Coventry CDP Final Report, 1975, p. 10.

One of the first writers to take up the typology was Chris Hamnett, in an Open University course book. He too adopted a structuralist model of urban problems, and in his writing the typology was part of a persuasive or proselytising strategy. He described the continuum of models, and suggested (in a question section for students) that attempts might be made 'to match up the various models of deprivation to conservative, liberal and socialist ideologies'. In concluding, he wrote:

> In this unit I have attempted to set out the case for a 'structural' explanation of deprivation in the inner city, in terms of the weak 'market' position of the deprived in the employment, housing and education markets ... [other models] ... could still be argued to be the 'correct' explanatory approach, although I hope I may have persuaded you otherwise.[28]

Councillor Young used the typology in a discussion of attitudes (in society at large and among local authority officials in particular) which could be identified with the culture of poverty model. He was concerned to demonstrate the effect which these attitudes could have in stigmatising the population of deprived areas, leading to injustice. He illustrated his article with an account of an incident which arose during the improvement of arrangements for dealing with refuse on a local authority estate. Bin recesses were to be replaced by receptacles which were to be sited well away from house windows. The tenants had been allowed to choose which of several receptacle designs would be adopted. The incident occurred when officers and members of the authority visited the project to inspect progress:

> Imagine our surprise on seeing that, although the bricking up [of bin recesses] had taken place, there were no bin receptacles – of any sort! As a result, the rubbish was strewn everywhere! The response of the Cleansing Director was that (a) the bricking up was only in three blocks, (b) when he saw clearly that this was not the case – to say that it was nothing to do with him, that it was the Planning Officer who was in charge of the whole exercise, and (c) that anyway all bins which had been inserted experimentally had been vandalised and that the area was one in which such vandalism was to be expected. On moving up the line of officers who were inspecting the area – particularly the landscaping – the Director of Planning's explanation was more plausible and coherent in that many of the bins placed in the three blocks had, in fact, been vandalised which had required new specifications to be ordered from the manufacturer and that in the meantime the bricking up could be halted only at the expense of a re-negotiated

contract! The real explanation, which required the joint might of the Chief Officer and the community worker to extract from the bureaucracy, was that (a) the manufacturers had delivered the wrong bin design – viz., one which the tenants had rejected, (b) only six instead of eighteen bins had been delivered, and (c) ONE receptacle had been damaged. I had been witness to the creation of a myth in front of my very eyes![29]

Once again the concern is with categories such as myth, illusion and explanation. Once again, the typology itself contains the position of the writer who uses it, and that position involves an almost evangelistic concern to enlighten or to disillusion.

The typology also suggests an explanation of cognitive disability at the corporate level. We might offer an hypothesis along these lines: 'the differing backgrounds of officers and members involved with the deprivation strategy, and the different political interests with which they naturally align themselves, lead them unconsciously to adopt attitudes towards the deprived which effectively "disable" them for the understanding and constructive analysis of proposals by officers and members from different backgrounds.'

The unconscious adoption of these attitudes would most probably be rooted in the primary socialisation of individual officers, and they might well be unaware of the ways in which these attitudes run counter to their best interests as professional staff. To use the typology with such an hypothesis seems all the more reasonable given its immediate context in the Coventry report:

The change in the way we defined the problems and saw the solutions has been a key part of our experience in Coventry. One of the remarkable features of the whole 'deprivation industry' is that differing underlying assumptions have not been made at all clear, and there has been a tendency to blanket our conflicting approaches. One of the signs of this is the way basic concepts (e.g. of deprivation, disadvantage etc.) are used loosely and interchangeably. We have found it useful for our own clarity to distinguish some of the differing explanations of urban problems along the lines of diagram 1 [the table on p. 20]. This is obviously a crude typology as the categories are not logically consistent or exclusive. However, it has proved a useful framework for disentangling some of the basic assumptions which we seem to have made about the problems at different stages.[30]

If researchers concerned with deprivation recognise in their own efforts at analysis a serious confusion of basic assumptions, then it is not diffi-

cult to see how a large institution (the staff directly involved with the
deprivation strategy in Strathclyde would number hundreds) can
attempt to tackle a similar problem of analysis and achieve, 'with the
best of intentions', a state of organised cognitive chaos. In Strathclyde,
of course, there was another level of complexity. The local authority was
conducting not simply an analysis of urban problems, but an analysis of
the response to urban problems, the sort of self-analysis at which the
CDP report hints.

This gives us a picture of society which begins to fit the problem of
non-understanding in Strathclyde. However much officers realise that
success for Strathclyde's deprivation strategy is in their own interests,
they are 'disabled' by their upbringing from acting in their own best
interests. Staff are defended from the implied charge of conspiracy
('obstructiveness', 'undermining of parts of the strategy') by being demonstrated to be 'victims' of a change-inhibiting ideology.

Limitations of the Coventry typology

The difficulty with the typology as it stands is its irrelevance to the central problem of a non-learning institution. It is not wrong, but it fails to
address the problem in Strathclyde, and fails more obviously the more
carefully that problem is construed. Strathclyde's deprivation policy
presupposes that the style of service delivery reflects attitudes which
need to change. Existing patterns of service delivery are seen as inac-
cessible not simply because of the physical location of officers, but because of an insensitivity to the real needs of clients (this emerges more
clearly in the chapter on Strathclyde's policy development).

Many officers and members in Strathclyde could see the problem of
non-learning in terms similar to those of the above hypothesis. The CDP
reports were widely known, read and understood, and the typology itself
was familiar to a number of officers. Unfortunately, this sort of awareness among a large number of officers and members, combined with
both their strenuous efforts to enlighten their colleagues and their frequent expressions of frustration and disillusion at the authority's failure
to learn, denies the illuminatory power of the typology and of the structuralist position of its proponents. The problem of a non-learning authority remains apparently untouched by all the self-critical and
self-analytical awareness which is evidenced. This, of course, does not
deny the illuminatory potential of structuralist models of society in
general, but *this* one does not work here. If the Coventry CDP team
could 'disentangle' their basic assumptions, why could the same process
of disentangling not work freely in Strathclyde? There is no reason to

see the 'ambiguous' position of the CDP workers in Coventry (financed and briefed by the state to do a job of analysis, which necessarily involved learning about the confusion of basic assumptions on the aetiology of deprivation) as fundamentally different from the position of officials in Strathclyde who were briefed to 'set their own house in order'.

What is needed is an explanation of the 'criticism blocking' function which prevented officers from learning about the destructive potential of their own basic attitudes towards deprivation. No such mechanism was proposed in any of the CDP material, nor in other writing, such as Dearlove's, which pointed to ideology. For example, any hypothesis based on the typology must focus on the socialisation of officers who are insulated from criticism; the texts from Strathclyde, which describe the intransigence of professionals in the face of the deprivation strategy, focus on the process of professionalisation. This is seen as a problem in all the local government professions (although some professions are chosen more often than others 'purely for example'). Primary socialisation is obviously relevant, and in other contexts one might simply respond by pointing to links between a certain sort of primary socialisation and a certain sort of professional management training. In the case of the Civil Service and central government, one might point to links with Oxbridge which have been well explored, and Oxbridge links with broader social and class structures. In Strathclyde this sheds much less light, and the variability of professionals' backgrounds is the more striking phenomenon. The focus on secondary socialisation or 'professionalisation' evident in the remarks of both Councillor Young and Ian Kilbride seems much more relevant, yet beyond their anecdotal observations there is no literature which looks directly at professionalisation in terms of its transformation of the individual's ways of learning and knowing.

It is interesting to look at Councillor Young's use of the dustbin incident, bearing in mind Ian Kilbride's comment about career prospects. Arguably what emerges most strongly from the incident is the inability of professionals to countenance the possibility that a mistake has been made, or to admit mistakes in front of other people. Staff dare not be associated with failure; they want a corporate initiative to work, but being part of the Council's corporate policy of critical self-analysis means trying to get a policy to work which has, as a central feature, the identification of failures with which the same staff may well have been associated. Similarly, Stan Hughes' policy proposal was blocked for reasons which apparently had nothing to do with deprivation nor with any officer's attitude to it. The failure even to discuss the substance of the proposal (whether because of an inappropriate presentation, an inappropriate reaction to appropriate presentation, or whatever) is the thing to explain.

So while obstacles such as those faced by Stan Hughes' proposal characteristically arise in the context of deprivation policy, they have, in a sense, nothing to do with deprivation at all. The problem is located in the rationality of the authority; as far as the authority is concerned it is a practical problem, a problem of discourse. As far as social theory is concerned the problem seems to centre on a weakness in the idea of ideology itself, a failure to deal sufficiently radically (or practically) with theories of knowledge.

RATIONALISING RATIONALITY: THE POSITIVIST DISPUTE

The literature which contributes most to a discussion of cognitive failure is that which occupies itself primarily with methodological issues in social theory, and with the philosophical roots of these problems. In particular we will consider the debate over positivism, and the dispute between Popper and the Frankfurt School. There are surprising parallels between issues in the positivist dispute and issues in Strathclyde, and the problem of rationality (or learning or discourse) which arises in Strathclyde is paralleled in the frequent failure of proponents of competing theories of knowledge to communicate effectively with one another.

For this reason the *Positivist Dispute in German Sociology* (the *Positivismusstreit*) is adopted as a central text for the book.[31] We will consider material from both sides of the dispute; the dispute itself is the focus.

The dispute is largely concerned with the sort of thinking which should be encouraged. Should we promote personal development, helping 'wisdom', 'insight', or some other personal or moral quality to be developed, or should we aim to produce accurate statements, clearly justified and expressed with a minimum of ambiguity; should we seek 'sensitivity' or 'precision'? In this context, how should we study the social world? Should we describe it as it actually *is*, building accurate statistical models which might then allow us to look at different options, planning rationally for the future, allowing discussions about what *should* happen to be kept distinct from our understanding of the present actual state? Or should we try, above all, to bring to the attention of an apathetic mass of people the truth about the inhumanity of the world as it departs so markedly from what it *should* be? Marx's thesis on Feuerbach is particularly relevant: 'The philosophers have only interpreted the world, in various ways; the point, however, is to change it.'[32]

It is difficult to identify any one central thread in the Positivist Dispute without, in effect, deciding in favour of one side, but a number of issues do emerge as significant for both sides. One is the role of value judgments; both sides are explicitly concerned with political questions. Dahrendorf is ready to speak of the philosophy of each side as having a moral or ethical dimension. Central to the value judgment question is the question of whether or not two distinct spheres can or should be identified – the world that *is*, and the world that *ought to be*. Is this separation of the two spheres a 'positivistically bisected rationalism' (as the Frankfurt School maintain)[33] – a sort of mutilation of humanity – or is 'the dualism of what is and what ought to be' (as Dahrendorf paraphrases Popper)[34] 'necessary for the improvement of the world'?

This follows Dahrendorf's summary of the dispute, and already there are problems. Arguably he misrepresents Adorno in particular; undoubtedly he is already talking a language which few local authority staff would be at home with.[35] However, two elements of his summary are particularly important here, one on the interconnections between issues in the positivist dispute:

> there is an inner connection between certain conceptions of the task of sociology, between certain epistemological and logical–scientific positions and between certain moral principles which also possess political relevance.[36]

The second points to the roots of Popper's and Adorno's views in what have become two distinct and often widely separated traditions in twentieth century social theory:

> the fundamental difference in the cognitive hopes and aspirations of Popper and Adorno becomes clear – a difference which permeated the entire discussion ... It is hardly necessary to mention the names of Kant and Hegel here.[37]

At this point it is useful simply to see that there are differences in philosophical, 'social–theoretic', sociological, moral and political views, that these different sorts of issues interconnect, that they determine thought at a very basic level, and that there are two fairly independent traditions, looking back to Kant on the one hand and Hegel on the other, which are often mutually incomprehensible. Even on this scanty characterisation of the positivist dispute – a dispute in social philosophy – it has something in common with disputes in Strathclyde over how criticism should proceed.

CRITICISM: THE UNWRITTEN RULES

One more step is necessary before the main hypothesis can be stated. That is to introduce the issue of rules governing officers' behaviour. Ian Kilbride's comments demonstrate that officers are part of a hierarchy of management to which they owe allegiance, which holds them accountable, and which offers them, subject to conditions, a degree of protection (if a department's man holds a department's line he will be defended by the departmental hierarchy). At a number of points, officers and members spoke of 'unwritten rules' concerning what an officer should or should not do. The rules frequently and explicitly addressed the problem of criticism both between and within departments.

Sometimes, in conversation with officers and members, these rules would be invoked to justify behaviour or to criticise it. At times they were characterised as a cover for inaction, at other times they were seen as being broken at the risk of chaos and the breakdown of communications. Often two sides would emerge: junior officers, or officers from one department speaking of another department, would speak of people 'dragging their feet' and using the rules to justify it; in reply, some officers would identify others as 'mavericks', irresponsible rule breakers.

One position would be fundamentally moralistic, emphasising what *should* be done, the other might at times be equally moralistic, but would typically emphasise what *could not* (technically) be done. At times the difference seemed to be between realism and idealism. At times it seemed as if the two positions were ends of a spectrum, and that, as with the CDP typology, the spectrum would correlate with a broad spectrum of political attitudes.

This leads to the sort of typology which the Coventry CDP had developed being recommissioned. The focus on urban problems, however, has to be replaced by a focus on the appropriate model for the conduct of criticism within a local authority.

Two basic positions emerged in Strathclyde over the status of the rules, and related to each of these positions there seemed to be a set of ideas about the nature of the problems which the deprivation strategy faced. The strategy might be confounded by the failure of certain officers to change their attitudes to earlier policies, or it might be confounded by the naïvety of other officers to technical–political problems connected, for example, with the internal workings of the Labour Group, or the legislation relating to a particular service department.

The value of the positivist dispute is that it gives a set of categories which can be used in a process of 'disentangling' similar to that which the Coventry team had done, yet at a much more fundamental level, more appropriate to the process of learning which is problematic in Strathclyde. So, the dispute in Strathclyde can be seen to involve two basic epistemological positions (theories of knowledge, or views about how knowledge should grow). One is identifiable with Popper's critical rationalism: realist, concerned with propositions, facts and theories, separating the world of 'is' from the world of 'ought'. The other is identifiable with Adorno's critical theory of society: idealist, necessarily iconoclastic, refusing the dualism of 'is' and 'ought'. The search is on, in effect, for Strathclyde's neo-Kantians and neo-Hegelians.

It emerges, however, that a third position is involved, the 'third man' of the positivist dispute,[38] which has a superficial similarity with Popper's position in that it separates 'is' and 'ought' and is concerned with propositions, facts and theories, but which (as this book argues) also has a fundamental affinity with Adorno's position in its attitude towards certainty and the capacity of human reason to achieve it. At any rate, this 'third man' differs from Popper and Adorno in valuing facts far more highly than theories. While this third man has a variety of names in the positivist dispute, he is simply called 'empiricism' in the body of the thesis.

THE BREAKDOWN OF CRITICISM: AN HYPOTHESIS

We suggest the following formulation: 'that the failure of individuals or departments in Strathclyde to manage the criticism of policy in a constructive manner reflects the different ideas held by these groups about the growth of knowledge, and the incorporation of these conflicting ideas in the local authority's policy documents and its unwritten rules for officers' behaviour.'

In other words, epistemology (theory of knowledge) is foundational not only for ethics and for political theory but also for practical political behaviour.[39] Conflicting theories of knowledge lead to conflicting analyses of policy and conflicting political behaviour; an institution which contains conflicting theories of knowledge cannot easily behave in a coordinated way.

This prompts a further question. If the hypothesis is correct, then the practical advice which would flow from it might be for the Regional Council to develop a consistent policy at an epistemological level. It would need to agree not only that the strategy on deprivation must be primarily self-analytic, but also that the analysis should be carried out in line with one consistent set of ideas. But which one, and how can that sort of choice be made? Can that sort of policy reasonably be implemented, or does it invade the rights of individual officers to their own views on matters of morality? Perhaps, however, it is not a matter of prescribing for one particular philosophy of knowledge, perhaps it is more a matter of trying to eliminate hindrances to pluralist debate. The point for present purposes is that the hypothesis carries with it problems of its own which require to be resolved at a philosophical level.

The book depends on philosophical issues having an inner connection with political and 'managerial' issues. This is important if the positivist dispute is to offer more than a mere illustrative analogy which just happens, by some metaphysical fluke, to provide a strange illumination of the internal processes of one particular institution. It is proposed that we take this connection (between epistemology and practical debate) as providing a guide for judging between philosophies. We ask, then, whether it is possible to establish, for particular philosophical positions, implications for open debate in a pluralist society.

This means that the task of analysis is not concluded at the point where conflicting theories of knowledge are identified in the local authority (although at that point the hypothesised solution to the empirical problem is corroborated). The book goes on to consider whether any particular theories of knowledge contain assumptions which on their own are sufficient to abort the process of policy criticism – that is, when translated into discourse or behaviour within the local authority. Are any of these theories or ideologies of such a nature that they lead inevitably to a breakdown of public rationality?

To pre-empt the philosophical discussion and the empirical analysis, the book proposes as a supplementary hypothesis, 'that this character of leading inevitably to a breakdown of corporate rationality can be found in the philosophical assumptions of two distinct groups of officers and members (broadly speaking, the 'feet draggers' and the 'mavericks'), in so far as these two groups adopt, respectively, empiricist and idealist positions'. Each is guilty of an hypostatisation (the attribution of reality to a non-reality) resulting from an over-estimate of the status of human knowledge or of the capacity of human reason. Each group, in carrying this empiricism or idealism through to behaviour within the local authority, is led into behaviour which militates against the open discussion of ideas, that is, behaviour which is dogmatic. This dogmatism, growing out of philosophical presuppositions which are basically metaphysical or religious, opposes a principle which is basic to both sides in the positivist dispute, namely that open and free discussion of ideas, however critical (in content, at least) they may appear to be of societal institutions, must be allowed to continue if genuine learning is to occur.

At the philosophical level, provided that it can be established that the two sides mean the same thing when they talk about encouraging free discourse, it is proposed that there is common ground between the two positions (of Popper on the one hand, and Adorno and subsequently Habermas on the other) and that criteria can be established which enable the process of criticism to be guided away from a necessarily destructive path. At the practical level this suggests simple and straight-forward recommendations which can be made to facilitate Strathclyde's work of policy criticism. These recommendations are, essentially, to promote a process of translation, breaking down the barriers between different professional languages, and revising the rules which defend these languages. Innocuous as this may seem, it does raise an argument against the continuation of existing systems of access to the professions, or against the continuation of what amount to professional monopolies.

What is ideally needed is a theory of 'culture', specifically of intellec-tual culture, which can link the historical traditions identified, for example, by Dahrendorf (Kant and Hegel) with the professionalism of officers in Strathclyde. Without such a theory, the idea of ideology is rather hollow. For this reason, a broad historical review is important. Ideally we would establish links between professional training and the different traditions of rationality. This opens up a large area of empirical research which it is simply not practicable to pursue here. Obviously there are strong links between the evolution of an intellectual culture in general and the development of a professional culture, but ideally these links would be explored and would mediate between the accounts we offer of traditions of rationality and of the breakdown of criticism in Strathclyde. The immediate task, however, is to establish the nature of corporate management structures in local government, and in Strath-clyde in particular, and to identify some of the institutional barriers to a general process of policy criticism across departmental boundaries. In part this is an examination of the nature of departmental boundaries themselves.

2 Strathclyde: management structures

This chapter looks at the current wisdom of the 1970s on the subject of local government management, and at the way it was applied in Strathclyde. This focus on 'management' issues tangles inevitably with political issues, those of status and power. In particular, then, this chapter looks at the status of senior local government officers, the Directors of key departments, and looks at the status of their 'professional judgment'. We also look (more briefly) at the role of the party group – which is the Labour Group in Strathclyde – and at the relationships which are envisaged between professional staff and elected members. The corporate planning movement challenged conventional wisdom in several of these areas, but, more significantly, it left several pieces of conventional wisdom quite undisturbed.

Within Scotland the key documents are the Local Government (Scotland) Act of 1973 – the Act which, in effect, created Strathclyde Regional Council, or at least told it what to do – and the Paterson Report. The Paterson Report pooled ideas from local authority officers and members who were involved in setting up Scotland's new authorities. It was one of the last in a line of proclamations of the virtues of corporate planning, and as such it has some national significance. As far as Strathclyde is concerned, the detailed advice which it contains on departmental structures and management processes was followed extremely closely. This means that in looking at Paterson's advice for local government management we are actually looking, in effect, at the management structures which existed within Strathclyde Regional Council in the period under study. A dissection of Paterson thus forms the core of this chapter, and when we have finished with that body we consider, by way of conclusion, the report of one of Strathclyde's own review groups, which looked at departmental structures in the Regional Council and proposed adjustments of the Paterson model in the light of experience. As a body of wisdom, the Local Government legislation and the Paterson Report are an often contradictory mass, and Strathclyde's experience quickly exposed some of the difficulties.

Before we tackle the Paterson Report, however, we need to consider briefly what is meant by the phrase 'corporate planning'. Hambleton's *Policy Planning and Local Government* is a useful guide; it is a general review of corporate planning in local government, and notes the marked convergence with deprivation policy. Hambleton describes corporate planning as follows:

> the two words 'corporate planning' communicate two fundamental ideas – that the local authority should consider its resources and activities as a corporate whole and that it should plan and review them in relation to the needs and problems of its environment. To appreciate these ideas it is necessary to contrast them with the traditional view of management in local government ... this tradition sees the central task of the authority as the provision of separate services directed at essentially separate problems. Further, it views the local authority as the passive administrative agent of central government – an agent which is incapable of mapping out its own future. Corporate planning presents a firm challenge to both of these traditions.[1]

Corporate planning is a reaction against 'the traditional view of management in local government'; it is a reform movement. The idea is also implicit that for the solution of any problem in the authority's area, detailed criticism of previous policies will be necessary. This criticism must be a process, not merely an event.

Hambleton reviews documents from government bodies in Britain which establish corporate planning as an ideal. Most of these relate to the reorganisation of local authorities in the 1970s. He points out the importance of the Paterson Report in Scotland: 'It was left to the Paterson Report ... to place official emphasis on the corporate planning process, which it saw as the "whole core" of the authority's activity.'[2] Before we can tackle the Paterson Report itself, however, we need to review the Local Government (Scotland) Act of 1973 (LGSA) to establish the responsibilities of the authorities for which Paterson was giving advice.

THE LOCAL GOVERNMENT (SCOTLAND) ACT 1973

The bulk of the Act amends or applies earlier legislation. It points out for each relevant strand of legislation which of the new authorities constituted in the Act is 'the authority'. To illustrate: 'The Education Authority for the purposes of the Education (Scotland) Acts 1939 to

1973 shall be a regional or islands council.'[3] Thus each strand of legislation is considered without any attempt to deal with the relationships between different functions which might develop within a particular local authority.

So, in deciding to coordinate particular functions, an authority is not guided by the Act, it is using its own discretion. Limits to that discretion are provided, if at all, by existing legislation. This legislation may require that certain actions be taken in fulfilment of a function. For example, 'Every education authority shall appoint a committee, which shall be known as the education committee, to which ... all their functions as such authority shall stand referred.' Similarly for social work, 'Every local authority shall establish a social work committee for the purposes of their functions under this Act.'[4] In some legislation this sort of requirement is extended. In the Social Work (Scotland) Act of 1968, for example, 'a local authority shall, in accordance with the provision of this section, appoint an officer, to be known as the Director of Social Work.'[5] Comparable provisions for other functions are rendered inoperative by LGSA, so the instances noted above (education and social work) are the two main limits to the Region's discretion, and the structures which the Region set up to discharge their functions under education and social work legislation were subject to the discretionary judgment of the Secretary of State. Otherwise the authority is left to determine a scheme of management as it sees fit. Thus:

> a local authority may arrange for the discharge of any of their functions by a committee of the authority, a sub-committee, an officer of the authority or by any other local authority in Scotland.
>
> A local authority appointing a committee, and local authorities appointing a joint committee, either under this Act or under any other enactment, may make, vary or revoke standing orders respecting the quorum, proceedings and place of the meeting of the committee, joint committee, or any sub-committee of any such committee, but subject to any such standing orders, the quorum, proceedings and place of meeting shall be such as the committee, joint committee or sub-committee may determine.
>
> Subject to the provision of this Act, a local authority shall appoint such officers as they think necessary for the proper discharge by the authority of their functions.[6]

To get some idea of the real force of the restrictions we need to think for a moment about the practicalities of service provision, or, more precisely, the practicalities of decision-making about service provision. Education and social work together take up the vast bulk of the Region's budget. There are 103 members of the authority, and, with reasonable rules on quorum, the cost in financial and management resources of steering all education and social work matters through the two committees as required by statute is not inconsequential. It takes up a large proportion of that part of the budget which covers services other than those delivered directly to the public. It also takes up a significant amount of members' time. It means, in effect, that there is little practical scope for setting up extra committees or departments which straddle traditional service boundaries, unless, perhaps, their business is to relate to only a tiny proportion of the services delivered by the authority.

But even if the resources were available, there would be a duplication of responsibilities in different committees. Enforcing the requirement that education and social work committees must deal with all matters relating to their respective functions would mean parallel discussions in the function-specific and the function-coordinating committees. It would generate absurd logical, procedural (not to say political) wrangles. Even within a politically stable authority like Strathclyde, the existence, in formal independence of one another, of Service committees, a Policy and Resources committee (a central coordinating committee) and the Labour Group meeting is sufficient to generate considerable tangling. And this discussion avoids the question of whether or not a strict interpretation of the legislation would not effectively rule out such function-coordinating committees from the word go. It is difficult to see how these considerations can but rule out the 'total' approach to either a particular spatial unit or a particular client group; it would, at least, be practically unworkable.

The most pertinent general comment on the Act so far is that it clearly leaves quite unchallenged the link, at least in education and social work, between professional interests and the structures within which thinking about service delivery should take place. The effective monopoly of senior officers is established in law, and this radically limits the opportunity for open critical debate on service matters.

THE PATERSON REPORT

The Paterson Report, *The New Scottish Local Authorities: Organisation and Management Structures*,[7] was produced by a committee of representatives from the pre-reorganisation local authority associations. There was a steering group of elected members, and an advisory group of officials, chaired by I.V. Paterson, then County Clerk in Lanarkshire. One of the members of the advisory group, L. Boyle, then Glasgow's City Chamberlain, became the first Chief Executive of Strathclyde Regional

Council. We will look first at the report's criticism of 'the traditional view' of local government organisation. A number of passages occur which have much the same character as Hambleton's, but which make the criticism more explicit. The following is an example:

> We believe that the traditional type of organisation does possess certain strengths, not least of which is its professionalism. The specialist approach to particular aspects of local government services has resulted in expert knowledge backed by a wealth of experience on the part of both elected members and officers always being available to meet the growing complexity of today's activities. However, this very professionalism has helped to foster the excessive departmentalism which is perhaps the main weakness in the existing management of local government in Scotland. ... 'There may be unity in the parts but there is disunity in the whole.'[8]

The report noted:

> the serious adverse effects resulting from insufficient coordination – housing developments lacking in community facilities; education and housing provision out of phase with each other; social work problems created by unilateral action taken elsewhere in the organisation; wasteful duplication of facilities.[9]

Paterson describes corporate planning as a process, where 'an essential characteristic of the process is its continuous or cyclical nature'.[10] The report identifies nine steps in the process; the following are the most relevant here:

- to consider the various means of achieving objectives;
- to evaluate the various means and ... decide on the best;
- in so doing to examine the interrelationships and interaction of the different departments of the authority;
- to carry out a systematic and continuous review of the programmes in the light of progress made and of changing circumstances.[11]

All this inevitably includes the criticism of current services. It is doubtless intended to be constructive criticism, directed at 'the best means' being identified for reaching a given end; but there can be no choosing a best means from several possibles (one of which will always be the status quo) without pointing out at least something as *not* the best. Nowhere does Paterson make this criticism of the policy status quo more explicit than in the passages referred to, and this may reflect a deliberate choice by the committee, but the implication is never far below the surface. It is unavoidably involved in the whole approach which the report recommends.

It is important to appreciate the degree to which, in understanding Paterson, we are understanding the early development of Strathclyde's internal structure. Some idea of this can be gained simply by comparing Paterson's recommendations for the terms of reference of the Policy and Resources Committee, the central coordinating element, with those adopted in Strathclyde.

Strathclyde: terms of reference for P&R

1 To guide the Council in the formulation of its policy objectives and priorities and for this purpose to recommend to the Council such forward programmes and other steps as may be necessary to achieve those objectives, either in whole or in part, during specific time spans. For this purpose also to consider the broad social and economic needs of the Council and matters of comprehensive importance to the Strathclyde Region, including the contents of structure and local plans, Regional Reports, transport policies and programmes and any other policy plans. To advise the Council generally as to its financial and economic policies.

2 Without prejudice to the duties and responsibilities of the service committees, to review the effectiveness of all the Council's work and the standards and levels of service provided. To identify the need for new services, the expansion of existing services, and to keep under review the necessity for existing ones.

3 To submit to the Council concurrent reports with the service committees upon new policies or changes in policy formulated by such committees, particularly those which may have a significant impact upon the policy plan or the resources of the Council.

4 To advise the Council on the allocation and control of its financial, manpower and land resources.

5 To ensure that the organisation and management processes of the Council are designed to make the most effective contribution to the achievement of the Council's objectives. To keep them under review in the light of changing circumstances, making recommendations as necessary for change in either the committee or departmental structure, or the distribution of functions and responsibilities.

6 To be responsible for the supervision and control of:
   (i) The Chief Executive's Office;
   (ii) Department of Policy Planning.[12]

Paterson: terms of reference for P&R

1 To guide the council in the formulation of its policy objectives and priorities, and for this purpose to recommend to the council such forward programmes and other steps as may be necessary to achieve those objectives, either in whole or in part, during specific time plans. For this purpose to consider the broad social and economic needs of the authority and matters of comprehensive importance to the area, including the contents of structure and local plans. To advise the council generally as to its financial and economic policies.

2 Without prejudice to the duties and responsibilities of the service committees, to review the effectiveness of all the council's work and the standards and levels of service provided. To identify the need for new services and to keep under review the necessity for existing ones.

3 To submit to the council concurrent reports with the service committees upon new policies or changes in policy formulated by such committees, particularly those which may have a significant impact upon the policy plan or the resources of the council.

4 To advise the council on the allocation and control of its financial, manpower and land resources.

5 To ensure that the organisation and management processes of the council are designed to make the most effective contribution to the achievement of the council's objectives. To keep them under review in the light of changing circumstances, making recommendations as necessary for change in either the committee or departmental structure, or the distribution of functions and responsibilities.

6 To be concerned, together with the appropriate other committees, in the appointment of heads of departments and any deputies.[13]

The two texts are clearly related.

PATERSON: KEY ELEMENTS OF STRUCTURE

This section is concerned primarily with the following elements of the overall structure which derive from Paterson: the Executive Office, the Management Team, the Department of Policy Planning and the Policy and Resources Committee.

The Executive Office

The Executive Office is the office of the Chief Executive of the Council, existing to enable him to carry out his function. Paterson outlines his function primarily in the terms of reference which are proposed for him, and these are reproduced here:

1 The Chief Executive is the head of the council's paid service and shall have authority over all other officers so far as this is necessary for the efficient management and execution of the council's functions, except where:
   - principal officers are exercising responsibilities imposed on them by statute;
   - the professional discretion or judgment of the principal officers is involved.

2 He is the leader of the officers' management team and, through the policy and resources committee, the council's principal adviser on matters of general policy. As such it is his responsibility to secure co-ordination of advice on the forward planning of objectives and services and to lead the management team in securing a corporate approach to the affairs of the authority generally.

3 Through his leadership of the officers' management team he is responsible for the efficient and effective implementation of the council's programmes and policies and for securing that the resources of the authority are most effectively deployed towards those ends.

4 Similarly, he shall keep under review the organisation and administration of the authority and shall make recommendations to the council through the policy and resources committee if he considers that major changes are required in the interests both of the authority and the staff.

5 As head of the paid service it is his responsibility to ensure that effective and equitable manpower policies are developed and implemented throughout all departments of the authority in the interests both of the authority and the staff.

6 He is responsible for the maintenance of good internal and external relations.[14]

In the body of the Paterson Report these terms of reference are stated to establish the Chief Executive as:

> an officer recognised as the head of the authority's paid service, accountable to the council for the provision of coordinated advice and the effective implementation of agreed policies and plans, and with direct authority over and responsibility for all other officers except where they are carrying out statutory duties or are exercising their professional judgment.[15]

He is not seen as the head of a department, but as being supported by a small group of heads of departments:

> it is vital to ensure that he does not become isolated but has at his
> disposal all the necessary facilities to keep himself fully informed and,
> in particular, to carry out this coordinative role in policy planning.
> His support will clearly come in large measure from the heads of the
> service departments and the central support services and from the
> policy planning unit where it exists.[16]

The Executive Office, then, exists to provide this sort of support to the
Chief Executive, and an Executive Office corresponding roughly to
Paterson's specification (with the addition of the Directors of Manage-
ment Services and Manpower Services) was adopted in Strathclyde.

The management team

Together with the Chief Executive and his office the Management Team
applies the principle of corporate management to the officers of the
local authority:

> we believe we can now take as read the necessity for a cohesive team
> of officers with an acknowledged leader working to a common set of
> objectives.
>
> The role of the officers' management team is to act as the focal
> point for the preparation and presentation to the council, via the
> policy and resources committee and the service committees, of co-
> ordinated advice on policies and major programmes of work. This im-
> plies a commitment on the part of all the members of the team to act
> with the wider objectives of the whole authority in mind, not being
> concerned solely with the activities and interests of their own particu-
> lar departments. We consider that this is a realistic and indeed essen-
> tial aim. ... It should be kept to a small number to facilitate discussion
> and decision taking.[17]

This group is seen as having functions distinct from those of the Executive Office. Paterson is at pains to establish this:

> We would underline strongly, however, that it should not be regarded
> in any way as diminishing the role of the service department heads in
> the Management Team.[18]

This introduces a fundamental weakness of the report; the distinctive
contribution of each element of structure to the overall process is left
strangely undefined. This seems to be why the distinction between the
Executive Office and the Management Team is asserted. The assertion

functions primarily to discourage what is an otherwise obvious identification of the same function as belonging to the two elements. Perhaps
in this light we can understand the comment from Strathclyde's own
Policy Review Group that Paterson 'proposed certain new organisational forms but was unable to provide much detailed advice on associated management processes'.[19]

It would seem reasonable, on the basis of the comments from Paterson noted above, to distinguish at least two processes or activities,
namely passing information, and making decisions. This seems inevitable if we are to make sense of the Paterson Report as it stands. The key
words in the descriptions of the bodies seem to be 'advice' and 'support'.
The Chief Executive as leader of the Management Team, and the Management Team itself, each have the function of giving 'coordinated
advice'. So, looking at the Chief Executive, he is 'accountable to the
council for the provision of coordinated advice' and 'He is the council's
principal adviser on matters of general policy.' Looking at the Management Team, it is 'the focal point for the preparation and presentation to
the council of coordinated advice' and 'it should be kept to a small number to facilitate discussion and decision making'.

In contrast, the Executive Office functions to support, and it seems
reasonable to take this support as being largely the provision of information. Thus, describing the Executive Office's function in relation to
the Chief Executive, 'it is vital to ensure that he has at his disposal all
the necessary facilities to keep himself fully informed'.

There are difficulties however, since this leads to several elements
having basically the same function. Thus, continuing to look at the Chief
Executive and his office, the picture is confused by the use of the phrase
'coordinative role', which follows the last quoted section; he is 'to keep
himself fully informed and, in particular, to carry out his coordinative
role in policy planning'.

It is possible to see this as describing the Executive Office as an information gathering service, and 'in particular' an information gathering
service with a remit to gather information particularly for the purpose
of coordinating policy planning. The problem is, of course, what other
sort of information would the Chief Executive want, since policy planning is so all-encompassing?

Alternatively, the phrase which describes the Executive Office as a
facility for helping the Chief Executive 'to carry out his coordinative role
in policy planning' may mean that the Executive Office has a function
over and above information gathering, and the only reasonable conclusion would be that it is thus given an evaluative or advisory function.
Unfortunately this makes its function identical to that of the Manage-

ment Team, where, as noted above, the evaluative function is explicit. Perhaps the Chief Executive is a sort of high-level 'fixer', and his office works by 'leaning' on departments to make them toe the corporate line. But then we hit the repeated boundary-setting which protects senior professional staff, as we shall discuss later, when they are exercising their 'professional judgment'. Repeatedly, at this crucial point, the 'key elements' are denied the necessary clout.

If we press on for the moment with the distinction between information-passing and evaluation, it does at least seem to provide a way of distinguishing between the Executive Office and the Management Team. This is also in line with Wheatley's comment, as in Paterson, which identifies 'intelligence' as 'the handmaiden of all the functions'.[20] Paterson refers to Wheatley's comment while stating the need for 'a central research and intelligence capability', and goes on to state that 'we have already implied in our outline description of a possible corporate process that the availability of reliable information is fundamental to effective policy planning'.

Paterson does not suggest an allocation of this 'capability'. The paragraph describing it immediately follows the prescription of a policy planning unit, but does not give any indication of whether the intelligence capability is to be part of the policy planning unit or a separate element altogether. However, a diagram does place under the Director of Policy Planning (or a member of the Executive Office) the three, apparently discrete, functions of policy planning, research and intelligence, and programme area team coordination.

This confusion of functions among the key elements clearly has at least some of its roots in what we have been calling the 'cognitive base'. The problem has to do with the process of information gathering or passing, and the related process of evaluating or deciding. This is undoubtedly an area in which theories of the growth of knowledge are involved. Moreover, the privileged position, relative to this corporate cognitive endeavour, of senior officers and their 'professional judgment' is already emerging as problematic, although here Paterson is more clearly following the lead given by statute.

The way to clarify this is, of course, to introduce the idea of a hierarchy of power, with departments defending interests and, for that reason, being selective about what sort of information they pass on, and to whom. What we are trying to do here is to show that, while Paterson itself tries to see things in terms not of power, but of rationality, its own cognitive base is simply not up to the burden placed on it. This does not demonstrate the inadequacy of rationality as a primary category for understanding 'what is really going on', it demonstrates the inadequacy of Paterson's conception of rationality.

The Department of Policy Planning

Paterson discusses a gradualist 'possible approach' to corporate management, and it is in this context that the policy planning unit is described. The approach is to characterise the whole authority, and these are its stages:

1 Production of a document summarising the authority's existing policies and activities (sometimes called a position statement);
2 Production of a statement of the council's policies, objectives and priorities for the future;
3 Identification of cases where shortfalls from the desirable level of service are known or suspected to exist;
4 From these, selection of key areas for investigation in depth by multidisciplinary teams (policy analysis or review);
5 Improved financial budgeting procedures, capital and revenue, on a rolling programme basis for at least five years forward;
6 Gradual build up of a comprehensive management information system; computer based and centred on the region, it should draw together into a readily usable form the mass of relevant information already available;
7 Initiation of research to fill information gaps;
8 Integration of all planning and budgeting into a unified system carried out on a cyclical basis in phase with annual estimates procedures.[21]

Against this background the policy planning unit is envisaged as part of the Executive Office. It is envisaged only for the larger regions. The following describes the unit:

First, we believe that there is a need for a policy planning unit as part of the Executive Office. The unit's role would be to service the Chief Executive and his Management Team and the policy and resources committee by providing detailed assistance in such tasks as:
● identification and formulation of objectives;
● evaluation of programmes;
● provision of specialist advice to programme area teams;
● monitoring and review of progress against plans;
● overall coordination of the policy planning process.
The unit would consist of a nucleus of permanent specialists together with a complement of staff seconded from the service departments as required.[22]

A 'programme area' is 'the grouping together, in some form, of activities which are closely related in terms of their purpose or end-result'; a programme area team is a 'multi-disciplinary' group of officers, set up where 'a number of departments fall within one programme area'. Members of teams could be 'seconded from relevant departments on a full-time or part-time basis'. Unfortunately, these sections do not describe what a multi-disciplinary team would *do*. The only clue is the comment in the fourth stage of the gradualist approach; this involves selection (from identified areas of service shortfall) of 'key areas for investigation in depth by multi-disciplinary teams; this stage is usually called policy analysis or review'.

The Policy and Resources Committee (P&R)

Paterson spends some time with the general issue of relationships between elected members and professional staff. The basic position is that 'The power of decision making must in the end remain with the council' (i.e. the elected members). This power is exercised on the basis of 'advice ... not solely from its own officers but also ... from an appropriate body of its own members'. But Paterson recognises that the distinction between advising and decision-making is not clear cut:

> The idea that policy is a matter exclusively for elected members and administration exclusively for officers is, in our view, unrealistic although it is disturbing to find, as the Bain Report comments, that 'many members and officers still see this as a sufficient description of their respective roles and one behind which they can shelter as occasion requires'. Bain recognised that both elements were present in different degrees at every stage of the management process, the balance on the scale shifting progressively from member control with officer advice at the 'policy setting' end to officer control with member advice at the 'execution' end.[23]

Complaining of excess member involvement in administrative minutiae, Paterson goes on to state that there is 'low-level decision making which could only remotely be construed as essential to the democratic process' and that 'The principle should be that issues are dealt with at the lowest level consistent with the nature of the problem.'[24] The P&R Committee is not the main decision-taking body; it is one of the advisory elements of the overall council structure. Given the degree to which Paterson's formula follows the Strathclyde Joint Advisory Committee, we quote in full:

> The functions of the policy and resources committee are well

described in the observation made to us by the Joint Advisory Committee of the Strathclyde Region. 'The Policy and Resources Committee should have more than a coordinating role. It should be responsible for identifying and setting out for consideration by the whole council the fundamental objective which the council should be aiming to achieve, charting the broad course to be followed and setting the policy guidelines. It should also be charged with responsibility for coordinating the activities of other committees and for recommending how disputes between such committees might be resolved. It should have a free-ranging remit enabling it to monitor and review the performance of service committees and departments towards the attainment of the Council's objectives.'[25]

The key phrases are 'setting out for consideration', 'setting the policy guidelines', and 'recommending'. These all reinforce the advisory conception of the Committee's function. The same tone is struck in the terms of reference, which speak of the Committee as a body 'to guide the council', 'to recommend to the council', 'to advise the council', and so on.

The submission from Strathclyde shows the same naïvety which appeared in the review of corporate planning nationally. It acknowledges that there will be disputes between committees. It gives P&R the job of 'recommending how disputes between such committees might be resolved'. Yet no guidance is offered on principles which might be applied to such cases of arbitration, although they are bound to challenge the autonomous area of 'professional judgment', or to be claimed to challenge it by defensive departments and their associated committees. This naïvety is surprising, and the question inevitably arises, given the awareness of the people involved with Paterson and the Joint Committee of the 'realities' of local government, how far is it genuine?

To continue, P&R is the vehicle for the submission of advice from the official side of the authority to the full Council. This advice is channelled to P&R through the officer-staffed 'key elements' and this accounts for the closing section of P&R's terms of reference which speaks of 'supervision and control' of these key elements. To talk of 'control' suggests a difference in the status of the advice which P&R gives when compared with the official advice. Yet P&R is in the same boat as the Chief Executive, given responsibility for controlling departments whose autonomy is asserted in the same document as is the need for them to be controlled and 'coordinated'. The tension is apparent when Paterson looks at committee structure:

the strengths of the specialist approach should be preserved in whatever new forms of organisation are finally implemented by the new authorities. We think it essential therefore that, within the framework of the overall policy plan, the service committees continue to be responsible for policy formulation and implementation within their own particular spheres of interest.[26]

Paterson quotes again from the Strathclyde Joint Advisory Committee:

The programme or service committees should not be subordinate to the Policy and Resources Committee and should enjoy the same right of direct access to the council.[27]

We can begin to make sense of this when we consider what Paterson and Wheatley have to say about the relationship between party politics and the internal structures of a local authority. This puts P&R, in particular, into a different light, and suggests that much of the limitation of its function so far identified is more apparent than real.

The Policy and Resources Committee is composed only of members of the majority party. It is dominated by leading members of the majority group, 16 members of the majority group Executive committee, and the five chairmen of the Resource committees. It is the party muscle, and a 'recommendation' is, for the majority party, virtually a ruling. Of course, no leadership will be totally free of constraint, and no sensible leadership will move without getting a good estimate of the feeling of the majority group meeting. However, assuming a largely coherent party group, and where that party holds a working majority, it is difficult to see how P&R can be other than the effective point at which council policy is produced. It is here, and in the party meetings, that the tensions are absorbed between departmentalism and the corporate approach. Only where a department is insulated from control by its own committee does a significant tension remain. It helps to look at what Paterson and Wheatley had to say on the subject of party groups. First, Paterson:

In any group of people there will be some who by virtue of their personal attributes will be the acknowledged leaders and opinion formers. In principle therefore the bulk of a policy and resources committee membership should be drawn from their ranks. We have recognised that the majority party group is in some cases the real decision-making body. Where this applies we believe it should be openly acknowledged and given recognition in the authority's procedures.[28]

This is in broad agreement with the Wheatley Report:

There is no doubt in our minds that, where there are party politics, the management body will normally be dominated by the majority party. Some may see this as a matter for regret. Others may welcome it on the ground that the work of local authorities may be expected to gain thereby in coherence and direction.[29]

To conclude on P&R, it is essential to point out how limited the legislative and prescriptive documents are for determining its real role. It is clear that P&R is the focus for discussion of general policy guidelines. While it does not formally control the work of the authority, it is the place where effective control can be attempted with the greatest hope of success.

PATERSON AND THE PROFESSIONALS: SUMMARY

Paterson's repetitive report, full of the vocabulary of coordination and weak on real efforts to tackle the problem of departmentalism, tries repeatedly to create 'functions', 'roles', 'elements' and 'structures' which can be charged with coordinating responsibilities. It looks as if this effort functions in reality as a cover for the impotence of local government as presently constituted in the face of the legally established autonomy of senior officers when they are either exercising statutory responsibilities, or doing things which involve exercising their distinctive professional judgment. (These two things are, in practice, more or less the same.)

Time and again, in reading Paterson, one is left with the impression that the document itself is only a token for the real process of discussion that must have gone on. One really wonders whether senior people from local government can have been so incoherent, or is there some still undiscovered truth, some cabbala, which could yet make the report intelligible? The final impression is much the same as that which Dearlove describes in his own survey of the reorganisation of local government:

> In my honest attempt to come to terms with management reorganisation I have read many pieces of work which sought to lay bare the essentials of what should be done. The more I read, the more confused I became. The whole thing kept slipping through my fingers ... Gradually I learned to stop worrying about my lack of ability to really understand the corporate approach. I came to realise that it was actually impossible to get to sure grips with it. A slippery lack of precision was the one thing that was of the essence. Vagueness was important in that it gave it a kind of featherbed resilience and a marked invulnerability to criticism.[30]

For all Paterson's 'slippery lack of precision' (let us call a slippery lack of precision a 'paterson'), the Report does advocate management as a rational, coherent process, and the vocabulary which is used flops back repeatedly to 'monitoring', 'review', 'judgment', 'evaluation', 'information', and so on. It is precisely in the use of this sort of vocabulary that the patersons are most apparent. Paterson is uncritical on issues of the growth of knowledge, and in that uncritical intellectual environment a looseness of thought remains unchallenged.

It does seem that Paterson assumes that 'information' is some neutral commodity which is gathered, like harvesting a field of corn, and brought into the corporate barn. When this information has been 'evaluated' it is turned into 'advice' (from officers) or 'recommendations' (from committees). To observe a broad empiricism here is not significantly to anticipate the philosophical discussion.

Similarly, it is as a block to this process of rationality that the privilege of senior officers' professional judgment stands out. It is central 'control' which is hindered, but it is a process of rationality which P&R or the Chief Executive cannot completely control, and it is the exercise of a particular sort of 'judgment' which is the prerogative of senior officers. Yet this idea of a unique sort of rational process, the exercise of 'professional judgment', goes unexplored and unchallenged.

Paterson, like the rest of the corporate planning movement, tries to promote the rational 'learning' authority without any coherent idea of how learning, or the growth of knowledge, can occur. For all this, the Report met with widespread appreciation.

STRATHCLYDE: REVIEW OF DEPARTMENTAL STRUCTURES

We need to consider the position in which the Regional Council found itself when the 1973 Act came into effect. A statement of this is provided in a report from an *ad hoc* study group on departmental structures, set up shortly after the authority was constituted. This Policy Review Group (or PRG), as it was known, was made up of elected members together with officials from a range of departments, and was itself, therefore, an example of the corporate approach.

1 In determining its overall and departmental management structures at reorganisation in May 1975, the Regional Council had to take account of several factors. Of these, the most important were:
   - the need to ensure that service to the public continued at a satisfactory level without interruption, despite the enormous practical problems involved in taking over the functions of a large number of former authorities;
   - the requirement to match in the staff of the former authorities

and, in so doing, to minimise disruption and widespread dispersal of people;

- the Council's wish to adopt the principles of the Paterson Report, which advocated a corporate approach to management and certain new organisational concepts.

2 The first two factors argued strongly for a significant element of continuity of existing and well-tried organisational patterns and processes, despite their acknowledged weaknesses. The Paterson Report, in contrast, proposed certain new organisational forms but was unable to provide much detailed advice on associated management processes since insufficient practical experience was available at that time from any reliable source.

3 The Council therefore adopted provisional (or 'interim') management structures and establishments which appeared to provide the best initial balance between these conflicting factors. At the same time, however, the Council also decided that the structures and associated issues should be reviewed at an appropriate future time when sufficient operational experience was available but before the provisional arrangements had become too firmly entrenched.[31]

Given that the recommendations of the PRG report were only implemented in 1980, and then not completely, the 'interim' structures referred to above are the ones in effect during the development of deprivation policy on which this book focuses. In fact, the review was partly contemporary with the development of the deprivation strategy, being initiated in November 1976, while the Regional Report, which outlined the deprivation strategy, was published in May 1976.

The PRG report approves of corporate management, at least as an ideal. Limitations to the implementation of corporate planning are noted, but the report affirms that, 'Despite these limitations, the benefits achieved from the corporate approach over the first two years have been very substantial.'[32] The report cites the production of the Regional Report, the Transport Policies and Programmes documents, 'the Council's initial approach to the alleviation of deprivation which attempts to marshall resources from several departments, and to direct them and coordinate them on an area basis', and 'improved management processes, particularly in the areas of evaluation of policy options and of budgetary procedures'. All of these, the report claims, were produced 'on a corporate basis'.[33] The group therefore sees its own role as to improve corporate functioning by the eradication of a number of specific weaknesses. There are four sources of weakness:

- the amalgam of new and traditional organisational forms set up at reorganisation, with the latter of necessity predominating;

- as a result, the continuation of traditional attitudes to management processes, to the detriment of the development of the required new processes;
- as a further consequence, the dispersal of integral parts of the total policy process across several departments, thus intensifying the difficulties of coordination;
- a tendency for policy formulation to become organisationally separate from implementation, with potentially adverse effects on monitoring and review.[34]

The first and second of these together reintroduce the idea of the corporate approach as a reaction against tradition. The two approaches, corporate and traditional, cannot really be harmonised – the one can only continue 'to the detriment' of the other. The second of the two paragraphs quoted above implies that attempts to harmonise the two had indeed been accompanied by conflict.

On the third and fourth of the paragraphs above, specific anomalies are noted to illustrate how 'the services directly associated with policy formulation, implementation' etc. are 'fragmented'.[35] These anomalies are largely duplications of functions which were seen as the province of the 'key elements' described earlier – but which were formerly related to individual departmental functions and were retained in their departmental location at reorganisation. They are relics of the traditional structure, it seems, which have to be relocated within the appropriate 'key element'.

Careful reading of the report, however, as it describes these anomalies, suggests that such a view would be misleading. Three paragraphs are given in full here to make this point. They are the first three of six paragraphs describing anomalies:

Basic data for policy formulation is provided by the research and intelligence function. Research and intelligence units exist in both Policy Planning and Physical Planning Departments. While the latter was set up primarily to provide data of relevance to land-use planning, it has become increasingly involved with socio-economic and demographic considerations and this trend seems likely to continue.

Similarly, the functions of the Regional Report section and the Economic Policy Group, both located within Physical Planning, relate more directly to strategic policy planning than land-use planning. Instances of 'policy' documents arising from the latter group, with no doubt good intentions but without prior consideration from an overall strategic viewpoint, further illustrate the difficulties caused by the fragmented organisational arrangements.

A long-term resources planning capability is being developed within the Department of Administration, organisationally divorced from both the Chief Executive, who carries overall responsibility, and from the Department of Policy Planning, one of whose prime functions is intended to be long-range planning.[36]

The problem is that particular sections of departments have reinterpreted their roles to achieve greater coordination of their own work with that of the whole authority. This is hardly corporatism which has not gone far enough; individual units have gone too far, and have encroached on the role of 'key elements', in particular on the role of the Policy Planning Department. The real issue seems to be centralisation versus dispersal. The centre should be controlling the separate departments, but to do this it needs virtually to 'absorb' these departments. Control is sought for the sake of coordination, although the character of the dispersed elements has also been developed for the sake of coordination.

This shows, for example, in the concern of the planning profession in recent years that physical planning should consider social issues, a concern which is largely responsible for the existence, as a (purely Scottish) policy vehicle, of the Regional Report. This concern developed out of an awareness that the narrow conception of physical planning as land-use planning leads to bad planning – planning, that is, 'without prior consideration from an overall strategic viewpoint'. Now, for the sake of coordination, the PRG seems set to revive the narrow interpretation of the role of physical planning.

Corporate planning came into vogue at a time when similar realisations were developing in other services. The question is really about who should do the 'consideration from an overall strategic viewpoint'. If Paterson gave the impression that everybody should be doing everything, then PRG supplies the corrective observation that not everybody can be in control. The conflict is one of authority, in particular of authority among professional staff. The conclusion of the report about these anomalies is that:

the existing structures at the centre of the Region represent a barrier to the full achievement of the benefits of a corporate approach in that:
- the individual elements of the process, from policy formulation through to monitoring and review, are dispersed across departments, thus negating the essential integrated and cyclical nature of the process;
- worse still, any one element can be found not just in one but in several departments.[37]

This clearly decides the issue in favour of centralisation. The background problem is ignored, namely that any such broadening of the central perspective must be achieved at the cost of a narrower perspective in the departments. Arguably the goal of overall coordination could be pursued in either way – although in the latter a wider discretion and greater authority would inevitably be delegated to officers nearer to the detailed work, or nearer to service delivery (and Paterson recommended this).

The recommendation of the PRG report, however, is quite consistent with its earlier conclusion. It involves the enlargement of the Chief Executive's Department to 'as a first step, incorporate the present Departments of Administration and Policy Planning and the Industrial Development Unit'.[38] In the longer term, parts of Physical Planning should also be absorbed.

The Management Team is dispensed with. It 'should not be part of the formal decision-making process'; it is seen as virtually redundant as a formal body. It does, however, survive in an informal role as the 'Chief Officers' Meeting'. One of its functions would be 'consideration of issues affecting all Regional Departments',[39] which raises the question of how this represents any real change. This is one of the very few patersons in the PRG report.

Although the overall implication of the PRG is that coordination should involve centralisation on the official side of the authority, this still ducks the main issue. Beefing up the Chief Executive's clout does nothing to minimise the force of legislation which, along with the political interests of professional staff, is what really strengthens the hands of departmental directors.

In this light, then, the most remarkable section in the PRG report is not about general structures at all, it is about education. It comes in that part of the report dealing with specific departments. The study on education concludes that the basic management structure is satisfactory. It goes on, having tackled the basic question in its remit, to a broader question of accountability. The relevant section is given here virtually in full:

> Traditionally [education authorities] have never involved themselves in matters of curricula and the control of standards; this applies not only in Strathclyde but generally throughout the country. The Review Group felt that, as a matter of policy, members should be concerned about what education is provided in schools and colleges, and whether it is adequate and efficient.
>
> The question of member involvement in detailed matters of curricula is an extremely complex one, not least because of the national

implications, and therefore not a subject on which the Review Group felt able to comment without much deeper investigation. The Review Group believes, however, that the Education Committee might consider the advisability of adopting a more positive role in this general area and, as a first step, might ask that head teachers and principals be requested to prepare annual statements of progress, developments, achievements and shortcomings in their school/college over the past year and a declaration of objectives for the forthcoming year. These school/college 'profiles' would provide a continual record of the school's performance and aspiration. While the prime purpose would be to promote accountability and good management, information from the profiles might also be published to promote public awareness of the activities of schools and colleges and their relevance to the local community.[40]

Given the limits placed on the Chief Executive's freedom to control the Director of Education when he is 'exercising responsibilities imposed by statute' or where his 'professional discretion or judgment' is involved, it is difficult to over-emphasise the radical character of this proposal. It does not even limit itself to areas where increased corporate working is appropriate – such suggestions are made in the next paragraph for three specific policy areas (truancy; welfare benefits; and provision for under-fives). The proposal is on a matter of education policy, relating to the management of educational institutions only, and addressed directly to the Education Committee to whom it is the Director of Education's traditional role to be the sole adviser.

Yet the proposal occurs logically. The key issue for the authority has been seen as central control. It is perfectly reasonable, then, that all departments should be opened up to review, and not only to 'once for all' review, but to a continuing process of review. If social service delivery in general must share some of the blame for the problem of deprivation, then review must involve criticism.

The 'school profiles' suggestion contains exactly this seed of criticism. It assumes that there will be 'shortcomings' in the school's performance, the status quo, as a matter of course, and it expects these shortcomings to be opened up for the whole authority, and for the community, to see and to criticise. All this is radical indeed, but it simply makes explicit a general principle which underlies the whole of corporate management. That principle is that the corporate approach is inseparable from policy criticism, and from open criticism of policy in specific fields by people other than those professionals who traditionally have had criticism of their own policy as their own prerogative.

Corporate planning, therefore, raises questions about informal politics and about the growth of knowledge; inconsistencies within the corporate planning literature over political issues mesh with inconsistencies over the growth of knowledge. A complex of issues emerges, centring on problems of criticism and control, of rationality and of power. The next chapter looks at policy statements and government initiatives in corporate planning and in deprivation policy, and identifies similar issues, particularly when questions arise over the relative importance of professional or non-professional judgment. The key question is: who is to decide what should be done about deprivation?

3 Strathclyde: deprivation policy development

This chapter introduces key deprivation policy documents from Strathclyde. It presents a significant portion of the text of the two main documents which we dissect later in the book. It sets the evolution of these documents against a background of deprivation initiatives, both national initiatives and projects on Clydeside. The chapter focuses on the relationship between professionals and the community, and on the debate over the causes of deprivation; are the deprived to blame for their own poverty, or should blame be placed on structures and attitudes (including professional attitudes) in society?

THE NATIONAL BACKGROUND

One of the earliest initiatives, on Educational Priority Areas (EPA), introduced the idea of a deprived culture. EPA was one of the first initiatives to promote positive discrimination for disadvantaged communities. It also pioneered the idea of 'action research'. The 'community' concern was explicit; the view was that the need for positive discrimination arose partly from a failure of communication between school and community and partly from children being 'severely handicapped by home conditions'.[1]

The Urban Programme, announced in 1968, made a derogatory assumption more prominent. It provided finance for projects in areas of deprivation. The areas were described as 'areas of special social need ... often scattered in relatively small pockets' of deprivation. This showed in:

> notable deficiencies in the physical environment, particularly in housing; overcrowding of houses; family sizes above the average; persistent unemployment; a high proportion of children in trouble or in need of care; or a combination of these. A substantial degree of immigrant settlement would also be an important factor.[2]

The language stops short of 'feckless', but not far short.

The initiative which most clearly brought the issue of cultural pathology to the fore was the Community Development Project. We will examine it in some detail, not least because of its particular influence in Strathclyde. Announced in 1969, CDP consisted of twelve projects in local authorities across Britain. The projects focused on narrow areas within a given authority's boundary. One of the projects was in Paisley, near Glasgow, and focused entirely on a single local authority housing estate, Ferguslie Park. Each project had two sides, an action team who worked in the area of the project and an academic research team appointed to monitor the project. A first source is the Home Office document describing 'Objectives and Strategy'. This states:

> that an experimental approach to solutions, using social science methods of enquiry and evaluation as a built-in support for social action constitutes a wise and worthwhile addition to traditional ways of tackling the problems of social welfare. As the more obvious problems, such as poverty at large within the community, begin to yield to familiar but essential long-term policies, problems are exposed which are of great complexity and difficulty.[3]

Four activities were necessary, therefore: 'description, communication, social action and evaluation'. In the description 'as accurately and comprehensively as possible' of the characteristics ('individual, family and social') of the area,

> it will be necessary to look behind the more obvious and familiar indications of social ill health, such as delinquency, bad housing, lack of success at school, etc., and to expose the reasons why there is a breakdown in communications ... between the neighbourhood and the services operating within it.[4]

This leads to a need to understand the way people communicate grievances, 'building them into symbols of their own social isolation', since,

> if ... the neighbourhood systems of communication could be better understood, and at least some of the symbols of social isolation which they define could be removed by social action, a start would have been made in establishing a more positive link between 'us' and 'them'.[5]

A strange community language, hidden from professional eyes, seems to be at the root of the problem. To illustrate this an example is given of a 'symbolic' grievance:

> one family advice centre met with little success in tackling what were

plainly the more important problems of its neighbourhood until it realised that the persistent refusal of a bus company to extend a bus route (to give the people better access to a cheaper shopping centre) had a symbolic meaning with the neighbourhood out of all proportion to its intrinsic importance. The removal of this grievance by the efforts of the social workers proved to be the point of breakthrough; the workers were accepted within the neighbourhood's own system of communication and it became possible for them to build bridges of understanding between the community and the social services.[6]

While welcoming the awareness of the need for 'bridges of understanding', it is impossible to avoid the conclusion that this passage presupposes the correctness of professional judgment ('what were plainly the more important problems') in contrast to the irrational 'symbolic' judgment of the community, 'out of all proportion to its intrinsic importance', that they needed a better bus service to get access to cheaper shops. The role of social action is clarified as 'reward'. 'Deprived and hence rather inarticulate people will not communicate, to the point where adequate description of their needs and problems becomes impossible unless their efforts to do so are rewarded by social action.'[7] The action, like the grievance, is symbolic, and the language echoes operant conditioning.

The project did intend to coordinate government action, however, and encouraged professionals to reflect on the impact of their work in communities. Staff were asked to consider the implications of their own action for the situation as dealt with by other services, and they were encouraged to question the 'relevance' of services to a particular community. For example, 'people in a deprived area will not regard as particularly relevant to the needs of their children a secondary school curriculum which would readily be accepted by people buying their homes on a suburban housing estate'.[8] As this example makes clear, however, 'relevance' is two edged, and can deny people resources as well as it can make appropriate resources more accessible.

The fourth stage, evaluation, was to provide the project team with 'evidence regarding the success or failure of their efforts to reach their chosen objectives'. For measuring success or failure, 'indicators which are likely to be helpful' were suggested. These indicators reinforce the 'culture of poverty' conception of deprivation. For example, under 'Indicators of improved personal care' were 'improvements in personal health care (improved nutritional habits; improved personal hygiene; increased use of family planning)'. Under 'Indicators of improved family functioning' were 'reduction in injurious family crises' and 'increased marriage and cohabitation stability'.[9] One wonders what view of the world sees family crisis and marital instability as a particular characteristic of the culture of deprived people. The *Inter-Project Report* of 1973 made this denigration of communities explicit, and rejected it:

> local teams have increasingly questioned and moved away from the original 'social pathology' assumptions of the experiment. They have begun to develop perspectives which better account for the unequal distribution of both private and public goods and services.[10]

They pointed away from the character of the community to a 'wider canvas of population movements, employment and housing changes'. The conclusions of the document are that:

> The problems of the 12 CDP areas are not reducible to problems of employment, housing, income and education. They are not isolated pockets suffering an unfortunate combination of circumstances. They are a central part of the dynamics of an urban system and as such represent those who have lost out in the competition for jobs, housing and educational opportunity. ... In the same way that problems are inter-related, programmes to solve them have to be complex and far reaching. The problems in these areas are not going to be solved by marginal rearrangements to take account of their special minority needs. From its small area base, CDP can map the points at which private and public policies are having negative and unequal effects.[11]

The tension between these different views of the problem of deprivation (and of the role of the CDP teams who had seen fit to point out the 'negative and unequal effects' of 'familiar general policies') was resolved by the Home Office, in the words of CDP, 'actively seeking ways to close down or curtail project activities'. Tensions between local projects and local authorities were seen in much the same light.

When the Inner Area Studies (IAS) initiative arrived it was run by management consultants. The projects were in relatively small districts within the local authority area, but the view that was present in the beginning of CDP, that these were atypical of the rest of society, was replaced by a view of the areas as suffering from problems caused by structures in society. Thus, in the Liverpool final report:

> The inner areas are not the cause of the deprivation found within them; responsibility for this must lie in the structure of our society, its economic relationships and institutions.[12]

This structuralism did not lead to the confrontation that characterised CDP relations with government. IAS sought programmes which could still operate within the basic governmental framework, but a major part of the task of government was seen to be the provision of the right environment for these programmes:

> we have referred many times in this report to the problem of attitudes; the insensitivity and remoteness of government; the failure to recognise, let alone tolerate, different values; the uncertainty, fear and anger and the deep-seated and growing sense of alienation from government on the part of many residents of the inner areas; the failure of elected representatives to do more than speak for a few individuals across the barrier between governors and governed.
>
> The political and administrative framework for regeneration must, therefore, seek to counter the entrenched attitudes in the rest of society towards so many of its residents; to do this will require strong, central authority to achieve the necessary degree of positive discrimination. Yet at the same time, the need for central authority will have to be reconciled with the equally pressing need for effective local responsibilities.[13]

Several key ideas for Strathclyde can be found in IAS. 'Sensitivity' is important, along with 'attitudes'. Criticism is now directed at local authorities, officers and members, and at their culture, not that of the deprived communities, as the deviant culture. IAS established that the 'familiar general policies' of the Home Office CDP document were not good enough, and, more than any earlier initiative, brought a CDP style of criticism on to the government agenda. The tension between central control and local responsibility is also pointed out.

The Glasgow Eastern Area Renewal (GEAR) Project, announced in May 1976, was also influenced by IAS. It involved a number of agencies, including the District and Regional Councils. In 1978, Hugh Brown stated the project to be 'a concerted programme for the comprehensive social, economic and environmental regeneration of the entire area'. The emphasis in GEAR was on the coordination of activities in consultation with local people:

> the best prospect, and perhaps the only one, will be through coordinated action in all the different spheres of activity ... Above all else, however, the actual process of change must be managed in a just and dignified manner which recognises the needs and rights of the individual.[14]

National initiatives and social pathology

To Lawless, the contribution of CDP to deprivation policy was considerable – he quotes Weightman's description of CDP as *'the* British attempt to tackle the deprivation of inner city and declining industrial areas'. Lawless continues:

> the team have stimulated the diffusion of structuralist arguments of deprivation ... It has done more than any other initiative to promote and examine a completely new vision of deprivation which, despite the disturbing nature of its profound implications, central government has found hard to ignore.[15]

Higgins, looking at four programmes, including EPA and CDP, picks out conflict as a major characteristic of them all. She is less optimistic:

> Conflicts arising out of the programmes ... have on the whole resulted from misunderstandings, bad planning and lack of vision. Where this has been the case the conflict has been destructive and has not helped the clients in the programmes. Change, it seems, necessitates conflict. Conflict, however, does not always produce desired change.[16]

In this context it is worth considering two further initiatives. Firstly, we can look at the Transmitted Deprivation Studies announced in 1972 by Keith Joseph, then Secretary of State at the DHSS. These were purely research projects; the central concept was the 'cycle of deprivation', the 'cyclical process of transmission of deprivation and social maladjustment from one generation to another'.[17] It was assumed that this process of transmission was internal to the family. The initiative bore fruit in the book by Rutter and Madge, *Cycles of Disadvantage*.[18] This had what Lawless calls 'embarrassing' consequences. He sees the major contribution to the demise of the 'culture of poverty' explanation in general as being made by Rutter and Madge's book. Yet this was among the most empirically focused and ideologically non-committal projects, and had no connection with 'action'. Secondly we can look at the CIUD (Census Indicators of Urban Deprivation) work by Sally Holtermann in the Department of the Environment. This must rank as one of the most significant initiatives in actually stimulating policy action and changes in resource allocation. The CIUD studies used 1971 census data 'to construct, at enumeration district level, indicators of deprivation which can be used to identify, as far as the limited nature of the census permits, and analyse the distribution of areas with the highest levels of deprived persons'.[19] The reports repeatedly stress the limitations of the method:

> it will be useful to repeat some of the limitations of our approach: we

have defined deprivation as lack of command over resources. We believe this to be the best workable definition although, depending on the broadness of the definition of 'resources', it might not cover all facets of life which would engender individual feelings of deprivation.[20]

Another characteristic (implicit) of the work is its adoption of a relative conception of deprivation, 'a low level of material welfare enjoyed by individuals (households or persons), measured against standards that we feel command a general level of acceptance as being reasonable minima in this country today'.[21] Perhaps here there is as much true sensitivity, a feel for individual 'feelings', as in any of the explicitly 'committed' reports, and in speaking of 'lack of command' over resources the powerlessness of deprived communities is highlighted. It is sad that this sort of work was so often crudely denigrated by advocates of conflict.

THE LOCAL BACKGROUND: CLYDESIDE

Before the reorganisation of local government several reports appeared from a variety of agencies highlighting the incidence of 'deprivation', 'need' or 'disadvantage' on Clydeside. Glasgow Corporation produced the *Areas of Need* report in 1972,[22] and a number of officers and members from the corporation moved across to Strathclyde at reorganisation. The members who made the move included Councillor Shaw, who became Leader of the Labour Group in Glasgow shortly before reorganisation, and who then became the first Convener of the Regional Council. The *Born to Fail* report from the National Child Development Study, published in 1973,[23] identified Clydeside as having a high incidence of need, and a CIUD report of February 1975 considered deprivation in the conurbations of Britain, highlighting a concentration of deprived areas in Clydeside.[24]

One of the most significant local initiatives was the West Central Scotland Plan (WCSP), a comprehensive land-use plan covering a geographical area broadly similar to the local authority area of Strathclyde. The WCSP team were an *ad hoc* body, drawn primarily from a background in physical planning, and interpreted their remit widely. Their report was produced in 1974, and included substantial analyses of the regional economy. Volume 4 of the report, *Social Issues*, which was based on 1966 (sample) census data, contained an analysis of deprivation within the region.[25] With the institution of Strathclyde, several members of the WCSP team moved into the new authority; two became Depute Directors of the Region's Department of Physical Planning, another became leader of the Regional Report team within the same department.

All these projects provided statistical analysis of deprivation as an areal phenomenon, using either census data or special survey material, and this provided guidelines for the Region's own analysis. The continuities of personnel, however, are just as significant.

There are other pre-reorganisation policy strands woven into the Region's documents, and again individuals provide connections. Councillor Young was Chairman of Social Services in Greenock and Port Glasgow before moving to the Region; his Director moved to become Director of the Glasgow Division of the Region's Social Work Department. In Greenock and Port Glasgow they had worked together on a policy of 'positive discrimination' towards deprived areas, and on a policy of community involvement in the solution of community problems. A 1973 report on the Greenock work indicates that they were giving emphasis to: 'the involvement of the community in social work, first as an educational process and secondly as part of a wider aim encouraging community participation in decisions.'[26]

As important as these initiatives, however, is the Gorbals Group, led by Geoff Shaw, a minister of the Church of Scotland. The group was established in the mid-1950s as a community ministry, based in a tenement flat in the Gorbals, with a communal lifestyle and a commitment to living out a radical form of Christian discipleship within the local community. Geoff Shaw's involvement with the Labour Party and in local government came as a result of his involvement with the Gorbals Group. Shaw produced a policy document for the group in 1955, and was still involved with it when he became Convener of Strathclyde Regional Council. His fight to have a new form of ministry accepted by the Church of Scotland was itself a challenge to professionalism directly comparable to that which he helped to lead in the Region. His 1955 paper states on behalf of the group that, rather than adopt a traditional ministry,

> In our consciences we have chosen the other way and have committed ourselves to a ministry to those who are far outside the Church. This small group must become the outward-looking nucleus of a Christian congregation – a congregation centred on the sacraments, on preaching and on worship, a congregation committed to carry the Gospel to the whole life of the community.
>
> The Church must cease to be an occasional visitor and must really learn to dwell among people ... especially, in our most pagan areas, we believe that this must start with ministers who will be prepared to leave behind the traditional building and the traditional privileges –

perhaps even reputation – and dwell in the midst of their people, because Christ first dwells there.[27]

STRATHCLYDE REGIONAL COUNCIL

On his election as Convener of the Council on 16 April 1975, Councillor Shaw spoke of the problems of deprivation faced in the Region, basing his account on two documents, the *Born to Fail* report and one of the CIUD papers. The minutes do not record the substance of his address, but it brought the following response:

> Bearing in mind that the Convener, in his inaugural address to this Regional Council, quoted some distressing facts about the deprivation of children in this Region contained in the authoritative publication 'Born to Fail', will he ensure (a) that every councillor gets copies of 'Census Indicators of Urban Deprivation: Working Note No. 6 – CIUD (75) 6', and of Glasgow Corporation's publication 'Areas of Need'?; (b) that immediate consideration of these reports is started in all appropriate committees; these studies to include an examination of the policies and actions which have dismally failed to cure this urban deprivation in the past and of the new policies and actions which will be necessary to speedily end this deprivation within Strathclyde?[28]

Councillor Shaw's reply to the question is minuted as follows:

> In reply, the Convener (1) stated that all members wishing copies of the documents referred to would have these issued to them, and (2) expressed the view that, although the document 'Census Indicators of Urban Deprivation' was a complicated statistical report, the information contained in it made clear the basic and well-known problems of the area.[29]

The next relevant minute is for the Council meeting of 16 May, the first after power was formally handed over. The following resolution was passed as an amendment from Councillor Stewart, from the Labour Group, to a motion from an SNP member:

> That this Council welcomes the Secretary of State's proposal to visit Melrose House on 27th June to meet representatives of the Regional Council to discuss urban deprivation and the added measures the Government could take to assist Strathclyde Regional Council to remedy the situation and re-affirms its view that the Census Report and other similar reports should be studied by all Committees and

that particular regard should be had to the areas of deprivation in the preparation and submission of the Regional Report to the Secretary of State.[30]

The Context Report: July 1975

The Context Report prepared the ground for the Regional Report, with an analysis of conditions in the Region and with policy suggestions. It incorporated the CIUD work, the *Born to Fail* data, and mortality data. It also built on the work of WCSP. The report was concerned with the position of the Region relative to the rest of Britain, and with the relative positions of areas within the Region. The conclusion of the analysis of indicators of deprivation is that:

> From the indicators examined it is clear that the Strathclyde Region suffers lower standards over a wide range of social indicators [than the rest of Britain. Also] there are marked disparities within the Region itself.[31]

The analysis is seen as supporting the decision of the council on 16 May. The 'policy considerations' section goes on to criticise past policy as having contributed to the problem of deprivation. The argument is this: firstly, poor job opportunities led to migration from the region; secondly:

> the population structure within different parts of the region shows the effect of planning policies over the last 25 years with movement from the older conurbation areas to new suburbs and the new towns.[32]

This created 'a severe population imbalance', most acute in Glasgow itself. Paralleling this 'imbalance' in population structure is an imbalance of housing tenure, with a low proportion of owner-occupation in the older conurbation area. Next, 'the imbalance in population structure and housing type in the region is mirrored by the incidence of urban deprivation'. The argument continues:

> Glasgow's problem, huge and complex as it is, arises from the lack of coordinated planning policies for the Region in the post war period. ... the density of development and the inadequate state of much of the housing stock necessitated wholesale clearance and overspill schemes. However, the implementation of these policies is one cause of today's problem: the solutions have discriminated against Glasgow and to a lesser extent some of the other older urban areas.

> It is these areas that have suffered most from the concentration of

investment and new development elsewhere in the region. The run down physical environment in areas of industrial decline and in the residential areas, and the lack of shopping, community and recreation facilities in these areas is perhaps as important a reason for the high rate of out migration from these areas and their 'poor' record of industrial attraction, as the economic decline and lack of job opportunities. These areas which include large tracts of post war local authority housing, as well as the older tenement areas and decaying town centres, are in marked contrast with the well provided suburbs and new towns.[33]

The proposed development strategy therefore emphasises 'positive discrimination' to redress imbalances, and a comprehensive approach, with community involvement, to 'grave imbalances' within the region.

> it is proposed to investigate the merits of adopting an area management application for more extensive areas of deprivation. Since many key issues underlining the problems of urban deprivation transcend the boundaries of service departments, an area committee system would be more responsive as a means of communication and hence public participation.[34]

Much of the time of staff in the Physical Planning Department between July and November was spent on further analysis of specific areas of deprivation. This analysis drew on 1971 census data, supplemented by data from the police and social work, and by fieldwork. It aimed to identify and delimit accurately discrete areas of deprivation; the result was a list of 114 areas across Strathclyde, subsequently known as Areas for Priority Treatment (APTs).

Policy and Resources Committee, 4 December 1975

The committee's recommendations were largely in line with the Context Report. On the APTs, the committee decided that there should be positive discrimination, but that it should be selective. Thus:

> the Council should concentrate their resources initially on a limited number of the worst areas and areas most at risk, and that the appropriate officials should accordingly be instructed to make a provisional selection of such areas and to report on the existing provision in these areas and possible projects therefor.[35]

The next recommendation set up a sub-committee of P&R to look at Urban Aid schemes for the deprived areas. These recommendations give the remits for two important organisational units, firstly, the Urban Deprivation Officer Group (UDOG, pronounced *you-dog*) and, secondly, the Policy and Resources Sub-Committee on Multiple Deprivation (or on Urban Aid) – this was usually known simply as the P&R Sub. Each was a key forum for the critical appraisal of policy. UDOG was composed of officers from a range of the Council's departments, and a similar set of officers reported to the meetings of the P&R Sub.

The Regional Report, May 1976

The Report retains the emphasis established in the Context Report. Of particular relevance here is the report's supplementary volume on urban deprivation, produced by the Physical Planning Department. The bulk of this volume simply presents the statistical analysis of areas of deprivation (the 114 APTs), with a 'factsheet' on each. The document also contains, however, sections which review 'existing policy approaches to deprived areas' and which discuss 'the problems of the APTs and policy approaches'. Section IV of the deprivation volume reviews national deprivation initiatives and their local manifestation. It also discusses a number of more localised initiatives. In particular, the comprehensive approach is pointed out in these schemes. The conclusion of section IV is that:

> several common themes can be identified. One of these concerns the complexity of the problems that are found whose overlapping nature requires that the areas be dealt with by local authorities on a more integrated basis. The Strone/Mauckinhill project in Greenock illustrates the type of special management structure which has been devised to provide such an integrated approach, and also to involve the community closely in the discussion and resolution of problems. ... 'community development' has been a major objective.
>
> Finally, the interaction of deprived areas with the wider community has been recognised, particularly by the Community Development Projects. Their work has shown them that many of the problems arising within their areas in fact have their origins elsewhere. Housing or employment problems, for example, can arise from the lack, or maladministration, of policies at the citywide or national level.[36]

The implications for action are, firstly, that there should be changes in management structure, or at least the addition of new elements to the overall structure of the authority. Secondly, there is a need for 'encouragement' and 'assistance' to be provided to the community with a view to local authority action in the area reflecting more fully the views of the community.

Section V makes proposals for implementing such a policy. Given the emphasis on an integrated approach, it is perhaps not surprising to find that there are recommendations for policy to be pursued within a range of departments. The importance of this still needs to be emphasised. It is one thing to say 'services should be more coordinated' – a fairly innocuous general statement with which few services will disagree; it is quite a different matter to say, for example, 'the education service should ...', when the person making the latter statement is not a member of the Education Department.

This is another example of the sort of comment which was found in the report of the Policy Review Group. There is a gradually more open statement of the critical presuppositions of the corporate planning movement. In the case of education, the problem is if anything more acute given the function of the Regional Report in a process of policy development, and given the section of the 1962 Education Act which safeguards the privileged position of the Director of Education in respect of comments relating to the 'promotion of Educational Developments'.

In the event, the recommendations for education and social work are unlikely to cause any embarrassment – relating as they do to shortfalls of staff and the need for recruitment. However, the potential is for more direct and pointed criticism to emerge, as for instance with regard to housing policy, where section V says that:

> allocation policies have operated in such a way that ghetto areas have been created which are unacceptable to the majority of prospective local authority tenants. Such areas have a growing problem of vacant dwellings, with the attendant problems of vandalism and disruption of tenants in adjacent properties. Moreover the visual effect of vacant housing in an area is likely to induce further difficulties in letting houses and in many cases local authorities have decided to demolish physically sound houses, ... Housing managers should be dissuaded from continuing with housing allocation policies which focus problems in certain schemes.[37]

Housing management is a District Council responsibility, which is why Physical Planning can get away with this comment. Had housing been a regional function, no document from another regional department could have been so outspoken, regardless of any precedent provided by PRG. The main element in section V, however, is its scheme of 'corporate management' for each of an unspecified number of deprived areas:

a management structure is suggested to enable Region and Districts to work together to tackle their common problems. ... The aim of the structure is firstly to allow a corporate approach with greater sensitivity to community interest.[38]

Four 'key elements' are identified: an 'Area Steering Committee', with members from Regional and District Councils, whose job is 'identifying issues and priorities' as various groups are 'feeding their knowledge and perception of problems into the Area Committee'; a 'Project Team' or 'Programme Group', meeting the need 'for all those officials concerned with the problems of APTs to work together'. The group members would work from an 'Area Office', the third key element, and:

This local office would enable the team to become aware of the important problems and issues within an area. The teams would also acquire knowledge through the expertise of their individual members, and eventually through their own specialised work in the area. As such, the team would provide an important source of information on the Area to the Steering Committee.[39]

The fourth element is the 'Management Team' of senior officials, which would 'advise the Area Committee on the viability and implications of its proposals, and would ensure that the technical views of each service department were taken into account in the consideration of any matter'.[40] This passage suggests something of the perceived nature of 'professional judgment' in its suggestion that, to protect departmental interests, it is important to take the *technical* views of departments fully into account.

There are still problems. Suppose an Area Committee suggests a change in local policy on education, how should the Education Department react? What are the implications if the criticism made locally has a general application; should the Education Department alter its general policy? As far as the authority as a whole is concerned, the local coordinating unit is just one more 'department', another discrete element within which devolved decision-making is in tension with central control. Guidance is given:

All proposals for action in an area would be discussed and approved in the first instance by elected representatives on the Area Steering Committee. The method of resolving problems will vary according to the type and severity of the issue in question. It is likely that some issues may involve management or administrative changes which could be resolved via the Management Team and the Service Departments and Committees. In some cases, however, the Area Committee will be involved in budgetary considerations, and these will have to be referred to the higher policy making bodies of the authorities concerned.[41]

This paragraph is the nearest in the whole volume to an explicit acknowledgment that conflict is likely. The implication is that, at least on 'budgetary considerations' (which crop up with virtually every policy proposal), the new elements should defer to the traditional structures.

UDOG's Multiple Deprivation Report, October 1976

This report was approved by the Council on 13 October, having had a 'preamble' added by the Policy and Resources Committee. The preamble makes it plain that the report is the definitive statement of the Region's deprivation strategy. After its adoption it was produced in quantity and circulated throughout the authority, becoming known as 'The Red Book'. The preamble describes the report as follows:

it identifies a large number of geographical areas in which many of the causes and effects of deprivation are compounded together to create a pressing need for priority treatment. It states that the main causes are:

1 economic forces – financial poverty coupled with non-existent or unsatisfactory job opportunities;
2 the operation of the housing market and of the social services, such as education and housing, which often tend to reinforce the problems;
3 certain managerial deficiencies of government and, in some instances, the attitudes and practices of departments.

All of these give rise to a vicious circle of hopelessness reflected by many in apathy, political alienation, delinquency, truancy and other problems of human behaviour. The project proposes no easy solution, nor does it pretend that the deeply intractable problems of urban deprivation can be solved by massive injections of finance. It does point to certain immediate steps which the Policy and Resources Committee now recommends to the Council as the first stage of the long haul towards community regeneration and the tackling of urban deprivation.[42]

The preamble notes prerequisites 'without which programmes of government expenditure will continue to fall short'. These are: firstly, 'real commitment' from officers, members and society; secondly, 'a readiness to learn from the mistakes of the past and to concede the existence of deficiencies in the way government delivers its services and relates to the public'; and thirdly, 'a concerted and sensitive effort on the part of all public agencies'. It then makes specific recommendations: firstly, that the analysis of deprivation in the report 'be accepted as reflecting the Council's view of the problem'; secondly, that the forty-five areas speci-fied (in line with the December meeting of P&R) should be given 'special consideration when allocating resources and preparing urban aid schemes'; thirdly, that a further selection take place to identify areas where 'coordinated arrangements' could be made.[43] These projects became known later as the Area Initiatives.

Moving on to the report itself, the first main section seeks to identify the problems found in deprived areas. The task

> is fairly straightforward for, given that the Council will wish to exer-cise its political judgment in determining the emphasis which it wishes to place on each of the factors involved, there already exists among members and officers a broad intuitive consensus, based on detailed local knowledge and the experience of previous remedial efforts, about what causes multiple deprivation.[44]

On the strength of this consensus the report proceeds to expound 'The major problems found ... in most multiply deprived areas'. Three types are identified. Firstly, there are problems relating to circumstances which apply nationwide; these are problems of poverty, of lack of em-ployment and of housing conditions. An example of the detail within these headings is:

> council housing schemes whose total environment is inadequate for a full social and community life; lacking in community facilities (e.g. play areas, shopping centres, schools, community centres, recreation facilities, health centres, entertainments, etc.).[45]

The second type of problem relates to 'difficulties arising from the atti-tudes, nature and scale of public services – health, education, police, social work, transport, leisure and recreation ...':

(a) inaccessibility of agency from field – general 'distance' of control of service delivery from recipients;
(b) lack of coordination of effort: no corporate approach;
(c) inadequately resourced services;
(d) insensitivity in service delivery: failure to deal in terms of people as opposed to tasks;
(e) environmental services unable to cope with difficulties arising from initial design and subsequent use;

(f) infrequent and expensive transport services.[46]

Thirdly, the report describes 'problems associated with the communities themselves'. There are 11 of these and the following are examples, but the report makes clear that its list is not exhaustive:

(a) sense of hopelessness: lack of knowledge and access to established machinery;
(b) increasing sense of dependence on outside agencies, linked often with frustration at lack of control over own affairs;
(c) truancy, under-achievement in schools and general lack of sympathy for education system;
(d) sense of anonymity and irresponsibility arising from the breakdown of older communities with redevelopment and population movement, from housing policies, from the concentration of disadvantaged groups like one parent families.[47]

The key recommendation in the report is that the local authority ought 'to "put its own house in order" – to provide the means whereby a corporate approach to the provision of services can be achieved'.[48]

The corporate approach can be expected to generate conflicts at a number of levels. In the description of 'Area Centres' the report calls for them to be, among other things, 'complaints centres', the complaints being about services, with a view to these services being more 'relevant' and 'accountable to the community':

> without prejudicing the role of the elected representative in receiving complaints about services, a clear and just procedure for dealing with complaints from the public should be devised and publicised.[49]

A conflict also occurs with departmental policies as they apply to the overall area of the authority, and as they apply to the area covered by the Area Centre. The resolution of this conflict as it manifests itself in individual staff members is seen as a task of training, and this becomes a primary function for at least some Area Centres:

> It should be recognised that area staff will be faced with two, possibly conflicting, obligations – their accountability to the corporate area group, as well as to their own departments. Many staff will not be convinced that a corporate strategy is either practicable or desirable, and many will be ignorant of its practical implications as well as of other departments with which they will be required to work in corporate harness. Training of staff will therefore be of crucial importance. There are a variety of ways of doing this, one of which might be to select examples where a corporate approach is working successfully

and use these in a programme of secondment, as training centres with a teaching unit attached to them. These teaching units would be designed to introduce staff to the practical workings of corporate strategies and to provide concurrent 'theoretical' instruction.[50]

The problem is one of education – requiring 'instruction', demonstration examples and a 'theoretical' input. It is also a problem of persuasion – staff are to be 'convinced'; but none of this can solve the problem of 'conflicting obligations'. The individual is the arena, and no amount of education of him alone will alter the basic conflict between corporate group and mainstream department.

'Community regeneration' introduces a conflict between professional and community perceptions of the needs of an area: 'The reactivation of community spirit in multiply deprived areas is perhaps the most difficult problem to face up to in terms of local authority decision-making processes and our traditional ways of tackling our problems.' What it needs is 'a willingness by the authorities to allow communities a genuine voice in the running of their areas':

> Committees and Departments will require to review their activities across the board to see if there are any areas in which communities could play a constructive role, either by carrying out directly activities normally associated with the local authority itself, or by taking at local level decisions which the local authority has taken in the past.[51]

The conflict is simply stated and the question is raised as requiring a decision from the Council. Here the issue is the relationship between professional and community views:

> does [the Council] wish to alter this balance so that, while still recognising the role that professional judgment has to play in resolving problems, it is prepared to offer an increased opportunity to local communities? ...
>
> How are Committees and Departments to be encouraged to overcome their natural reluctance to relinquish, even slightly, the design and quality standards which seem to them appropriate in favour of the perhaps lesser standards which communities may request?[52]

Criticism is to be valued. The basic problem becomes: how should criticism be rendered constructive?

> efforts to encourage communities to articulate their feelings will almost inevitably give rise to a greater degree of criticism of local authorities and central government than is experienced at present. Members will require to determine what attitude they would take to

such criticism – certainly it could be alarming initially to members and officers working in the field, but, more positively, it could be recognised as a valuable source of feedback on what is actually happening in each community. This does not mean to say that unjust or ill-informed criticism should be accepted and again it would fall to members at the local level to ensure by setting problems in their context that any criticism made is constructive and formulated in the light of the fullest possible information available.[53]

The relation of this process of criticism to the idea of learning is even more apparent when the report speaks of community regeneration as 'a long term process and an educative exercise in the broadest terms':

> There is a crucial need for the frankest possible discussion within the council to ensure first a clear political commitment to whatever approach emerges and secondly that this is understood and accepted at all levels of implementation.[54]

This is the main contribution of the report. There are also calls for action to support and promote employment, and to petition other agencies for action on issues which have a nationwide character, but the emphasis is on 'putting our own house in order'. This is a process of achieving continuous constructive criticism of local authority policy. In advocating this process the Red Book acknowledges 'professional standards' in a manner which appears most orthodox, yet it is a direct challenge to the traditional management of local government services.

Areas of Need – The Next Step

This is the title of UDOG's report of April 1977. It picks up some of the questions left hanging by the Red Book. For brevity it is referred to as 'the *AoN* report', or simply '*AoN*'. The section which we are particularly interested in is 'A Policy of Coordination'. This specifies areas where a coordinated approach of the type outlined in the earlier documents will be implemented. As before:

> It is a question of how best can the people, their elected representatives and officials get together to carry out, continuously, a critical review of how services respond to the needs of the community on a day to day and development basis.
>
> If communities are to have more control over their own development as the joint approach implies then all the participants must be able to speak with authority. As many decisions as possible must be taken and implemented at the local level.[55]

This means that 'departments will require to encourage initiative in and give increased responsibility to their own local officials' and 'these local officials must be encouraged themselves to respect, to respond to and encourage initiatives from local communities'.[56] The approach is re-emphasised as a process of training, it should 'deepen understanding' and 'heighten awareness', and the positive role of criticism or conflict is reaffirmed:

> in fostering initiative and delegating authority to members and officials the possibility of conflict between area and centre, and amongst groups and individuals at local level is recognised. It is believed the positive aspects will be greater than the drawbacks.[57]

On the assessment of needs in the area, to be done by the officers' group as a joint 'exploration' with the community, it is explicitly acknowledged that 'this assessment may necessitate a critical evaluation of present policies and ways of providing services'. On the question of 'community control', for instance:

> it would be naive to assume either that officers across the board will be immediately responsive to the idea of transferring, however gradually, any of the present functions to the community (since, to many, this will seem like 'working themselves out of a job') or that communities will necessarily be willing or able immediately to take on increased responsibility for managing their own affairs.[58]

However, in spite of the difficulties, a move is to be made in this direction. The report indicates that negotiation should take place on this transfer of authority or control to the community and from the professional staff. In saying this the *AoN* report answers 'Yes' to the Red Book question, 'Does the Council wish to alter the balance between community and professional judgment?'.

AoN recommends arrangements for such a corporate approach. The idea of a local manager reappears; he is to be known as the 'coordinator'. There is also to be a local consultative group, including elected members, and a local officer working group – all as outlined in the Regional Report. The oversight of the different projects on a region-wide basis will be the work of a sub-committee of P&R, serviced by the Policy Planning Department with Policy Planning in turn supported by UDOG.

The local members and members of the P&R Sub will provide an extra communication channel, by virtue of being members of the Labour Group. In addition to this informal link an official channel is provided by the coordinator, responsible to the Chief Executive via the Director of Policy Planning, and by liaison staff seconded to Policy Planning from mainstream departments. Besides all this a 'forum' is recommended, where:

> Representatives from each scheme will meet to exchange ideas and learn about each other's successes and failures. This will be done bi-annually or more often if required. The aim is to bring together policy makers, community representatives and officials in the centre and division in a conference, seminar type, setting. This would complement the more formalised report and monitoring carried out by committees and departments.[59]

The report indicates resources for the schemes. Firstly, these are to be from mainstream budgets, reflecting the fact that 'The alleviation of deprivation is at the heart of the Council's strategy.' Secondly, there is a note about increased urban aid finance. Thirdly, there are to be 'further monies made available from the £250,000 established to assist Community Councils'. Fourthly, 'there will be an examination of the distribution of existing resources', with a view to redeployment:

> An exercise will be carried out, initially on a sample basis, to establish if existing levels of service are properly matched to needs. This does not imply a reduction of necessary resources but an examination of over-provision.[60]

Finally, the prospect is indicated of support for capital projects and, once the schemes are running, of finances for area committees themselves. The section closes with a recommendation that the schemes should be subject to careful evaluation:

> As the approach proposed is experimental, it is recommended that an attempt be made to monitor and evaluate whatever takes place. There is a close relationship between the training programme and evaluation, and both may require assistance from outside agencies in the initial stages.[61]

These, then, are the major statements of deprivation policy from Strathclyde Regional Council. The element of policy especially focused on – the Council's 'house ordering' – is the major strand, acknowledged as such in Councillor Young's 1979 paper to the Labour Group.

Summary: Strathclyde's policy statements

The basic management task which the Council is set by its own policy documents is the task of managing criticism. They are to keep it from decaying into destructive conflict and to ensure that it leads to the construction of improved policy – improvement as perceived by local communities. Attitudes and traditions, perspectives and traditional understandings, are to be changed as a matter of policy.

In the *AoN* document the relationship between power and rationality is close. For example, the process of critical review is one in which 'all the participants must be able to speak with authority', and it is a process of debate or shared review which aims to increase 'community control'. Access to the review is access to a decision-making process. But the document still avoids a clear indication of which of the two perceptions, community or professional, will be decisive.

Against this background we can usefully consider the importance of the philosophical dimension of this book's investigation. To stay with Strathclyde, we have Councillor Young's account (in chapter one) of the inspection of a site where new waste disposal methods were being introduced. He describes the incident as 'the creation of a myth' and works through false explanations to extract 'the *real* explanation' (his emphasis).

The word *real* crops up repeatedly in connection with problems of analysis in local government. This book simply aims to take the word seriously. We suggest, in effect, that there are conflicting views of what 'the realities' really are, and that these are fundamental to the conflict which develops inevitably between different attitudes to the conduct of a process of policy criticism such as the Red Book and *AoN* initiate.

The problem of 'reality' is one of the foundational problems of philosophy. Philosophical traditions exist which approach the problem in diametrically opposed terms, seeing change as the fundamental reality to be grasped, or seeing stable entities as the basis of a right view of the world; some seeing material objects as the most real, and others seeing them as the least real. In particular the world-views of the religious and the technician clash forcefully. Without some exploration of this background we have little hope of understanding why professional culture has such difficulty in taking non-professional views seriously.

4 Traditions of rationality

The book is concerned with the conduct of criticism in pluralist societies. Strathclyde Regional Council provides a microcosm which can help us think about what we might call 'public rationality', rationality in public life in the broadest sense. It is in this broad societal or humanist sense that, as we stated in the introduction, the book is an exercise in critical theory. The philosophical issues considered in this chapter are important in their own right, they do not merely provide background material for the analysis which is to follow. Although the bulk of the book is directly concerned with local government decision-making there is a sense in which the analysis of Strathclyde's policy-making serves simply to support the philosophy. This is to affirm two things; firstly, that non-professional philosophy is important. Lay people, such as the officers and members of Strathclyde, can contribute to philosophical debate. They may contribute in non-philosophical terms, perhaps, but their contribution is no less important for that. Secondly, it is to assert that philosophy can never be a purely theoretical pursuit; it is not, *de facto*, completely insulated from the wider world and in many ways the ramifications of a particular philosophy for popular culture or practical politics are more important than its purely academic ramifications.

This means that philosophy and empirical analysis are inseparable, quite apart from the mediating role of methodology. What is needed is not so much a methodology as a method of drawing together, or translating between, practical life and the world of overtly philosophical philosophy. If, as we put it in chapter one, the search is on for Strathclyde's neo-Hegelians and neo-Kantians, we need some help with their identification. This is best provided on the basis of a broad survey of ideas about the growth of knowledge.

This chapter provides such a survey; it identifies two key traditions, one from Plato to Hegel, and another from Aristotle to Kant, the dialectic tradition and the analytic. Other significant dichotomies arise, however, notably rationalism opposed to empiricism, and the secular opposed to the religious. The confusing relationships between these different dichotomies stem largely from the fact that, for the greater part of the development of European thought, theology has been a major presence; it is now, of course, in eclipse. Nevertheless, we highlight it in this review, partly on account of its significance in the history of ideas, and partly because of the importance of theological ideas to key actors in Strathclyde, particularly to the first Convener of the Regional Council, Geoffrey Shaw. More importantly, a consideration of the relationship between philosophy and theology allows us to explore issues concerning dogmatism and open debate which are central to the philosophical discussion in the next chapter.

On the basis of this survey, chapter five tackles the Positivist Dispute directly, and then goes on to develop a way of examining texts from Strathclyde.

CLASSICAL THOUGHT

For Popper and Habermas, the main protagonists in the subsequent analysis, the classical tradition provides important themes against which their own positions are defined. It is here that the foundations of both the analytic and the dialectic traditions are found and basic options are mapped out for logic and metaphysics.

One difference between Athens of the fourth century BC and Strathclyde of the twentieth century AD is the absence of a system of slavery in Strathclyde. Yet this veils a similarity, that of the existence in both cases of a large proportion of the population who are economically disadvantaged, and who take little or no part in the formal political process. Any move to extend the base of participation in the critical analysis of society and politics, or to question the prerogative of an elite who have a privileged status when it comes to making judgments on ethical or practical matters, is a challenge to political interests. This was true for Socrates, who believed that even a slave, a non-professional, could learn to reason, and we have already seen in Strathclyde that widening participation in the policy-making process threatens the established roles of elected members and the privileged status of professional judgment.

Plato

We can take Plato as a foundation for the dialectic tradition. His theory of forms is a model for understanding the world in general, the world of tables and chairs, for example, as much as the world of moral qualities. This clearly indicates the continuity of the moral and the physical landscape as Plato conceived it.

It is vital to appreciate the inversion which has taken place such that today we tend to think of the physical as the most real, and the ideal, or the theoretical, as less real, to be tested in the real world of practical implementation. For Plato the form, the invisible idea which the craftsman follows when he draws up his plan and then cuts the wood to build the physical object, is more real than the physical object which appears at the end of the work. The physical chair is only an 'appearance' modelled on a reality which cannot be grasped by any of the senses of touch, smell, taste, etc. This makes understanding the *real* world a difficult business, a struggle, or, we could say, a *dialectic*.

The well-known Cave illustration from the *Republic* makes a good source. Plato describes men chained in a cave in such a way that they can see nothing but shadows cast in front of them by the light of a large fire behind them. The shadows are of figures cut from wood, figures of men, carried by living men who converse as they carry the figures. 'Will not the chained men think', says Plato, 'that the shadows are the reality, that the shadow figures are the source of the voices?'

> Suppose that a man is freed from the chain, will he not realise eventually, after a struggle, his former state of deception? And suppose that he leaves the cave, and sees not only the fire and the carriers of the cut-out figures, but sees the real human society, men walking and talking, in the light of the sun. Will he not now see his former state as one of complete deception, and even the understanding he reached, seeing only the fire and the people carrying cut-outs, as defective?[1]

The proposition that there are degrees of reality and truth, with increasing authenticity further from the physical, is explained in the account of the Line, which immediately precedes the Cave.[2] The Line is often held to be clarified by the story of the Cave. In fact the two accounts are, on this issue, exceedingly difficult to reconcile. As a further clarification of the Line, the Cave is a failure. Its value is in its emphasis on the role of criticism in dialectic learning.

Thus the prisoner who goes through this journey of cognitive emancipation goes through a painful process, painful for himself and others. At each stage he leaves the comfort of an understood world for confusion while he grapples with the next layer of reality. So he is 'forced' to look into the firelight, then someone has to 'drag him away forcibly up the steep and rugged ascent' to the outside world. (Why 'steep and rugged' when the illusion can equally well be constructed in a cave having a gradual and smooth connection with the outside world?) The man suffers 'pain and vexation'.[3] The conclusion of the story has him returning to the Cave:

> He might be required once more to deliver his opinion on those shadows, in competition with the prisoners who had never been released, while his eyesight was dim and unsteady; and it might take him some time to become used to the darkness. They would laugh at him and say that he had gone up only to come back with his sight ruined; it was worth no-one's while even to attempt the ascent.[4]

Learning precipitates a conflict of understandings, and with the conflict of understandings, a conflict of people. In Plato dialectic is this difficult journey through superficiality and misconception to a grasp of what is most real. The difficulty is unavoidable. If Plato's conception of learning is at all close to the truth then it is hardly surprising that a review of local government learning about deprivation should describe officers as 'unsure of the validity' of their 'intuitive notions' about deprivation.

Dialectic is a social process; it is also an internal and individual process. The fruit of the process cannot be encapsulated in any fixed statement, the fruit is a new sort of person. This leads to a problematic status for propositions. No verbal formulation of knowledge can share the necessarily personal quality of true knowledge. Because knowledge is also social, we try to communicate it, and we have no means apart from words. All the words can do is put 'out there' some sort of clues in the hope that the idea will be caught but at the risk of degrading the knowledge and rendering it illusory. The moment of grasping, of intuition, is a completely immanent event, a moment of 'seeing the light' which produces a changed life.

The changed life is marked by a commitment to opposing the current understanding of society, whether that is held by individuals or enshrined in social institutions. To be in the dialectic tradition is to hold such a commitment to challenge. As Horkheimer, one of the founders of the Frankfurt School, expresses it in his essay, 'Traditional and Critical Theory':

> If activity governed by reason is proper to man then existent social practice, which forms the individual's life down to its least details, is inhuman, and this inhumanity affects everything that goes on in the society. ... Critical thought has a concept of man as in conflict with himself until this opposition is removed.[5]

Quite clearly the authors of the report from the Coventry Community

Development Project and of *Gilding the Ghetto* place themselves in this tradition, and we will re-examine CDP texts in this light as a preface to the closer examination of Strathclyde texts.

Aristotle

Aristotle provides an analytic counterpoint to Plato's dialectic. One of the striking characteristics of his work is its range. He is credited with the first steps in formalising logical analysis, but the logical analysis is tied to a general interest in metaphysics. He worked on ethics and politics, and did empirical research in zoology and botany, where he is responsible for some of the earliest of anatomical work to be grounded in careful dissection. His fundamental interest is outlined in the *Metaphysics* as the study of 'Being as Being'.

For Aristotle, wisdom is the goal of philosophy, and wisdom is largely concerned with the knowledge of causes in general, and the final cause of things in particular: 'it is the first principles or ultimate causes of things for which we are looking.'[6] A little later he adds to the phrase 'being as being' the rider, 'i.e. substance together with its essential attributes'.[7] This might lead us to believe that he has in mind a 'scientific' project which, while broader perhaps than the typical modern scientist's research programme, can nevertheless be equated with the modern scientific enterprise taken as a whole. So it is interesting to see his *Physics* preoccupied with an attempt to prove the existence of the unmoved first mover as the ultimate cause of the physical universe. Traditionally this has been seen as an attempt to establish the existence of a God such as could naturally fit into the centre of a fully developed Christian theology. Thus, for example, Aquinas' commentary on the *Physics* closes with the following passage:

> He proves that the first immobile mover must have infinite power ... And thus the Philosopher ends his general discussion of natural things with the first principle of the whole of nature, who is over all things, God, blessed forever, Amen.[8]

What we are confronting is a broad and continuous ontology (understanding of what is really real) with no barrier between what we might today regard as separate spheres of enquiry, the theological and the scientific. The most consistent interpretation of Aristotle's work is to see a natural and all encompassing curiosity. He writes, 'All men by their very nature feel the urge to know.'[9] It is clearly an autobiographical comment.

So Aristotle examines those axioms which all sciences must take as fundamental, and he sees this as the task of philosophy. This leads him into logic: 'Evidently, then, it belongs to the philosopher, who studies the nature of substance in general, to study also the bases of syllogism.'[10] 'Syllogism' here means logic in general. This leads almost immediately to his view that:

> the best established of all principles may be stated as follows: The same attribute cannot at the same time belong and not belong to the same subject in the same respect ... It is impossible for anyone to believe ... that the same thing can be and not be ... Therefore everyone in argument relies upon this ultimate law.[11]

Aristotle regards this as self-evident: 'what principle, I ask, is more self-evident than the law of contradiction?' Nevertheless, he attempts a proof. At the end of the exercise, having convinced himself of some success, he concludes: 'still we have already found something more constant and true; which enables us to avoid the extreme view that makes definite thought impossible.'[12]

What was most unthinkable to him was that thought (we could equally well say 'debate') should break down into incoherence. To challenge the principle of contradiction was to challenge rationality itself. He turns to attack thinkers who had made such challenges, notably Protagoras and Heraclitus, and his attack aims to show 'what absurdities follow from denying it'.[13]

This is a foundational concern for the analytic tradition, and there is a marked similarity between this text in Aristotle and an early essay by Popper, 'What is dialectic?'.[14] The paper is concerned to establish the principle of non-contradiction and, like Aristotle's *Metaphysics*, it turns quickly from a logical demonstration of the 'absurdities which follow' to an attack on the principle's challengers.

Like Aristotle, Popper singles out the Heraclitean tradition, with Hegel as a modern representative of it. Like Aristotle, Popper is concerned to avert the danger of a collapse of rational debate. Lukasiewicz points out that in the course of Aristotle's argument his purpose undergoes a change, and the same can be said of Popper's article:

> Aristotle is no longer concerned to prove the Law of Contradiction in all its generality, but only to discover some absolute and non-contradictory truth which will show the falsity of the contrary of the Law of Contradiction – the thesis that 'the same property at the same time belongs to and does not belong to every object'.[15]

Such a thesis would inevitably produce the collapse of rational argument. But the thesis is not necessarily implied in the decision of an individual writer to challenge the application of the principle of non-contradiction to specific issues. The enterprise upon which a Heraclitus or a Hegel might be engaged is not (by their localised challenges to the principle of non-contradiction) automatically rendered unintelligible even to those who uphold the universality of the principle.[16] Taken to extremes (as they often are), arguments of *reductio ad absurdum* can all too easily backfire.

Lukasiewicz identifies in Aristotle a sympathy for the idea that, in the light of the changeability of the observable world, it may seem that an object has two contradictory attributes at the same time. The confusion thus generated may well reflect not just sloppy thinking but a fundamental problem rooted in the potential existence of attributes which are not presently manifested. In the course of his argument at this point in the *Metaphysics* Aristotle concedes something important. He is attacking the Protagoreans and Heracliteans, and their adherence to the observation of the world of appearances being in a state of flux or change, and being the most real world. Aristotle concedes that on this issue it is a matter of degree which is at question:

> The sensible world immediately around us is indeed subject to generation and decay; but this is a practically negligible part of the whole, and it would have been more reasonable to deny all change in the universe on the grounds that the greater part is unchanging, than to posit a state of universal flux because a mere fraction of the whole is subject to change. ... We must try to convince our opponents ... that there is an unchanging reality.[17]

Aristotle is aware that he has a problem understanding change.[18] To put it crudely, how can he deal properly with the present (much of which will continue while change occurs) and at the same time deal properly with the potential (some of which will undoubtedly be present in the future)?

Where change is seen as necessary – as it is in the context of social policy-making – this problem assumes much greater proportions than it has when the aim is simply to account for the observed world, and the tension is perhaps all the greater between the two basic positions. On the one hand there is the pressure to be a 'maverick', pushing for change at all costs, or seeing change as inevitable; on the other hand there is the concern of the 'feet-draggers' with the stability and preservation of the institutional framework. Aristotle, on this analogy, is a foot-dragger, and some of his frustration with the maverick Heracliteans can be heard in the frustration of Strathclyde's alleged foot-draggers when they describe the behaviour of the Regional Council's mavericks.

THE JUDAEO-CHRISTIAN TRADITION

As we have seen, Councillor Shaw's concern for deprived people flowed directly from Christian belief and significantly influenced the form of Strathclyde's emerging deprivation policy. For this reason we need to establish a basis for identifying religious language in Strathclyde texts. The search is also on for Kantians and Hegelians, however, and we will contend later in this chapter that Hegel can usefully be approached against a background of Christian theology. For both these reasons, then, we need to introduce the Judaeo-Christian tradition.

There is a more fundamental reason, however, for looking at an overtly religious tradition. The book is concerned with public debate or discourse in the widest sense, and therefore with the problems raised by the coexistence of dogmatism and tolerance, pluralism and evangelism. These issues recur when dealing with the Positivist Dispute and when dealing with Strathclyde texts. If we are to deal properly with the language or rhetoric of these texts, we need to be familiar with the language and vocabulary of religious thought and with the issues which traditionally mark points of conflict between religious and anti-religious ideologies.

We can use the Solomon narrative as an introduction. Solomon, as king, was a political and economic leader, and a central figure in the Israelite cult. As a charismatic leader he embodied justice for his people. There is thus a link between the Judaeo-Christian conceptions of wisdom and of political life, in which political life does not merely call for technical ability (what we might call 'management') but also demands what we would call 'ethical' judgment. The incident of the child claimed by two women illustrates personal judgment within the framework of the Law *(Torah)*. In the central account of Solomon's early reign he oversees the building of the temple, in the process establishing trading links and political alliance with a neighbouring power. On the completion of the temple he takes a leading role in worship. Yet, within the narrative, the most concise account of his wisdom is as follows:

> God gave Solomon wisdom and very great insight, and a breadth of understanding as measureless as the sand on the seashore. Solomon's wisdom was greater than the wisdom of all the men of the East, and greater than all the wisdom of Egypt. He was wiser than any other man, including Ethan the Ezrahite – wiser than Heman, Calcol and Darda, the sons of Mahol. And his fame spread to all the surrounding nations. He spoke three thousand proverbs and his songs numbered a thousand and five. He described plant life, from the cedar of Lebanon to the hyssop that grows out of walls. He also taught about animals and birds, reptiles and fish. Men of all nations came to listen to Solomon's wisdom.[19]

This demonstrates an identity of enterprise between Israelite tradition and wisdom-seeking outside the cult of Yahweh. It also shows that 'breadth of understanding' is central to wisdom. These aspects of the tradition belong together and are most naturally understood in the light of what we might call a broad ontology. We would find such an ontology in the Judaeo-Christian tradition by looking at the first two chapters of Genesis and noting the range of objects considered there as fully real. There is a convergence, or at least a parallelism, with the ontological breadth of the Aristotelian tradition. For both Aristotle and Solomon an almost naïve curiosity could be understood as both a search for and an expression of wisdom.

Alexandria to Cordova

An important contention later in this chapter is that the Enlightenment breaks an earlier consensus of theological and philosophical openness, what we describe as the consensus of a broad ontology. To indicate this consensus it is not sufficient to show a broad ontology in the classical tradition and a parallel breadth in the Judaeo-Christian tradition; we need to show these traditions meeting, and together meeting with Islam.

Alexandria is where Jewish Religion meets Greek Philosophy. Many diaspora Jews sought, in a Hellenised world, to make an accommodation to Greek thought, and Alexandria became the centre for this activity. Around 250 BC the translation of the Jewish scriptures into Greek began. While this was undertaken primarily for the sake of Jewish believers who had lost Hebrew, it also introduced Jewish beliefs to the Greeks.

We can look briefly at Philo, a Jewish scholar of the time of Christ. His work was in the form of commentary on Jewish scriptures, and in his commentaries he developed a synthesis between Greek thought, primarily Platonic, and Jewish belief. Thus, on Genesis:

> It consists of an account of the creation of the world, implying that the world is in harmony with the Law, and the Law with the world, and that the man who observes the law is constituted thereby a loyal citizen of the world, regulating his doings by the purpose and will of Nature, in accordance with which the entire world itself is administered.[20]

Philo upholds his belief in one God, the creator of the world, who has revealed his will to man in the Law *(Torah)*. Nevertheless, the passage might almost be taken as a statement of the classical conception of citizenship. It envisages the study of the observable world with a view to absorbing the orderliness of nature and becoming a good citizen living in harmony with the physical world and with other citizens. It underlines the broad ontological congeniality outlined above in comparing Aristotle and Solomon. In common with the classical and the Solomonic traditions the range of studies in Alexandria was broad, including geography, astronomy, medicine, mathematics, grammar and rhetoric. The openness of the tradition is perhaps best seen in relation to Philo's conception of human freedom. It is rooted in God's creation of humanity as, above all, rational. There is a clear connection between moral choice on the one hand, and the explorations of empirical research on the other:

> The special prerogative which man has received is mind, habituated to apprehend the natures both of all material objects and of things in general ...
>
> For God had made man free and unfettered, to employ his powers of action with voluntary and deliberate choice for this purpose, that, knowing good and ill and receiving the conception of the noble and the base, and setting himself in sincerity to apprehend just and unjust and in general what belongs to virtue and what to vice, he might practise to choose the better and eschew the opposite.[21]

The phrase 'of all material objects and of things in general' summarises the broad ontological attitude.

The Alexandrian tradition continues into the Christian era, surviving the Islamic conquest of North Africa (Alexandria capitulated in AD 641) and eventually merging with Islamic scholarship in Baghdad at around 900. The openness of the tradition continues in the Translation Movement in Baghdad, with its emphasis on the translation and criticism of Aristotle. This tradition is continued by the Islamic scholars of Cordova, in Umayyad Spain, right into the twelfth century. Ibn Roshd (Averroes) was 'the Commentator' who, in thirteenth century Paris, was quoted by Aquinas in the *Summa Theologiae*. In Renaissance Italy, Islamic scholarship provided many of the early sources for classical texts which had otherwise been lost. In the sixteenth century, Scottish medical students used Islamic texts. It is tragic that the openness and pluralism of these traditions should have been denied by Western historiography (Christian and secular together) and have been sunk in easy caricatures of 'Scholasticism'. It is important to note, however, the tension between philosophy (or *falsafah*) and theology (or *kalaam*) in both Christian and Islamic traditions, and the redactions consequent upon this tension.

Seen as a whole, the history of ideas from Greece and Israel via Alexandria and Cordova is astonishingly open, however marred by outbreaks of violence from a wide range of cultural roots. The Enlightenment, and more recent empiricist (particularly Humean) traditions rooted in the Enlightenment, are responsible for a tragic narrowing of vision. The truth is that there was considerably more light – in the form of open, pluralist, rational scholarship – *before* the Enlightenment than the Enlightenment tradition has allowed.

THE ENLIGHTENMENT

If Strathclyde's problem of non-learning is caused by dogmatism, then it is the Enlightenment which introduces the problem most starkly. Equally importantly, however, the Enlightenment has the same significance for the Positivist Dispute as does Classical thought. It provides a series of views against which both Popper and Habermas define their own positions; this is just as Dahrendorf has indicated, as we saw in chapter one.

The pre-Enlightenment consensus of a broad ontology was not an ideological uniformity, then, and this is often adduced in the Enlightenment as evidence of intellectual darkness and the need for light. Yet the more variation one identifies the harder it becomes to identify the beginning of the Enlightenment. We will start with Hume, when the loss of the consensus is apparent; a respect for Aristotelian logic persists, but respect for metaphysics is replaced by a direct and dogmatic attack upon it.

In the *Enquiries* we encounter the Enlightenment belief that through the exercise of rigorous reason, turning aside from the 'easy philosophy', centuries of human groping in the darkness can be dispelled. Practitioners of the 'easy philosophy' are described in the opening of the *Enquiries* as:

> alluring us into the paths of virtue by the views of glory and happiness, ... They make us feel the difference between vice and virtue; they excite and regulate our sentiments.[22]

Followers of the contrasting practice, the philosophy which Hume aims to establish as legitimate,

> endeavour to form [man's] understanding more than cultivate his manners. They regard human nature as a subject of speculation; and with a narrow scrutiny examine it, in order to find those principles, which regulate our understanding, excite our sentiments, and make us approve or blame any particular object, action, or behaviour. They think it a reproach to all literature that philosophy should not yet

have fixed, beyond controversy, the foundation of morals, reasoning and criticism.[23]

The historical comment of that last quotation, 'a reproach ... that philosophy should not yet have ...' develops by the end of the section into an optimistic call:

> we have, in the following enquiry, attempted to throw some light upon subjects, from which uncertainty has hitherto deterred the wise, and obscurity the ignorant. Happy, if we can unite the boundaries of the different species of philosophy, by reconciling profound enquiry with clearness, and truth with novelty! And still more happy, if, reasoning in this easy manner, we can undermine the foundations of an abstruse philosophy, which seems to have hitherto served only as a shelter to superstition and a cover to absurdity and error.[24]

Against this background the well-known conclusion to the *Enquiry on Human Understanding*[25] can be seen to direct the attack as explicitly as Hume dared against theology's 'sophistry and illusion'. This is just as much a break with tradition as with faith. Two observations are apposite here: firstly, that Hume is stating a principle which has become the guiding principle of empiricism. It is substantially the same assertion as that made by Ayer in *Language, Truth and Logic*:

> The traditional disputes of philosophers are, for the most part, as unwarranted as they are unfruitful. The surest way to end them is to establish beyond question what should be the purpose and method of a philosophical enquiry ...
>
> We shall maintain that no statement which refers to a 'reality' transcending the limits of all possible sense-experience can possibly have any literal significance; from which it must follow that the labours of those who have striven to describe such a reality have all been devoted to the production of nonsense.[26]

The latter paragraph is parallel to Hume's 'sophistry and illusion' passage. Secondly, however, and far more significantly, in attacking tradition Hume and Ayer are concerned not simply to overthrow past confusion and ignorance, but to outlaw disagreement on substantial philosophical issues. Thus the 'reproach' is that philosophy has not so far 'fixed, beyond controversy, the foundation of morals, reasoning, and criticism' (Hume); or the aim is to establish 'beyond question, what should be the purpose and method of a philosophical enquiry' (Ayer).

This is a strangely abiding feature of Enlightenment thought, and it requires us to think carefully about the constraints on open debate of various traditions. One of the enduring features of the pre-Enlightenment consensus was the tension between philosophy and theology, *falsafah* and *kalaam*, or between open enquiry and the tradition itself (Aristotelian or Judaeo-Christian). The Enlightenment clearly found this capacity for containing sharp controversy on fundamentals within a broad agenda to be something undesirable. The empiricist tradition in particular has attempted to reproduce within the constitution of the enterprise of reason itself the constraints on scholarship which before the Enlightenment came from the institutional or political context within which scholars worked. To some degree this puzzle of the Enlightenment's embarrassment over controversy is explained by its desire to perform a grand-scale *reductio ad absurdum* against the Judaeo-Christian tradition in particular. But it goes much further than this.

It is not simply that metaphysics is proscribed, there is the beginning of a consistent attempt to drive a sharp wedge between 'emotion' and 'reason'. In the passages quoted above from Hume, for example, the 'easy' philosophers make us 'feel' vice and virtue, or they 'excite our sentiments', while the genuine philosopher tries to form 'understanding' rather than to 'cultivate manners'. To present these two as necessarily opposed separates Hume from the classical as much as from the Judaeo-Christian tradition.

What we have, at least, is the root of the widely held scepticism of popular culture, 'If I can't see it, I won't believe it'. However much it logically rebounds on itself, this view is central to popular culture and to professional culture. That the proposition functions in popular culture as an obstacle to theoretical criticism or ethical thought is inseparable from the empiricist enterprise. Social function here exactly mirrors the logical content and explicit motive of empiricist philosophy.

Kant

Kant and Hegel have become flag-bearers for traditions which seem at the moment to be widely divergent. Yet they shared attitudes towards tradition which are as significant for understanding their work as the attitude, which they both also shared, that a new era had dawned, consigning much of the earlier march of reason to the museum. We will attempt to relate both of them to earlier and broader traditions of rationality.

We can relate Kant to earlier traditions by using his own brief remarks at the end of the *Critique of Pure Reason*. The issue is the source of human knowledge:

In respect of the origin of the modes of 'knowledge through pure reason', the question is as to whether they are derived from experience, or whether in independence of experience they have their origin in reason. Aristotle may be regarded as the chief of the empiricists, and Plato as the chief of the noologists. [Noologists are those who refer the origin of ideas to the mind alone, independent of experience.] Locke, who in modern times followed Aristotle, and Leibniz, who followed Plato ... have not been able to bring this conflict to any definitive conclusion.[27]

The 'definitive conclusion' mentioned here is what Kant hoped to supply. In this he was motivated by the same desire to settle matters once and for all which we noted above in Hume and Ayer. It would be easy, in this context, to present Kant as having resolved the problem in the Humean manner, by simply caricaturing metaphysics; certainly it is easy to present Kant as more of an Aristotelian than a Platonist. In the preface to the *Critique of Pure Reason*, for example, is evidence of Kant's impatience with controversy linked with the most unqualified approval of analytic logic: 'since Aristotle it has not required to retrace a single step.'[28]

In fact Kant took Leibniz seriously. Nothing shows this more clearly than the central question of the *Critique of Pure Reason*: 'How is a priori synthetic knowledge possible?' Hume's philosophy denied that any a priori knowledge could possibly exist which was truly synthetic (that is, which could say anything about the world 'out there', which could have reference beyond itself).

Kant's solution was a set of categories which were innate, but which could only be fulfilled in experience. Without the categories, experience would be a disordered jumble; without experience, the categories could provide no knowledge of the external world. In this Kant set out with the assumption that the world was fundamentally stable, and that the Aristotelian principle of non-contradiction was axiomatic:

> The Highest Principle of All Analytic Judgments, the universal, though merely negative, condition of all our judgments ... is that they be not self-contradictory; for if self-contradictory, these judgments are in themselves, even without reference to the object, null and void.[29]

He does not defend this, he merely assumes it and its self-evidence (following Aristotle). Significantly, however, Kant held consistently to the view that this was an analytic principle; it could give no 'positive information'.[30] In particular, Kant opposed the modification of the principle of non-contradiction to include statements about time:

> Although this famous principle is thus without content and merely
> formal, it has sometimes been carelessly formulated in a manner
> which involves the quite unnecessary admixture of a synthetic ele-
> ment. The formula runs: It is impossible that something should at one
> and the same time both be and not be.[31]

This formulation gives an apparent limitation to the principle, but in
fact merely confuses the issue by trying to say something positive (synthetic) about two different points in time. Nevertheless, Kant himself
put forward a superficially similar proposition: 'Only in time can two
contradictorily opposed predicates meet in one and the same object,
namely, one after the other.'[32] The point is that, within Kant's system,
change in the world is problematic. Kant allows that contradiction may
occur in reality, and this has to render problematic the way we speak
about contradictory realities. A synthetic proposition which says something true about a contradictory reality is always going to be capable of characterisation as an analytic statement which contravenes the
principle of non-contradiction.

For Kant this was not a problem; he thought that mathematics or
physical science would occasionally throw up contradictory propositions, and that therefore he should concede the possibility of contradictions in reality. His system never seriously explores the problems such
contradictions might generate. This sheds some light on Popper's essay,
'What is Dialectic?'. Popper's formulation of the principle of non-
contradiction is very like that which Kant condemns. This allows us to
introduce Hegel. For him the problem of contradiction was more acute
given his interest in the historical development of thought; change was
a central concern.

Hegel

There are two fundamental obstacles to the appropriation in Britain of
Hegelian thought. Both are unnecessary. Firstly, there is the tendency
to approach Hegel solely via Marx. This generates a string of misconcep-
tions. Hegel's thought is markedly divergent from Marx's on the subject
of religion. Hegel's Christian belief, and its place in his thought, is still
under-examined. This separates attempts to comprehend Hegel from a
vocabulary or tradition which is still, in Britain, relatively well understood, that is, Christian theology. Arguably, Hegel's thought evolves
against a background of Christian theology (or of Hegel's dispute with
it).

Secondly, there are obstacles arising from the incomplete nature of English translations of Hegelian work. Much scholarship which interacts with Hegelian thought has created a Germanic English style, with compound words constructed from what is really a rather limited English vocabulary. There is little attempt to use English idioms to express ideas which were first articulated in German. This pseudo-Germanic cage in which Hegelian thought has been trapped is a tragic and often farcical construction.

The analysis in the rest of the book attempts to demonstrate a broadly Hegelian character in the policy adopted by Strathclyde Regional Council towards deprived areas, or in the attitudes of individuals who were involved in policy development. For such a thesis to stand, it is essential that the possibility be established of Hegelian ideas finding expression in relatively colloquial English.

We can approach Hegel via Judaeo-Christian thought. To pick up the Solomonic wisdom discussed in the early part of this chapter, Solomon's breadth of interest is a natural reflection of the breadth of the Creation stories in Genesis. These assert the goodness of creation, and open up a whole world for exploration. In them, humanity is presented as created in the image of God and out of the dust of the earth, a living soul in the same sense that the animals are living souls. Humanity is given the responsibility of agency on behalf of God.

One of the first tasks for human agency is a cognitive task, recognising and naming the diversity of created things. This account of human agency, rational and creative in response to divine rationality and creativity, yet under the authority of the creator, is followed by the account of the temptation and fall.

The fall is presented as an act of rebellion, a denial of the authority of God. This attitude is not merely intellectual, but results immediately in broken human relationships which reflect the broken relationship between God and man. Male–female relationships are characterised by oppression, and violence takes a prominent place, culminating in the story of the Flood: 'Now the earth was corrupt in God's sight, and full of violence ... So God said to Noah, "I am going to put an end to all people, for the earth is filled with violence because of them."'[33] Violence and oppression result from the perversion of the creation role of humanity. Gracious rule becomes oppressive and exploitive; friendship with a personal God (who, in the narrative, feels distress) turns to enmity which, given the transcendence of God, can best express itself in attacks on God's more tangible image-bearer.

This produces a fundamental ambiguity in the Christian tradition. The world and humanity within it is intrinsically good, because created by a good God. Nevertheless, the tragedy of the fall affects creation comprehensively; it becomes true of man that 'every inclination of the thoughts of his heart was only evil all the time'.[34] This emphatic comprehensiveness (every, only, all) still does not preclude the narrative speaking of humanity as in the image of God: 'Whoever sheds the blood of man, by man shall his blood be shed, for in the image of God has God made man.'[35]

Similarly, redemption is achieved once and for all time by Christ's death. Yet it is also to be worked out in temporal existence by the increasing conformity of the redeemed community to God's will, and it is only to be achieved at the future consummation of human history when the risen Christ returns and humanity is judged in his presence. The kingdom of God is both present and future. At the moment, it both is and is not. Correspondingly, humanity is at present accurately understood as *not* being something which it was, and will be, and ought to be. Humanity is still inhuman (which raises difficulties for those Christians dedicated to the principle of non-contradiction). This gives genuinely Christian thought an unavoidably dialectical character.

We can now turn to Hegel, using the *Lectures on the Philosophy of World History*. The first thing to establish is that Hegel is considering human history, and a particular concept of humanity underlies his enterprise. This is the traditional conception of humanity as rational: 'man is a thinking being, and it is this which distinguishes him from the animals. All that is truly human, as distinct from animal – feeling, knowledge, and cognition – contains an element of thought.'[36] Hegel identifies the basic categories 'under which the historical process generally presents itself to thought':

> The first category comes from our observation of the changing individuals, nations, and states which flourish for a while, capture our interest, and then disappear. This is the category of change.[37]

This puts Hegel firmly in the camp which Aristotle is attacking in his discussion of the principle of non-contradiction. It is a fundamentally contrasting viewpoint to that expressed in Aristotle's comment that 'We must try to convince our opponents ... that there is an unchanging reality.' The second fundamental category is rejuvenation. Change is largely the result of the destruction of earlier human achievements. Hegel argues that, tragic as this destruction is, it often leads to a new phase of growth:

> The negative aspect of the idea of change moves us to sadness. It oppresses us to think that the richest forms and the finest manifesta-

tions of life must perish in history, and that we walk amidst the ruins of excellence ... But the category of change has another, positive side to it. For out of death, new life arises.[38]

There is a basic understandability here, and, however such ideas have been abused, there is an agreement with unsophisticated human experience, even 'common sense', which belies the verbalism of much Hegel scholarship. Local government officers and members in Strathclyde are not Hegel scholars, but their language and culture is not, on this reading of Hegel, incapable of containing an appreciation of Hegel's concerns. Hegel's third category is reason. It is in introducing this that Hegel brings into the picture what is perhaps the central element in his system, the commitment to seeing the process of change, decay and rejuvenation, as a single story:

the immediate result of these intriguing speculations is that we grow weary of particulars and ask ourselves to what end they all contribute. We cannot accept that their significance is exhausted in their own particular ends; everything must be part of a single enterprise. Surely some ultimate end must be promoted by this enormous expenditure of spiritual resources ... We feel the need to find a justification in the realm of ideas for all this destruction. This reflection leads us to the third category, to the question of whether there is such a thing as an ultimate end in and for itself. This is the category of reason proper; it is present to our consciousness as a belief that the world is governed by reason.[39]

This is a common human reaction; when confronted with destruction in history we say, 'it just doesn't make sense' and we ask 'why?'. Hegel himself connects this question ('whether there is such a thing as an ultimate end in and for itself') with the Christian doctrine of providence, in which he professes a personal belief:

For divine providence is wisdom, coupled with infinite power, which realises its ends, i.e. the absolute and rational design of the world; and reason is freely self-determining thought, or what the Greeks called '*nous*'.[40]

He presents his view of world history as an exercise in theodicy, the problem of upholding the goodness of God in an evil world:

From this point of view, our investigation can be seen as a theodicy, a justification of the ways of God ... It should enable us to comprehend all the ills of the world, including the existence of evil, so that the thinking spirit may be reconciled with the negative aspects of existence; and it is in world history that we encounter the sum total of concrete evil.[41]

It is in this context that we must see Hegel's conviction that 'the sole aim of philosophical enquiry is to eliminate the contingent'. That is, it is philosophy's job to 'make sense' of the world's propensity for destruction or oppression. 'Making sense' here has to be understood in a way which preserves its naïve or non-professional connotation – it has to provide an answer to a sense of dismay which is immediate, not articulated in terms drawn from academic theory. It also has to be intellectually rigorous. In some ways this sort of 'making sense' is not unlike a government's task of policy-making; a policy must satisfy the requirements of statute and polity, and it must survive scrutiny by political opponents within and without the party; it must also command the consent of a non-professional public.

In both contexts, the political and the philosophical, making sense of a problem implies both an intellectual resolution and a practical resolution, and this dual resolution is perhaps best contained in the word 'answer'. An answer is the right (propositionally correct, two and two make four) response to a problem; an answer is the right (practically effective) response to a problem.

That, at least, is a Hegelian view. At this point we can turn to consider the Positivist Dispute, introducing the thought of Popper and Habermas more directly.

5 The Positivist Dispute

This chapter has two main functions, and its two sections correspond to these functions. Firstly, it reviews the Positivist Dispute, introducing the 'critical theory' of the Frankfurt School on the one hand, and Popper's 'critical rationalism' on the other. The two sides in the dispute are both considered in relation to the problem of finding an appropriate method for the study of society, and we propose a way to resolve some of their differences. In the course of this discussion a third philosophy of knowledge – empiricism – is described and rejected. In this first section the chapter deals with philosophy simply as philosophy, and one important concern is to provide a sort of 'translation' between the different positions, particularly between critical theory and critical rationalism.

Secondly, the chapter characterises the three theories of knowledge for the purpose of identifying them in Strathclyde texts. This characterisation provides a basis for the exposition of those texts in subsequent chapters, and consequently the concern here is to clarify the distinctive vocabularies and emphases of each of the three philosophical positions. It is also important to translate between the language of professional philosophy and 'lay' or non-professional language.

The characterisations of critical theory, critical rationalism and empiricism which emerge, however, do not have a purely methodological function. Their philosophical importance is as great as the more overtly philosophical conclusions reached in the first section of the chapter, since they provide the bridge between these philosophies as academic theories on the one hand and as a practical polity on the other. If the ramifications of a particular philosophy for popular culture and practical politics are the most significant of its ramifications, then exploring the 'translatability' of philosophical language into ordinary language is of great importance. If a particular theory of knowledge becomes embedded in general culture such a translation *will* occur – whether it is a good translation or a poor one by academic standards – and the theory of knowledge cannot avoid being judged by the political behaviour which it generates. We do, however, distinguish between those practical ramifications of a particular philosophy which are more or less inevitable, and those which reflect its corruption.

THE FRANKFURT SCHOOL: THE CRITICAL THEORY OF SOCIETY

We can begin by looking at Horkheimer's essay, 'Traditional and Critical Theory'. Horkheimer outlines a 'way of knowing'. This is counterposed to 'traditional' empirical science, which works within a framework of 'an essential unchangeableness between subject, theory and object'.[1] Horkheimer's critical theory is dialectical:

> in genuinely critical thought explanation signifies not only a logical process but a concrete historical one as well. In the course of it both the social structure as a whole and the relation of the theoretician to society are altered, that is, both the subject and the role of thought are changed.[2]

There is an obvious connection with Marx here, which Horkheimer acknowledges. There is also an explicit dependence on German idealism, first on Kant's affirmation of the character of knowledge as a human production, which Horkheimer sees as paving the way for a 'protest' against 'the adoration of facts and the social conformism this brings with it'. More directly Horkheimer depends on Hegel, who saw 'the cunning of a reason that is nonetheless world-historical and objective', and whose eschatological view of human history is absorbed into critical theory.

This striving for a future goal is central to critical theory. There is a conviction that 'the free development of individuals depends on the rational organisation of society', and that true 'humanity' is in conflict with 'existent social practice', and there is a consequent recognition that, for critical theory, 'its goal is man's emancipation from slavery'.[3] The result is that a tension is generated within the critical thinker; he is part of an inhuman society, at the same time he is struggling with society – and himself – to produce a more humane world. This tension (or dialectic) is basic to the critical thinker's identity. Horkheimer's statement of this proves to be vital for the subsequent analysis of Strathclyde texts, so we give it here quite fully:

> The scholarly specialist 'as' scientist regards social reality and its

products as extrinsic to him, and 'as' citizen exercises his interest in them through political articles, membership in political parties or social service organisations, and participation in elections. But he does not unify these two activities, and his other activities as well, except, at best, by psychological interpretation. Critical thinking, on the contrary, is motivated today by the effort really to transcend the tension and to abolish the opposition between the individual's purposefulness, spontaneity and rationality, and those work-process relationships on which society is built. Critical thought has a concept of man as in conflict with himself until this opposition is removed. If activity governed by reason is proper to man, then existent social practice, which forms the individual's life down to its least details, is inhuman, and this inhumanity affects everything that goes on in the society.[4]

At issue is the real character of 'social reality'. Is it truly 'extrinsic' to the individual, or is the true nature of man such that to see him as an isolated social unit is to be under an illusion? The corollary to this is the view of the individual. The traditional thinker sees himself on the one hand 'as' scientist and on the other hand 'as' citizen, and the two aspects are separated. This separation corresponds to the separation of 'fact' (the domain of the scientist) from 'value' (the domain of the citizen). Habermas describes a similar condition when he speaks of a 'positivistically bisected rationalism'.[5]

We can go immediately to two key phrases from Adorno in the *Positivist Dispute*. Firstly, 'the experience of the blindly dominating totality and the driving desire that it should ultimately become something else'.[6] Adorno sees the great failure of positivism (meaning the same thing as Horkheimer's 'traditional science') to be in shutting itself off from this experience. To Horkheimer and Adorno, facticity, the idea of a fact as an objective thing extrinsic to the thinker or knower, is a vital part of the positivist's mechanism for shutting himself off from this experience. Arguably this experience is very like the widespread experience of ordinary people in a world where things seem to be wrong, crazy or unbearable. Secondly,

> positivism ... will only allow appearance to be valid, whilst dialectics will not allow itself to be robbed of the distinction between essence and appearance.[7]

Taken with the passage from Horkheimer, these phrases give a concise account of the Frankfurt School's conception of dialectical philosophy and critical social thinking. In their eyes, the two activities (philosophy and the critique of society) are identical. This philosophy is rooted in an ontology which is broad, and fundamentally collectivist. As with the Christian conception of humanity, the Frankfurt view of society sees it as something which both is one thing and ought to be another. This character of *ought-to-be-something-different* is central to a right description of what society presently *is*.

Unavoidably, then, critical theory has a religious character. Adorno objected to 'the scientistic habit of stigmatising dialectics as theology, which has crept in through the back door, with the difference between society's systematic nature and so-called total thought'.[8] We might well reply that to be labelled a 'theologian' is not necessarily to be 'stigmatised'. It is simply to practise secular dogmatic metaphysics rather than religious dogmatic metaphysics to see theology as intrinsically a worthless intellectual exercise.

But in fact it is not Adorno's concept of 'totality' which marks him out as religious so much as his insistence on an immanent critique. That is, he has a view that society will be transformed for the good as a result of a new consciousness arising amongst men and women, this consciousness being produced by an immanent 'conversion' experience which re-orients the whole life of the individual. It is the claim to have had that experience, and that the experience is the one necessary experience for human thought, which makes Adorno religious. The structure or 'shape' of critical theory is also markedly parallel to a remarkably orthodox Christian theology; there is a doctrine of judgment (criteria by which the world should be judged, and is being or will be judged) or of authority (the compelling force which must shape human life) and there is a doctrine of salvation (emancipated humanity). It may be theology without God, but it is certainly theology.

So we can move from the description of critical theory's aims to the view of factual analysis of society as avoiding this imperative confrontation with reality. In Adorno's memorable phrase, factual analysis 'slides off its [totality's] back without any impact'.[9] Similarly Habermas comments in *Legitimation Crisis* on Luhmann, an apologist for systems theory:

> The pattern of systems rationality is suited for empirically substantive theories about object domains in which unities that are clearly demarcated from their environment can be identified.[10]

That is, it is suited to analysis which slides off society's back, which leaves it unchanged. Already the Positivist Dispute shows parallels with arguments about deprivation policies; John Edwards and Joan Higgins comment (see chapter one) on the illusionary or diversionary character of statistical or quantitative assessments of deprivation. Their comments might reasonably be characterised as an accusation that such measures of deprivation are calculated to slide off society's back.

The Frankfurt School and the problem of method

The problem of method arises from two concerns, with communication and with right people. The concerns are two sides of the same coin; the true nature of human life will only be found when people think and act and, in particular, *debate* humanly. This is a problem we saw earlier with Plato, and which he articulates most directly in the *Seventh Letter*. He describes tools which can help lead to an apprehension of the truth, the tools being names, definitions, representations and knowledge:

> the soul is searching for knowledge of essential being, but what each of the four offers it, whether in words or in actual practice, is not what it is searching for, but something which, whether it is expressed in words or displayed in visible form, can be easily refuted by the evidence of the senses.[11]

The four tools are each by 'very nature defective', and in the last analysis all the educator can do is move from one to the other, hoping for the best, knowing that many people will never 'see'.

> It is only when all these things are rubbed together and subjected to tests in which questions and answers are exchanged in good faith and without malice that finally, when human capacity is stretched to its limit, a spark of understanding and intelligence flashes out and illuminates the subject at issue. That is why any serious student of serious realities will shrink from making truth the helpless object of men's ill-will by committing it to writing.[12]

This is very like the comment in Adorno and Horkheimer's *Dialectic of Enlightenment*:

> The dilemma that faced us in our work proved to be the first phenomenon for investigation: the self-destruction of the Enlightenment. We are wholly convinced – and therein lies our *petitio principii* – that social freedom is inseparable from enlightened thought. Nevertheless, we believe that we have just as clearly recognised that the notion of this very way of thinking ... already contains the seeds of the reversal universally apparent today.
> There is no longer any available form of linguistic expression which has not tended to accommodation to dominant currents of thought.[13]

If we are suspicious of 'object domains in which unities that are clearly demarcated from their environment can be identified', how do we ever manage to do empirical research? Without empirical research, critique unfortunately lacks bite, and policies remain as generalisations which cannot be implemented. Without empirically focused language, translation is almost impossible, either between ideologies, or from policy statement to practice.

Habermas offers a solution which follows the work of Claus Offe in suggesting that we look for indicators of the repression of debate. One of these indicators is the existence of 'rules of exclusion codified in a political system'.[14] This has a clear link with Horkheimer's essay:

> the critical activity of which we are speaking is wholly distrustful of the rules of conduct with which society as presently constituted provides each of its members. The separation between individual and society in virtue of which the individual accepts as natural the limits prescribed for his activity is relativised in critical theory.[15]

This does suggest a solution to part of the problem of method. But not a complete solution. In the appendix to *Knowledge and Human Interests (KHI)*, Habermas reaffirms his central thesis, and claims for it an identity with 'the concept of theory that has defined the tradition of great philosophy since its beginnings'. That concept of theory is of an attitude of mind that seeks to free itself from 'mere human interests' and that bases itself on Ideas. The knowledge which arises is 'the *only* knowledge that can truly orient action'.[16] He is explicit about the *a priori* character of his philosophy, which sees the world developing to a future state in which the Idea of autonomy and responsibility is fully realised and individuals are freed from oppressive constraints to a pure and undistorted social life:

> The human interest in autonomy and responsibility is not mere fancy, for it can be apprehended *a priori* ... Taken together, autonomy and responsibility constitute the only Idea that we possess *a priori* in the sense of the philosophical tradition.[17]

The key to this self-discovery is reflection on language:

> what raises us out of nature is the only thing whose nature we can know: language. Through its structure, autonomy and responsibility are posited for us. Our first sentence expresses unequivocally the intention of universal and unconstrained consensus.[18]

Habermas reaffirms the dialectical or evolutionary character of human history as a development towards unconstrained communication, and thus gives philosophy the central task of uncovering the various ways in which that development has been hindered:

> only when philosophy discovers in the dialectical course of history
> the traces of violence that deform repeated attempts at dialogue and
> recurrently close off the path to unconstrained communication does
> it further the progress whose suspension it otherwise legitimates:
> mankind's evolution towards autonomy and responsibility.[19]

All thought either helps or hinders this evolution, which is still posited
as an *a priori* Idea. It is in this light that Habermas' acceptance of Offe's
search for 'codified rules of exclusion' makes sense. Habermas concludes that the goal of philosophy is not to achieve a method for the
sciences which is purged of all 'knowledge constitutive interests', but to
achieve a method which favours the emancipatory cognitive interest and
which inhibits or criticises all other cognitive interests. So the last substantial attack in *KHI* is on 'the illusion of pure theory'. The real failure
of theory is that it failed to purge itself of a connection – which existed
even in the classical conception of theory – with repressive interests. The
interest was evident in the concern for stability in the Greek city state
and the attempt to protect this stability by locating the task of over-
coming societal contradictions (and the tension created by a contingent
natural environment) within the individual. Habermas thus accuses
classical philosophy of promoting an ontology which would serve this
purpose. If we remember Aristotle's comment that 'we must try to convince our opponents that there is an unchanging reality', then we can
perhaps see Habermas' point. But his closing sentences bring back the
problem of method. His case against the philosophy of knowledge de-
molishes the foundations of the whole tradition which has its roots in
classical thought and which sprouts afresh in Kant–Hegel–Marx. So:

> Philosophy remains true to its classic tradition by renouncing it. The
> insight that the truth of statements is linked in the last analysis to the
> intention of the good and true life can be preserved today only on the
> ruins of ontology.[20]

Habermas never resolves the question of ontology. He strives against
idealism, but realises that rigorous materialism leads almost inevitably
to a form of empiricism. In this light his comment on Apel's 'cognitive
anthropology' is revealing. One senses Habermas to be in an unguarded
moment of reflection, and that his comment really applies much more
widely. He says of Apel's work that,

> while it stresses the rejection of the idealistic premises of an abso-
> lutist transcendental philosophy, [it] dissembles the fact that prop-

ositions about the human species ... can only be grounded in a history of the species or of social evolution.[21]

What follows has to be taken as a comment on anthropology in general (anthropology as the broad philosophical and even theological enterprise which attempts to understand humanity):

> Anthropology faces the inevitable dilemma of either making empirical generalisations about behavioural characteristics and therefore being too 'weak', or making ontological propositions about human essence and therefore being too 'strong'.[22]

We could say 'dogmatic' instead of 'strong'. Habermas does not resolve this dilemma, nor does he seem to see it as providing a critique, by its very existence, of the central concerns of *KHI*. Habermas is quite open about the *a priori* character of his thought. He makes this explicit in discussing the Idea of autonomy and responsibility as a basis for the historical imperative. He is left with a metaphysical theory, and a dilemma; to be too 'strong', or too 'weak'? It is the dilemma of the wise preacher, who has an inward commitment to dogmatics, but who recognises in his audience the imperative of apologetics.

Habermas fails to radicalise totally his own critique of philosophy. To do so would leave him without any properly grounded concept of deliverance, face to face with a 'blindly dominating totality' which simply *is*, and which mocks (to personalise it) any attempt to speak of 'right'; not quite 'might is right', but certainly 'might is, and why should you think you can do anything about it?' This sort of rigorous existentialism seems unthinkable to him, but to reject it makes him a fully fledged metaphysician. As we have already indicated with regard to Adorno, that is a far from dishonourable position.

The question remains, then: is there any method for learning which can function effectively in a pluralist society, where dogmatism will abort discussion, which does not depend on rules which produce the 'systematic deformation of dialogue', and which allows participants to hold views on grounds which other participants may see more as 'faith' than as reason?

POPPER AND THE PROBLEM OF METHOD

The Hegel–Marx critique of Kant builds on what it sees as his greatest contribution, the establishing of all knowledge as a human product, reflecting human consciousness, not at all a 'thing in itself'. This rejects the Kantian divorce between things as they appear and things as they are in themselves. As Adorno comments, dialectic 'will not allow itself to be satisfied with appearances'. Popper, in contrast, accepts the Kantian distinction. In refusing to blur the distinction between subject and object, Popper allows knowledge to change without the subject changing. This neutral, non-transforming knowledge is, of course, exactly what Habermas wants to avoid. For Popper it opens up a no man's land between the internal consciousness of a living human being and an external world of things in themselves. Popper develops this 'no man's land' into his 'world 3', a world of propositions, hypotheses and theories with an existence independent of the individuals who formulate them. He comments:

> The laws of nature are our invention, they are animal-made and man-made, genetically *a priori* though not *a priori* valid. We try to impose them upon nature. Very often we fail, and perish with our mistaken conjectures. But sometimes we come near enough to the truth to survive with our conjectures. And on the human level, when descriptive and argumentative language is at our disposal, we can criticise our conjectures systematically. This is the method of science.[23]

This is the method of apologetics as distinguished from dogmatics. It recognises that to assert human responsibility in the all-society-encompassing way which Habermas does is to recognise the responsibility of the other person in the dialogue to make up his or her own mind. When society is the focus (object) of dialogue we must beware the oppressive potential of a conception of knowledge which lays on the knower an imperative to pursue transformation of the object with the same zeal as he or she is driven to pursue the transformation of the subject. It is this imperative which tempts Habermas to dogmatism, to be 'too strong'. To continue Popper's comment on Kant:

> When Kant said that our intellect imposes its laws upon nature he was right – except that he did not notice how often our intellect fails in the attempt: the regularities we try to impose are psychologically *a priori*, but there is not the slightest reason to assume that they are *a priori* valid, as Kant thought.[24]

The only 'reason' which could establish *a priori* validity would be an onto-logical assertion, itself ungroundable – an assertion of a fundamentally metaphysical character. What in Popper's view can be demonstrated is that the third world, of theories, has an independent existence such that we can interact with it and improve it:

> everything depends on the give and take between ourselves and our

work; upon the product which we contribute to the third world, and upon that constant feed-back that can be amplified by conscious self-criticism. The incredible thing about life, evolution, and mental growth, is just this method of give and take, this interaction between our actions and their results by which we constantly transcend ourselves, our talents, our gifts.[25]

Popper is referring here to what can be seen in looking back over the growth of human knowledge – the growth from Newton's physics to Einstein's is one of his favourite examples. Self-transcendence depends on imaginative criticism; we transcend ourselves

> by trying to think of circumstances beyond our experience; by criticising the universality, or the structural necessity of what may, to us, appear (or what philosophers may describe) as the 'given' or as 'habit'; by trying to find, construct, invent, new situations, that is, test situations, critical situations; and by trying to locate, detect and challenge our prejudices and habitual assumptions.[26]

We could say, by challenging 'reifications'. It is a matter of whether or not you can do better than you are already doing and know that you have done better. Theories differ in the degree to which they generate further observations, or have interesting consequences. They can be assessed in the light of these ramifications. These latter can be assessed in the light of an intersubjective ethics (either of a 'decisionistic' nature or the fruit of collective will formation). In fact, this assessment of the ramifications of theories is exactly the sort of exercise which Habermas carries out in *KHI* – philosophy as critique. In the last analysis, of several competing theories, none will be capable of being demonstrated as true in an apodictic sense, but one may still emerge as preferable to the others.

The business of deducing ramifications and subjecting them to the widest possible range of criticisms is what Popper is speaking of when he talks of imaginative criticism. It is a process which depends on language, the independent verbal character of knowledge, and on a wide variety of sources of criticism. It is thus a process which ought to thrive on the sort of pluralism by which critical theory is threatened (because, as prone to making statements which are 'too strong', it is itself a threat to a truly open and pluralist debate).

The problem is that while Popper may have moved us away from a philosophy which is apt to monopolise debate in a dogmatic fashion, he seems to have done it by giving us a philosophy which can only debate with a selected group of agnostics. We are freed from a philosophical dictatorship only to be subject to an oligarchy of the non-committal.

Agnosticism can be maintained as dogmatically as any metaphysically 'committed' philosophy, and the systematic deformation of discourse, which Habermas eventually recognises his own position as apt to produce, finally returns. The problem here is Popper's tendency to treat metaphysicians as neophyte scientists, which virtually amounts to: 'You are making sense so long as you don't mean what you intend to mean.'

If Popper could overcome this tendency he could perhaps happily debate with holders of metaphysical theories which are committed to certain things being true, even if those 'things' are not empirically falsifiable. The question becomes: 'are there grounds for debate between holders of different metaphysical theories?'

Popper tackles this in an essay in *Conjectures and Refutations*, 'The Problem of the Irrefutability of Philosophical Theories' (the word 'philosophical' here amounts to 'metaphysical').[27] But the seed of a solution is evident in the comment on self-transcendence noted above, where Popper notes that we must try to 'think of circumstances beyond our experience'. What we need is a recognition of common elements of human experience, and that these can act as a common ground for theories which, while they 'go beyond' the consensus of what constitutes human experience, yet remain in touch with experience. Experience (which includes more than physical sensation and the ability to number, extending to emotional experience, for example, of joy or distress) provides a ground for translation between metaphysical theories.

This goes beyond Popper, however. In the essay referred to he faces the question of whether or not there can be grounds for disagreeing with a theory even if it cannot be refuted. His solution is actually very straightforward:

> every *rational* theory, no matter whether scientific or philosophical, is rational in so far as it tries to *solve certain problems*. A theory is comprehensible and reasonable in its relation to a given *problem-situation*, and it can be rationally discussed only by discussing this relation.[28]

Although it extends Popper's thought to say that the experience of distress in the face of a contingent world is a coherent 'problem-situation', his thought does logically bear this extension, from which it is arguably only a translation to the Frankfurt problem of a 'blindly dominating totality'. It is simply to draw human experience, the subjective world, explicitly into the 'nature' upon which Popper, following Kant, speaks of our intellect trying to impose laws (or simply, an *understanding*).

This avoids saying, 'You are only making sense if you don't mean what you intend to mean.' It amounts to: 'You are making sense when you can express your views in terms which I use myself, and I make sense when I express my views in terms which you use.' It lays down principles for all who would participate in debate, and only because these would, if disregarded, ensure the end of the debate. It amounts to an agreement not to be dogmatic in debate, but allows for dogmatics, or 'preaching' as an adjunct to debate. It is an attempt to persuade preachers to give a place to apologetics. It is not a codification of rules of exclusion.

In practice the central principles concern translation. Translation is a facilitator of debate, exploring the common basis in experience of different vocabularies and categories. This is what we have tried to do in this chapter. The method is simply exposition and criticism, in the medium of language and in the light of tradition, of substantive theories. It is a method of critique which seeks to avoid solipsism and unnecessary neologism. It tries to talk the same language as those whose work it criticises. By a rather long route, then, we arrive back at traditional standards of debate. We are left with the old tools, the deduction of consequences from propositions, the search for integrity in theoretical structures, and so on. We are also left with a long textual tradition which can provide a shared vocabulary and iconography. These tools are to be used in a process of imaginative criticism.

As an illustration, we can find common ground between Popper and the Frankfurt School, identifying them as sharing an empirically identifiable problem, namely the distortion of discourse by forceful means. At the end of the *Positivist Dispute* Popper says this:

> Man has achieved the possibility of being critical of his own tentative trials, of his own theories. These theories are no longer incorporated in his organism, or in his genetic system; they may be formulated in books, or in journals; and they can be critically discussed, and shown to be erroneous, without killing any authors or burning any books; without destroying the 'carriers'. In this way we arrive at a fundamentally new possibility; our trials, our tentative hypotheses, may be critically eliminated by rational discussion, without eliminating ourselves. This indeed is the purpose of rational critical discussion ... if the method of rational critical discussion should establish itself, then this should make the use of violence obsolete; critical reason is the only alternative to violence so far discovered. It seems clear to me that it is the obvious duty of all intellectuals to work for *this* revolution.[29]

This can be compared with a brief passage, which we have already considered, from the appendix to *KHI*:

Only when philosophy discovers in the dialectical course of history the traces of violence that deform repeated attempts at dialogue and recurrently close off the path to unconstrained communication does it further the process whose suspension it otherwise legitimates: mankind's evolution towards autonomy and responsibility.[30]

Both passages contain metaphysical theories, both assert that mankind should progress towards unconstrained communication or an open society (to translate). Both clearly identify violence as an evil. There is little difference between Popper's 'possibility' and Habermas' 'evolution', or between Habermas' 'autonomy and responsibility' and Popper's 'rational critical discussion'. Both identify the same brutally empirical problem, and the onus is laid, by each, on the same empirically identifiable group ('all intellectuals' and 'philosophy', taking the latter as those who actually practise it) to practise/live/work for the solution of that problem. The two passages genuinely translate one another. This convergence between Popper and Habermas is even more apparent, however, in their strikingly similar method of exposition and critical review of key texts in the European tradition from classical times onward. This latter evidence is so strong that it is easy to miss it.

So, if Popper's position is chosen as a method for social analysis it can only be justified as a better 'faith', as slightly less dogmatic. Indeed, the form of Popper's critical rationalism which is chosen is a Frankfurt form, chosen in recognition of the validity of Habermas' characterisation of the dilemma (too strong or too weak). It also recognises the importance of Habermas' concern to identify the empirical indicators of repressed debate. Rather than talking of 'Popper's position', then, we can characterise the position as Socratic. It is a faith, above all, in human rationality as having a non-dogmatic character:

> Socratic intellectualism is decidedly equalitarian. Socrates believed that everyone can be taught ... And his intellectualism is also anti-authoritarian. A technique, for instance rhetoric, may perhaps be dogmatically taught by an expert ... but real knowledge, wisdom, and also virtue, can be taught only by a method which he describes as a form of midwifery. Those eager to learn may be helped to free themselves from their prejudice; thus they may learn self-criticism, and that truth is not easily attained. ... The true teacher can prove himself only by exhibiting that self-criticism which the uneducated lacks. 'Whatever authority I may have rests solely upon my knowing how little I know.' ... How did Plato convert this doctrine? At first sight it might appear that he did not alter it at all, when demanding that the sovereignty of the state should be invested in the philosophers;

especially since, like Socrates, he identified philosophers as lovers of wisdom. But the change made by Plato is indeed tremendous. His lover is no longer the modest seeker, he is the proud possessor of truth. A trained dialectician, he is capable of intellectual intuition, i.e. of seeing and of communicating with the eternal, the heavenly forms or ideas. Placed high above ordinary men ... Plato's ideal philosopher approaches both to omniscience and to omnipotence ... It is hard, I think, to conceive a greater contrast than that between the Socratic and the Platonic ideal of a philosopher.[31]

It is the dialectical 'gadfly' of the *Apology* which Popper has in mind here, rather than the master of dialectic from the *Republic*.

At this point we can draw some tentative conclusions on the ontological issues which underlie the chapter. At the end of the day the subject/object distinction is both upheld and rejected. That is, it is held to allow of movement in only one direction across the divide, but it is held to require that movement. The object must be able to modify the subject (I must be open to change my understanding) but the object must be allowed to resist modification (I can't force you to change to accommodate my insights). We are back with something embarrassingly like traditional liberalism.

With this conception of the subject/object relationship comes an apparent separation of questions of 'fact' from questions of 'value', of empirical questions from metaphysical. These distinctions are not upheld on the basis of any reified 'rules of logic'; they are upheld as a reasonable solution to the practical problem of finding a method for social analysis. 'Practical' here has both senses together ('ethical' and 'technical', rather as Solomon's solution to the problem of the two mothers is both ethical and technical). This basis is at root metaphysical, but its roots are in a metaphysics which is committed to human reason as necessarily non-dogmatic and yet non-relativistic. Any claim to absolute knowledge, or to its possibility, can only be made on grounds which are metaphysical. It can also only be denied on metaphysical grounds. If such knowledge ever appears, of course, it might well prove to be intrinsically persuasive and unconcerned to be recognised as 'absolute'. We live in hope.

A consequence of such a theory of communicative behaviour would be to make empiricism a difficult position to hold (although attempts to argue for it would be welcome). It is an issue over which Popper and Habermas have expended a great deal of effort.

Excursus: arguments against empiricism

The first argument against empiricism is its dogmatism. This is immediately apparent in the example of logical positivism, arguably the most coherent and philosophically articulate empiricism. If we take the basic tenet that 'all propositions which are not empirically verifiable, and not tautologous, are meaningless' and the well-known observation that this tenet itself is a proposition which is neither empirically verifiable nor tautologous, then it is clear that the basic tenet is held on grounds which are, to its holders, not defensible by reason alone; that is, it is held on grounds of *a priori*, metaphysical 'faith'. Thus far, of course, it is like Popper's system. It is unlike his, however, in its denial of meaning to other metaphysical systems. The basic tenet is one which must lead to dogmatism. It must make statements which are 'too strong'.

Empiricism can, however, be criticised on other grounds, and two quite different ones can be demonstrated. The first is from Popper; his 'experiment' (a corroboration seeking experiment!) on observation is a useful vehicle. It is in the course of a lecture:

> My experiment consists of asking you to observe, here and now. I hope you are all cooperating, and observing! However, I fear that at least some of you, instead of observing, will feel a strong urge to ask: 'WHAT do you want me to observe?' If this was your response, then my experiment was successful. For what I am trying to illustrate is that, in order to observe, we must have in mind a definite question which we might be able to decide by observation.[32]

Popper is here identifying theories as the motive for our observations. The empiricist's idea of observations as primary is refuted by the discernible fact that observations are always preceded by a structure of interests or expectations. To use Habermas' terms, observation is always oriented by a knowledge-constitutive interest.

A second ground on which to refute empiricism is Hegel's refutation of sense-certainty. Hegel was aware of the aims of empiricists to get a 'pure' starting point for knowledge building. He shared the same aim: 'Our approach to the object must be immediate [in the sense of 'without any distorting medium'] or receptive; we must alter nothing in the object as it presents itself.'[33]

Hegel's main reason for rejecting sense-certainty was just this fact of its uselessness for any method without a medium. The *This* of immediate perception is an attempt to abstract radically the object from all reference systems (which could be called theories) – hence the avoidance of phrases like 'this red ...' etc., where language, or its terms, presupposes universal ideas (like 'redness' or whatever). But the *This* ends up being as universal a term as any possible; every place is *this* place to the person who is actually observing it, every thing is *this* thing.

As soon as the individual observer tries to build his generalisation, relying even only on his own record of observations (memory or notes), he uses language, and language presupposes universals. The proposer of sense-certainty finds that his basic observations are, in the pre-theoretic stage, cast in or mediated by terms which presuppose generalisations.

Empiricism thus collapses in on itself given only its own premisses, as did the metaphysically dogmatic form of critical theory (which was dependent on ontology yet which could be maintained only on the ruins of ontology).

IDENTIFYING THE THREE PHILOSOPHIES

To return to the main argument, then, three different philosophical positions emerge: Popper's critical rationalism, the critical theory of the Frankfurt School, and a naïve empiricism. A similarity also emerges between the direct and immediate character claimed by both empiricism and critical theory for the most fundamental observations which can be made and which should be determinative for all secondary statements. Put differently, both say something about the nature of authentically rational and human experience at a foundational cognitive level, and want their own 'something' to be given a particularly authoritative status. This gives both philosophies a confidence in their 'knowledge' which is seen (from a roughly critical rationalist position) as misplaced. Their tenacious upholding of the quality of this knowledge as somehow apodictic is a metaphysics with necessarily dogmatic consequences. It is also important not to lose sight of the similarities between critical rationalism and empiricism – their shared valuing of unambiguous propositions, their shared commitment to analysis and to the Aristotelian principle of non-contradiction, and a shared respect for the achievements of physical science.

This identification of the three positions leads to a number of vocabularistic 'indicators'. These, combined with a few simple ground rules for their application, form the basis of the exposition in the empirical chapters which follow. The need for ground rules arises from the ambiguity of language, including the ambiguity of individual words. Consider the word 'really', for example. It can have ontological overtones; a confrontation between officers is *really* a clash between two different interests or *really* a childish tiff between two immature people or *really* just the result of some accidental misunderstanding, but it cannot, in this sense of the word, be all three at the same time. Yet 'really' can carry the sense of simple true statement of fact, so that the officers can really be representing two conflicting interests, be immature personalities and be the unfortunate victims of misunderstanding, all at the same time; and all this can really happen on Tuesday. So the word can be used by a questioner who is concerned to reduce events to a level where they can be explained by some all-dominating reality, some fundamental principle, or it can be used to make a simple factual inquiry. It can be part of the idealist's question, part of the empiricist's question, or part of the critical rationalist's question.

We should also bear in mind that it is unfair to read on to individual authors or interviewees a coherent epistemological position, as if they were capable of articulating a consistent epistemology. But it is equally unfair to read on to them an incoherent philosophical position, as if the categories used in the exegesis were apodictic. Then again, the explanation of non-constructive criticism in Strathclyde depends partly on there being identified a general 'mush' of conflicting philosophical assumptions in the shared attitudes of local authority staff. These considerations combine to reduce the degree to which individual words occurring in a text can be used to identify particular philosophical views in its author.

The solution to this problem, in so far as it is soluble, depends on the use of context – primarily the textual context, but also the social or historical context. Thus there is a basic ground rule that individual words are set in context for the sake of exegesis ('a text taken out of context becomes a pretext') and this has practical implications for the presentation of textual data. It lays a responsibility on those offering such data to present it, as far as possible, in continuous passages giving a reasonable amount of material before and after the phrases under examination. That is, it is important to avoid as far as possible the presentation of text in discrete 'particles' – individual sentences or phrases, 'proof texts'. It was with such considerations in mind that an effort was made in earlier chapters (which depended heavily on exposition) to present sufficient of the context of a statement to enable its exposition to be criticised without the critic having to establish for himself an entire text.

The three philosophical positions were thus identified largely on the basis of vocabulary but, as a prior stage, three key concerns of theories of knowledge were identified. Firstly, a concern with propositions, a concern either to establish accurate propositions or to criticise propositions. Secondly, by contrast, a central concern with persons or *praxis*, a concern to promote the development of 'right' people or to criticise people. Thirdly, a concern with criticism itself, a conviction that it is necessary or valuable.

These three concerns combine in different ways to form the different philosophical positions; very roughly, the first and second characteristics together suggest naïve empiricism, which tries to avoid the third characteristic, so that 'it is a bad thing when people get facts wrong'. The second and third characteristics together suggest critical theory, which sees propositions as having little intrinsic value, so that 'it is a good thing when people who are wrong are criticised'. The first and third combine to suggest a critical rationalist position, which tries to focus criticism on propositions, not on people. The three characteristics can be arranged in a triangle, such that the sides of the triangle correspond to the three philosophical positions, thus:

Characteristics of the three philosophies

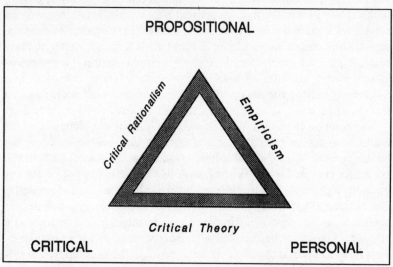

The angles represent characteristics of philosophies – a concern for right propositions, a concern for right persons or *praxis*, a concern to criticise existing institutions or ideas. Each of the three philosophies identified shows the characteristics at the two angles which its side connects, and is wary of a position which majors on the characteristic at the opposite angle.

The triangle is not presented as anything of great analytic power, nor is it vital to the argument of the book overall; it is more to say, as with the CDP typology, that it proved to be a useful device for sorting out the different positions. It was particularly useful in an environment in which given pieces of vocabulary, by virtue of their ambiguity, could not on their own be treated as particularly powerful indicators of a particular philosophical position. It allowed the concerns and corresponding vocabularies of the different philosophies to be identified as follows.

Empiricism

The valuable propositions are observation statements or 'facts' which are not mediated by any theoretical structure, but which form blocks 'out of' or 'on the basis of' which theoretical statements are 'built', 'developed' or 'constructed'. The less bias in the construction of these theories the better. The bias amounts to a partial treatment of the issue, presenting only some of 'the facts' rather than all of the facts. 'The facts' are neutral, pre-theoretic and 'given', (the 'extrinsic' of Horkheimer's essay); they are there simply to be 'collected' or 'gathered'. This identification corresponds to Horkheimer's identification of empiricism or positivism, and to Popper's 'bucket theory of the mind'. As far as the texts are concerned, it is the use of the words 'fact' or 'factual' which is central, but this needs to be seen in the context of an opposition to theoretical statements which are not based on fact or which are 'biased' and prior to the collection of facts.

Taking up the connection with natural language, one of the valuable things to emerge from the Frankfurt School is the occasional translation of their concerns into ordinary speech, and Popper's writing more often has this happy character. For present purposes a translation from Adorno is particularly valuable. He is talking about 'reified consciousness' (Horkheimer's 'traditional' way of thinking) and he comments: 'Reified consciousness automatically turns upon every thought which has not been covered in advance by facts and figures, with the objection: "where is the evidence?".' It is a useful characterisation of crude empiricism.[34]

Critical Theory

The behaviour *(praxis)* or character of people in society is the key thing, and therefore the predominance of ethical or moral statements is an identifying characteristic; a preoccupation with words such as 'should', or 'ought' or 'must' – words which suggest norms – is an indicator. A blurring of the distinction between matters of fact/positive theory/the world that 'is', on the one hand, and matters of value/normative theory/the world that 'ought to be' is another; it is a softer indicator, given its greater reliance on context, but perhaps for that reason also more reliable. A consequence of this 'is'/'ought' blurring, which stems from an ontology where reality has a fundamentally moral character, is a tendency to reductionism and a corresponding preoccupation with the words 'real' or 'reality'. As an indicator for critical theory, 'the real' corresponds roughly to 'the facts' of empiricism.

Related to this ontological preoccupation is another indicator, namely the blurring of a distinction between subject and object. This latter may lead to a prominent use of words like 'sense', in the way that, for example, Schliermacher's theology considers not 'God' but a 'sense of God'.

Critical Rationalism

The value of propositions is shared with empiricism, although critical rationalism places a higher value on theoretical statements, with observations statements seen as means to an end. Another key difference between critical rationalism and empiricism appears when a faulty or inadequate statement is identified. For the empiricist it implies that a mistake or error has been made by someone who is therefore at fault. Critical rationalism does not deny the concept of personal culpability, but looks more naturally to the content of the statement than to its provenance. The key to this is the view of all knowledge as conjectural and dependent on theories, the manner of whose invention or appropriation is as mysterious a thing as it is irrelevant to the analysis of their content or function.

The 'ought' and 'should', therefore, which were taken as indicators of critical theory when directed at people, are indicators of critical rationalism when they are directed primarily at statements. The strict distinction between 'facts' and 'theories' which was basic to empiricism virtually dissolves, and the concern is simply with statements. The goal is the production of general statements, but the relationship between making specific observations and producing general propositions is more dynamic – it leaves, for instance, a great deal of room for imagination, whereas empiricism discourages it. Speculation or conjecture is important and valuable to critical rationalism, and this, with the caution which stems from the awareness of knowledge as conjectural, may be indicated by a generally tentative hypothesising, 'this may be the case ...'. At the same time, there is a concern, shared with empiricism, to make accurate statements about a world which actually is, and which 'is' independently of any knowing subject.

Perhaps the most characteristic language of critical rationalism, however, is the language of 'learning from our mistakes' and therefore seeing mistakes as, in a sense, valuable because, although they identify inaccuracies, the fact that we are aware of them demonstrates that our knowledge has grown.

These, then, are the three characterisations. They are not absolute, but they do provide a guide to the *sort* of translations (of philosophies) which we might expect to find in practical discourse. Faced with real policy texts, and the language of policy makers, we will need to make running adjustments to our own translations. At any rate, we are now in a position to begin work on the policy-related texts. The next two chapters present those texts and proceed to their exposition.

6 Strathclyde policy documents: text and exposition

INTRODUCTION

This chapter presents the two main statements of Strathclyde Regional Council's deprivation policy – the document called *Multiple Deprivation* and known as the Red Book, and the *Areas of Need* report, or *AoN*. The policy context of these reports has already been outlined in chapter three, where their proposals are considered as part of a sequence of policy initiatives from central government and from a range of government agencies in Glasgow and Clydeside.

Besides these two documents, however, we consider *Gilding the Ghetto*, from the national Community Development Project (CDP). Although this is not a Strathclyde text in the obvious sense, we have already seen that CDP was an important influence on the evolution of deprivation policy within Britain, and this influence was marked in Strathclyde. CDP is acknowledged in early deprivation texts from Strathclyde (the Regional Report, for example, see chapter three) and we have seen that Councillor Young makes use of CDP material when writing about related issues (stigmatisation and the bin myth). We also noted, in reviewing the dialectic tradition (in chapter four), that the CDP literature stands within that tradition as clearly as any of the material from the deprivation industry, and that it warrants a re-examination in the light of the philosophical discussion of chapters four and five. *Gilding the Ghetto* was one of the most influential of the CDP reports, and is taken here as representative of CDP in general.[1]

All the documents presented in this chapter have thus appeared in chapter three, with more or less of their text being quoted. Each of these documents is now being considered as empirical material rather than as part of a background survey.

GILDING THE GHETTO

The report sets the problems of urban areas, and government response to these problems, in the context of a straightforwardly Marxist analysis of the capitalist state. Projects aimed at the problem of deprivation are seen as the state's attempts to restructure its management of a problem which is basically unchanging. This restructuring is seen as simply the latest phase of a flexible response, similar to the restructuring which occurred with the construction of the Welfare State. The problem is one of legitimation, of maintaining a consensus within society such that the operation of capital can continue unchallenged. Thus, the penultimate paragraph of a review of change in the 1960s:

> The changes in the nature and organisation of the state ... should not be mistaken for a change in its basic role. Its areas of activity and the range of its workers may have expanded, and certain circumstances may have altered, but its task remains the same and its institutions are governed by that task. As in the nineteenth century, it has on the one hand to ensure the continuing profitability of private capital; on the other it has to deal with the consequences of the way capital operates. With the working class both the source of profit for capitalism and the greatest threat to its existence, the state has to be constantly sensitive to working class demands while at the same time ensuring that any unavoidable concessions interfere as little as possible with the long term interests of capital. Between these two tasks lie the contradictions for the state. And in the 1960s and seventies as always it was these which governed the initiatives of the time.[2]

This, of course, is not a particularly original opinion, nor was it when the report was first published; its insistence on the irrelevance of the category of change is perhaps the only significant departure from a fairly orthodox institutionalised Marxism. The value of the report, at least for this research, is in its account of the analysis which went on in connection with these projects, both by the uncritical social scientists who were involved, and by members of CDP teams. The remaining extracts focus on these two groups respectively:

> The economist had been able to build up a framework of theory that commanded widespread support and acceptance, irrespective of its accuracy. The restructuring of British capitalism to ensure profitability was meeting with little opposition, although it was clearly not in the interests of people in the older industrial areas who saw their jobs being lost and their neighbourhoods declining. Why shouldn't the social scientists do the same and provide the state and particularly

local government – which was having to pick up the pieces on the ground – with a rational, objective and scientific research framework in which to develop solutions to the urban problem? ... So the poverty initiatives emphasised survey techniques, statistical analysis and computer models. With touching faith the social scientist, with his finely calibrated measuring instruments, was expected to provide the precise answers to the problem. ... Social scientists no longer needed to speak of the 'wretched, defrauded, oppressed, crushed human nature lying in bleeding fragments all over the face of society ...' nor did the media have to operate with the crude explanations used by the church in the nineteenth century:

> The rich man in his castle,
> The poor man at his gate,
> God made them high and lowly
> And ordered their estate.
> *All things Bright and Beautiful ...*

Instead they had the 'objective' scientific language of multiple deprivation and stratification systems to draw on and had developed complicated methods of proving that the class division between labour and capital no longer exists.

It was this ideology or system of ideas which the state mobilised in the form of the Poverty Programme to counter the day to day experience of working people in the inner cities. The initiation of the different policy initiatives was itself part of the process. The existence of special projects, government departments etc. to deal with the 'cycle of deprivation', 'social pathology' and their like clearly proved that these things exist. The institutions were the definitions made concrete.

Thus the CDP brief carried home the idea that there's nothing wrong with the social services, but there is a minority who fall outside its efficiency. Built into the National Project's very existence, its twelve small area teams, was the proof that the unlucky minority live in isolated pockets dotted around the country in what are in effect very special social circumstances. These were the 'areas of special social need' constantly referred to by the Home Office and the Department of the Environment. This idea of poverty affecting only small groups in marginal areas is a powerful one, for it immediately reduces the scale of the problem. It also carries the implication that those who live outside these areas share no common interests or problems with the deprived within. The working class are effectively split in two and the scene is set for convincing those within that their problems have nothing to do with wider economic and political processes.[3]

The conclusion of the document, looking back over its own account of the policy initiatives, includes the following:

The state's fight against urban deprivation has been exposed, like the 'emperor's new clothes', as empty rhetoric. But just as no one was foolhardy enough to laugh at the emperor, we too would be rash to disregard the reality behind the packaging of the Poverty Programme. The basic dilemma for the state remains the same – how best to respond to the needs of capitalism on the one hand and maintain the consent of the working class on the other ... This is the wider reality which puts the Poverty Programme in its proper perspective. For what kind of a 'Welfare' State is it which, at a time when economic recession is causing additional hardship, particularly among the people living in 'areas of special social need', cuts back the services on which people depend?... It is not surprising, then, that in the final analysis the 'deprivation initiatives' were not about eradicating poverty at all, but about managing poor people.

The story of the Poverty Programme reveals the nature of the state's interests and activities quite clearly. The Programme has evolved as a testbed for new ideas and strategies for dealing with the working class. As such, it also provides a framework both for understanding better the ways in which the state operates and for locating the weaknesses and contradictions within the state's structures and activities. In this report, we have concentrated on drawing out the broader strands of the state's interests and objectives. In doing so we have run the risk of presenting the state as a monolithic force.

As workers for the state ourselves, we are aware of the extent to which this is an oversimplification. Our experience in CDP makes us acutely conscious of the range of opinions represented within the state structures ... It is also clear, with increasing public expenditure costs, that [many] of the workers employed by it are in opposition ... The resistance of state workers to low wages and, more recently, the threat of redundancy and increased workloads yet lower standards, has been one of the most important recent developments in working class organisation.

But the struggle of state workers is not simply about wages and conditions of work, or restoring the level of services of a few years ago. The issues raised in this report show that it has to be about the content of the work we do, too ... For CDP workers, the contradictions involved in being state workers paid to analyse the causes of poverty, meant that effective organisation of all the twelve projects, across the institutional barriers drawn up by the Home Office, was essential both to protect our jobs and to extend our understanding of the problems we were employed to deal with. This has enabled us to develop our analysis of the reality which faces people in the areas of industrial decline and reject the definitions of the problems handed to us by the state. We have only been able to do this because we have fought for the right to control our work – what we do, for whom we are doing it and why. Breaking the geographical boundaries ... not only helped us to reject the small area focus we had been given, but also to resist Home Office attempts at control, when our employers reacted to this analysis.

For other state workers, working in the health service, public transport, education, housing and other services, there are possibilities for similar activity once the contradictory nature of state services is recognised and the decision is made to work towards providing a service in the interests of the working class, not capitalism and the state.[4]

The most striking characteristic of the text is the repeated insistence on a particular view of 'reality'. In the section quoted there are several different phrases which convey this. Thus the 'basic role' of the state continues unchanged in spite of changes in its 'nature and organisation', its 'areas of activity', and so on. Its 'basic' role arises from the fact that the 'basic dilemma for the state remains the same'. The social scientists' explanations, like the economists', are illusory by virtue of their avoidance of these 'basics'. Thus they 'command widespread support and acceptance irrespective of their accuracy', or they 'developed complicated methods of proving that the class division between labour and capital no longer exists', or else they offered 'a system of ideas mobilised to counter the day to day experience of working people'. By contrast, the CDP analysis 'exposed' the 'empty rhetoric' by uncovering 'the reality behind the packaging', the analysis 'reveals the nature' of the state's intentions. This view of the initiatives is 'the final analysis', since it is an analysis of 'the reality which faces people' or it has made clear 'the wider reality which puts the Poverty Programme in its proper perspective'.

The dispute is explicitly over what *really* exists. It is about 'basic' realities. It is unavoidably an ontological dispute. This recognition of the 'contradictory nature' of the state leads on to a related ontological assertion, namely that the state's workers share the contradictory nature of the state in their own being. Thus, while the social scientists in general continued in their objectivist illusion, the CDP workers realised 'the contradictions involved in being state workers paid to analyse the causes of poverty'. The growth of their understanding was directly linked with their struggle with these 'contradictions involved in being', and with the state itself. The workers of different projects thus organised 'across the institutional barriers drawn up by the Home Office', they 'broke' the geographical boundaries between projects, 'rejecting' the small area focus, and 'resisting' Home Office attempts at control. This activity was inextricably linked with 'extending our understanding of the problems' and 'enabling us to develop our analysis of the reality'.

Understanding the object is understanding oneself, and to grow in understanding of the object is to struggle directly with it. The phrase 'contradictory nature' reflects this; thus 'nature', which suggests issues of being or identity, has a characteristic, 'contradictory', which suggests speech, statement or proposition, or else a habit of opposition to a discrete and separate entity. This merger of issues appears again in the passages which address the state workers and their 'contradiction in being'. 'Contradiction' in the CDP text appears to be a similar thing to Horkheimer's 'tension', seen as basic to the experience of the critical theorist:

> The identification, then, of men of critical mind with their society is marked by tension, and the tension characterises all the concepts of the critical way of thinking. Thus, such thinkers interpret the economic categories of work, value and productivity exactly as they are interpreted in the existing order, and they regard any other interpretation as pure idealism. But at the same time they consider it rank dishonesty simply to accept the interpretation; the critical acceptance of the categories which rule social life contains simultaneously their condemnation.[5]

These ontological assertions suggest an epistemology which is closer to the critical theorist position than to either empiricism or critical rationalism. The CDP report also expresses a concern with right behaviour. The closing paragraphs are an appeal to state workers, who are to 'fight' and to 'act collectively to change'. The social scientists, whose work is described as intended 'to counter the day to day experience of working class people', are condemned on moral grounds. Their results are not assessed for their accuracy as statements of fact (the CDP view of the irrelevance of this exactly parallels the lack of concern with accuracy which they identify in those who sought to use economics and social science to generate consensus) but are assessed purely functionally. The social scientists themselves 'no longer needed' to use language with emotive ethical and anthropological (remember 'too strong') overtones – 'wretched, defrauded, oppressed, crushed human nature' – and by implication they were glad to draw instead on 'objective scientific language'. The personal focus, a concern with right behaviour and a belief in the irrelevance of accurate propositions, then, also underlies the report. The failure to make a distinction between ethical issues and matters of fact, which is observed here, cannot be avoided once the ontological reduction has taken place. All issues are in their proper perspective when set in the context of the most basic realities, and the subject/object distinction is blurred. The interesting point here is the degree to which the CDP report, without explicitly attempting to articulate an ontology or a theory of knowledge, has developed an ontologically and epistemologically consistent position.

The metaphysical character of the text leads into what is virtually a religious theme. Now that the fundamental 'reality' is 'exposed' or 'revealed', the time has come for state workers to recognise this reality and to make a decision to work in a direction opposite to that in which they previously worked (by virtue of their uncritical collaboration with the state). This is a theme of 'enlightenment' exactly as the Frankfurt School sees it, something which must produce a behaviour *(praxis)* in conflict with an earlier conformity. There is a parallel with the theological idea of 'repentance' – the New Testament uses the word *metanoia*, a change of mind *(nous)* or direction. This is the point at which a concern with change emerges in CDP, and what they are urging on their readers is unavoidably analogous to a form of religious conversion. In this light it is interesting to consider a brief passage from Habermas' *Legitimation Crisis*:

> The fundamental function of world-maintaining interpretive systems is the avoidance of chaos, that is the overcoming of contingency. The legitimation of orders or authority and basic norms can be understood as a specialisation of this meaning-giving function. ... The 'meaning' promised by religion has always been ambivalent. On the one hand, by promising meaning, it preserved the claim ... that men ought not to be satisfied with fictions but only with 'truths' when they wish to know why something happens in the way it does, how it happens, and how what they do and ought to do can be justified. On the other hand, promise of meaning has always implied a promise of consolation as well, for proffered interpretations do not simply bring the unsettling contingencies to consciousness but make them bearable as well – even when, and precisely when, they cannot be removed *as* contingencies.[6]

Clearly this identification of the role of religious meaning-giving systems is similar to that of the CDP report in its comments on 'All things Bright and Beautiful'. As the report does, so Habermas goes on to speak of the role of the sciences as meaning-giving systems usurping the place of religion in society. However, Habermas is prepared to notice that it is their meaning-giving function, rather than their religious or scientific character, which gives these systems their dangerously 'ambivalent' role. He is at this point on the verge of facing the fact with which he more fully comes to terms in, for example, the appendix and postscript to *Knowledge and Human Interests*,[7] namely that a non-metaphysical view of the world must reckon with the fact that it simply *is*. There is in fact a close similarity, deeper than a parallelism of vocabulary, with Popper's strictures against giving 'meaning' to history.

What the CDP writers have to face is that such an analysis (of religious and scientific meaning-giving systems) is as telling a criticism of their own work (as basically metaphysical) as it is a criticism of explicitly religious religion or scientistic science. Meaning-giving systems, if reasonably well constructed, are very powerful devices, regardless of their truth or flavour. To argue with CDP on their own ground, the widespread acceptance of *Gilding the Ghetto* among state workers whose activity does not threaten state structures (which widespread acceptance it is not the aim of this book to establish beyond Strathclyde) is the strongest possible demonstration of the fact that their own meaning-giving account of the deprivation initiatives has the same ambivalence which can be identified in religious systems. In this light the CDP view of the irrelevance of the accuracy of social scientists' work makes perfect sense.

CDP and the Home Office

To close the CDP exposition we compare the Home Office view of CDP, as expressed in the *Objectives and Strategy* text,[8] with the view offered in *Gilding the Ghetto*. On the question of social pathology, as considered in chapter three, the contrast between the two texts is marked; assessed in terms of their conception of knowledge, it is the similarity of basic assumptions which stands out. Both *Gilding the Ghetto* and the Home Office document present a particular view of reality, pressing this as the *real*, and dismissing contrasting views. Thus the Home Office document describes a situation in which 'plainly the more important problems' of a neighbourhood were regarded as unimportant by the community, who gave one particular superficial problem 'a symbolic meaning out of all proportion to its intrinsic importance'.[9] *Gilding the Ghetto* identifies this pressing of a particular view of reality, seeing deprivation policies as intended 'to counter the day to day experience of working people'; the text goes on to press its own 'analysis of the reality which faces people',[10] and clearly this too is consciously offered as a significantly more sophisticated view than that articulated by working people on the basis of their day to day experience.

To be fair to the Home Office document, it is closer to *Gilding the Ghetto* at several points than the mythology of CDP would suggest. The document speaks of 'remedying whatever can be remedied without large-scale development', which encourages a cynical view of the project, but the text goes on immediately to speak of 'doing so in a way which progressively builds up the capacity of the neighbourhood to express its needs and feelings; at the same time ... building up the capacity of the statutory services to respond with greater understanding'. Similarly the document notes that the public 'do not draw sharp distinctions between the roles of different services',[11] and then goes on to note the fragmentation of services described in the Seebohm report, making it clear that this fragmentation (characterised as it is by sharp distinctions between the roles of different services) is harmful. These latter themes in the Home Office text suggest a concept of community regeneration not unlike that found in the Strathclyde policy documents, with the same awareness of the value of 'feelings' and with a view of the need to improve professional 'understanding' which seems, in context, to have overtones of sensitivity as much as of scientific analysis.

STRATHCLYDE TEXTS

The next set of texts is drawn from the two key policy statements in Strathclyde. The first is the Red Book on 'Multiple Deprivation', produced by UDOG and adopted by the Council in October 1976.[12] This document has three parts: a preamble setting out the Council's adoption of the report, with resolutions for the implementation and further development of the deprivation strategy; a brief paper (two sides of A4) identifying forty-five 'areas for priority treatment'; and a longer paper (sixteen sides of A4) setting out in general terms a view of the nature of deprivation and of the approaches needed to tackle it. The exposition focuses on the longer of the two papers.

The second document is *Areas of Need – The Next Step (AoN)*, produced in April 1977.[13] The bulk of the document (Section III, taking up five sides of A4) proposes the adoption of a corporate and 'sensitive' approach to management in seven areas chosen from the earlier forty-five, setting out the framework for special projects in these areas, which came to be known as the 'Area Initiatives'.

A substantial body of text will be established for both documents before starting the exposition; this involves presenting a large number of key passages, setting these in the context of a coherent and relatively detailed description of the documents in their entirety – a fuller description than was required for the exposition of these same documents within a more traditional framework of ideas in chapter three.

Multiple Deprivation (the Red Book)

The preamble provides a brief summary of the report:

> It identifies a large number of geographical areas in which many of the causes and effects of deprivation are compounded together to create a pressing need for priority treatment. It states that the main causes are:
>
> 1 economic forces – financial poverty coupled with non-existent or unsatisfactory job opportunities;
> 2 the operation of the housing market and of the social services, such as education and housing, which often tend to reinforce the problems;
> 3 certain managerial deficiencies of government and, in some instances, the attitudes and practices of departments.
>
> All of these give rise to a vicious circle of hopelessness reflected by many in apathy, political alienation, delinquency, truancy and other problems of human behaviour. The report proposes no easy solutions, nor does it pretend that the deeply intractable problems of urban deprivation can be solved by massive injections of finance. It does point to certain immediate steps which the Policy and Resources Committee now recommends to Council as the first stage of the long haul towards community regeneration and the tackling of urban deprivation.
>
> We are clear that there are certain prerequisites without which programmes of government expenditure will continue to fall short; these are:
>
> ● real commitment from politicians and officers in government and from society at large;
> ● a readiness to learn from the mistakes of the past and to concede the existence of deficiencies in the way government delivers its services and relates to the public;
> ● a concerted and sensitive effort on the part of all public agencies, relating to the different levels of factors involved.[14]

In the main paper, the task of analysing the problems of deprived areas is seen as having two stages:

> ● the identification in general terms of the problems found to some

degree or other in virtually all multiply deprived areas, so that agreement can be reached on the broad nature of the principal causes as a basis for action;
- a closer look at each individual area ultimately selected for priority treatment to see which of the problems identified in the first stage are of greatest significance in that area ...

Dealing with the first stage is fairly straightforward for ... there already exists among members and officers a broad intuitive consensus, based on detailed local knowledge and the experience of previous remedial efforts, about what causes multiple deprivation.[15]

The report then goes on to identify the 'major problems found, to a greater or lesser extent, in most multiply deprived areas', classifying them under, first, nationwide issues (poverty, employment problems, housing problems); second, 'difficulties arising from the attitudes, nature and scale of provision of public services'; and third, 'problems associated with the communities themselves'. Examples of these problems as given in the document are listed below. From the first group, employment problems:

(a) high rate of long term unemployment;
(e) lack of job satisfaction;
(h) social problems connected with unemployment (which tend to reinforce the effects of other problems) – apart from hardship involved, feeling of frustration, bitterness or apathy and hopelessness over time, the inability to cope with work routines and the disciplines involved in holding down a full time job.[16]

From the second group:

(a) inaccessibility of agency from field – general 'distance' of control of service delivery from recipients;
(d) insensitivity in service delivery: failure to deal in terms of *people* as opposed to *tasks*.[17]

From the third group:

(a) sense of hopelessness: lack of knowledge and access to established machinery;
(b) increasing sense of dependence on outside agencies, linked often with frustration at lack of control over own affairs;
(h) sense of anonymity and irresponsibility arising from breakdown of older communities with redevelopment and population movement, from housing policies, from the concentration of disadvantaged groups like one-parent families.[18]

The report emphasises the arbitrary nature of this classification: 'It should ... be underlined that these are interconnected and often mutually reinforcing strands of a larger complex problem.'[19] In the light of these problems, then:

> Clearly, the first thing for any local authority to do in combating deprivation is to 'put its own house in order' – to provide the means whereby a corporate approach to the provision of services can be achieved ...
>
> It is therefore clear that deprivation can only be tackled effectively by a coordinated response of members and officers from central and local government closely involved with the community in an educative, regenerative process (and this cannot be all in one direction). It is unlikely, however, to have significant impact unless accompanied by certain additional and, in Scotland, largely untried initiatives which it is hoped the council will discuss in some detail, with a view to deciding to what extent it is prepared to take action on these.[20]

The last of these initiatives is:

(e) recognising that the reactivation of community spirit in these areas has a major role to play in their regeneration.[21]

The community regeneration theme is expanded in subsequent sections of the report. Before doing this, however, the report outlines ideas for 'Area Centres': 'To enable the working of services to be relevant, resourced, coordinated, known by and sensitive to the community', centres should be developed for 'information, publicity, advice and complaints'. One of the functions of these centres, when working well, will be the training of staff so that they are capable of delivering a relevant or sensitive service:

> It should be recognised that area staff will be faced with two, possibly conflicting, obligations – their accountability to the corporate area group, as well as to their own departments. Many staff will not be convinced that a corporate strategy is either practicable or desirable, and many will be ignorant of its practical implications as well as of other departments with which they will be required to work in corporate harness. Training of staff will therefore be of crucial importance. There are a variety of ways of doing this, one of which might be to select examples where a corporate approach is working successfully and use these in a programme of secondment, as training centres with a teaching unit attached to them. These teaching units would be designed to introduce staff to the practical workings of corporate

strategies and to provide concurrent 'theoretical' instruction.[22]

The section on Area Centres closes with a comment on 'Research and Evaluation':

> It is essential that the effectiveness of corporate approaches in deprived areas be measured through a deliberate programme of ongoing research by those involved in the project ... very serious consideration should be given to the appropriate forms of research as soon as possible.[23]

Of the remaining five sides of A4 in the report, four and a half are taken up with the issue of 'community regeneration' or 'the reactivation of community spirit'. It is seen as 'perhaps the most difficult problem to face up to in terms of local authority decision-making processes and our traditional ways of tackling our problems'. Success is seen as dependent on two key factors: the 'participation and support of the local community in the planning and management of operations', and the allowing of 'a genuine voice in the running of their areas' to the local community to 'promote a spirit of self-confidence' and encourage self-help.[24]

The potential for a conflict of opinion between professional staff and the local community, and the difficulty of managing such conflict, are both discussed. Given the centrality of this issue for the book, and the fact that this discussion in the policy document is virtually the climax of the whole statement of strategy, it seems reasonable to give the relevant section of text in full:

> In the past, local authority departments have been accustomed to planning and delivering services without prior consultation. Such consultation as has taken place has tended to be on the basis of already developed plans, and in cases where conflict has arisen between the standards of the council and the wishes of the community, the balance has generally swung in favour of the professional view. What the council requires to decide is:
>
> • does it wish to alter this balance so that, while still recognising the role that professional judgment has to play in resolving problems, it is prepared to offer an increased opportunity to local communities (principally through the medium of the Community Councils, or their sub-groups relating to multiply deprived areas) to articulate their own views of their problems and to play an increased role in determining the planning and delivery of services in their areas?
>
> • how are Committees and Departments to be encouraged to over-

come their natural reluctance to relinquish, even slightly, the design and quality standards which seem to them to be appropriate in favour of the perhaps lesser standards which communities may request?

Efforts to encourage communities to articulate their feelings will almost inevitably give rise to a greater degree of criticism of local authorities and central government than is experienced at present. Members will require to determine what attitude they would take to such criticism – certainly it could be alarming initially to members and officers working in the field, but, more positively, it could be recognised as a valuable source of feed-back on what is actually happening in each community. This does not mean to say that unjust or ill-informed criticism should be accepted and again it would fall to members at the local level to ensure, by setting problems in their context, that any criticism made is constructive and formulated in the light of the fullest possible information available.

Constructive criticism depends on the provision of as full information as possible to communities at the earliest possible stage. This in turn implies a willingness on the part of officers as well as members to make themselves accessible to local groups.

Information and encouragement by local members may not be enough – some areas may need the temporary appointment of a catalyst to reactivate community feeling and stimulate the development of longer-term leadership from within the community itself ...

Community regeneration is a long term process and an educative exercise in the broadest terms. It involves the mobilisation of all the local authority officials within the area in the role of community development officers, involving a commitment to people rather than tasks. It implies a sense of responsibility for and commitment to the community.[25]

The concluding paragraph of the whole document also makes clear that the idea of 'regeneration' is basic to the strategy:

It should be borne in mind that the comprehensive regeneration of multiply deprived areas and the communities which live in them is fairly new ground for local authorities. There is no expert on deprivation, no 'Director of Deprivation' with a body of knowledge and experience enshrined in a department to which recourse may be had for technical advice upon which political decisions may be taken. It is essentially a human problem, consequently complex, requiring a coordinated effort from the activities of all the Council's committees. There is a crucial need for the frankest possible discussion within the Council to ensure first a clear political commitment to whatever approach emerges and secondly that this is understood and accepted at all levels of implementation.[26]

Areas of Need – The Next Step (AoN)

The second document continues with broadly the same concerns, namely for community regeneration through coordinated and sensitive service delivery achieved on the basis of community participation in service development. Given the nature of the policy, no clear blueprint for all the different initiatives can be laid down:

> It is not proposed to lay down a particular solution. It is a question of how best can the people, their elected representatives and officials get together to carry out, continuously, a critical review of how services respond to the needs of the community on a day to day and developmental basis. How this is to be done may differ from one place to the next. Any solution should be shaped by, provide for and foster continuous active community participation.[27]

The report expands on how this 'getting together to carry out a critical review' should work:

> Simple coordination is not enough, all officials ... serving a specific area must achieve a unity of approach, an identity of purpose ...
>
> The work of developing this policy of mobilisation, understanding it in depth and relating it to the every day duties of each official must be seen as part of a training scheme. This programme, to put over the policy, deepen understanding, heighten awareness, sharpen responsiveness and foster initiative, would be conducted within the community and offered to staff, councillors and local people. It will bring out the strong element of delegation of power and the clear political commitment to the approach.
>
> (In fostering initiative and delegating authority to members and officials the possibility of conflict between area and centre, and amongst groups and individuals at local level is recognised. It is believed the positive effects will be greater than the drawbacks.)
>
> Coordination also means that key personnel in an area will require to be specially selected for aptitude and commitment. This may require the transfer of staff with these particular qualities into deprived areas from elsewhere.[28]

This can be seen as a programme for learning at a local level. The implications for the authority as a whole, as a body concerned with corporate learning, are briefly indicated:

Representatives from each scheme will meet to exchange ideas and learn about each other's successes and failures. This will be done bi-annually or more often if required. The aim is to bring together policy makers, community representatives and officials in the centre and divisions in a conference, seminar type, setting. This would complement the more formalised reporting and monitoring carried out by committees and departments ...

As the approach proposed is experimental, it is recommended that an attempt be made to monitor and evaluate whatever takes place. There is a close relationship between the training programme and evaluation, and both may require assistance from outside agencies in the initial stages.[29]

EXPOSITION: THE RED BOOK AND *AoN*

Looking at the two documents and comparing them with the CDP report, there is a glaring contrast. Neither of the two sources (Strathclyde and CDP) set out to articulate an ontology or a philosophy of knowledge, yet the CDP material emerges as remarkably consistent on these issues. The Strathclyde material is full of inconsistencies. There are elements in it which suggest critical rationalism (learning from mistakes, for example, which arguably is a central theme); there are elements which suggest critical theory, and even elements which could be reconciled with a naïve empiricism.

Of the three positions, the last mentioned, empiricism, is the least represented. The methods chapter identified the words 'fact' or 'factual' as helpful indicators, and neither of them occurs even once in the complete text of both documents. The only hint of empiricism is in the comment on criticism, where the importance of criticism being properly grounded is stressed. In the methods chapter we noted the importance in empiricism of emphasis on 'the facts', in the sense of a complete set of observation statements. In this sense, failure to take into account all the facts implies a deliberately partial or biased analysis. Such analysis leads to criticism which is unfair. So it is perhaps significant that the report disapproves of 'unjust or ill-informed criticism', and emphasises the need for criticism to be formulated 'in the light of the fullest possible information available' or 'as full information as possible'.

There is evidence of a critical rationalist approach to the problem; the phrase from the Red Book, which became a watchword for the authority's whole strategy, 'putting our own house in order', suggests a fundamental acceptance of past mistakes, and an effort to learn from them. This idea of learning from mistakes is made explicit in the preamble to the Red Book, which talks of the need 'to learn from the mistakes of the past and concede the existence of deficiencies'. The distinction between the world as it is and as it ought to be is also clear, thus 'criticism of local authorities and central government ... could be recognised as a valuable source of feedback on what is actually happening in each community'. The idea is that people involved in the different schemes should 'learn about each other's successes and failures', and 'that an attempt should be made to monitor and evaluate whatever takes place'.

The critical review of policy which the documents emphasise is not seen as uncovering final answers which can then be enshrined in policy, rather the documents seek to establish criticism as a normal and day to day process within communities and amongst staff. In this they are orthodox corporate planning documents, children of their time. Thus the range of people involved in an area (community, councillors and officials) 'get together to carry out, continuously, a critical review', and the community participation in this process should be 'continuous'. Similarly, the inter-project review procedure is presented as a process to be followed indefinitely rather than up to a certain point where all the answers have been found. This debate on the basis of shared information leading to a continuous development of policy – a process which is open in the fullest sense (no groups excluded and no time limit set) – has a thoroughly critical rationalist character. Popper's emphasis on the conditional or provisional nature of knowledge, and on the centrality of criticism by learning from mistakes, emerges in the Strathclyde documents at a number of points.

The character of the debate envisaged in the policy process is also Popperian, however, in its rejection of reductionism. The complexity of the problem is emphasised, and a wide range of factors is identified in its aetiology. Thus, 'many of the causes and effects of deprivation are compounded together' and it is 'underlined that these are interconnected and often mutually reinforcing strands of a larger complex problem'. The factors which are identified include isolated empirical variables, many of them amenable to statistical analysis; there is a clear assertion, therefore, of the positive value of 'the facts' (compare Adorno's 'where are the facts?' comment[30]). This factual information is important for identifying which problems are the most important in particular small areas, just as much as it is important for building up a picture of 'causes' of deprivation. Indeed the emphasis in the documents is on this application of separable factors to an analysis of small discrete areas (so that the analysis can slide safely off totality's back, as Adorno or the Coventry CDP team might say).

All in all there is a marked contrast between the approach in the reports and the emphatic and ontologically based reductionism which was evident in the CDP report, and which led in that report to a clear denunciation of the use of scientistic methods, seeing small-area-based analysis as fundamentally illusory.

In spite of the evidence of a critical rationalist and a naïve-empiricist character to the documents, however, it is possible to identify a critical theorist position and, seen in the light of indicators of critical theory, some of the evidence of critical rationalism becomes more ambiguous than it seems in the presentation above. The centrality of 'criticism' or 'critical review' has already been pointed out but, as the methods chapter made clear, 'criticism' is, on its own, too ambiguous a word to serve as an indicator. The debate between Popper and the Frankfurt School amounts to a debate over the right way to conduct criticism in society.

In both documents it is clear that one of the major problems which needs to be overcome in order to tackle deprivation is the 'attitude' of local authority staff. 'Attitude' is something which a person has; a policy only has one in a secondary sense (the policy is personalised for the sake of argument, or it embodies the attitudes of those responsible for its development, institutionalising a personal judgment made in the past or functioning by referring matters to the discretionary judgment of some authorised person). Both documents can be summarised as assertions that the problems connected with deprivation (or those which the Council can tackle) are problems of human behaviour, both in communities and amongst staff. What is therefore needed is a change in attitudes amongst the people already involved in an area, or else (in the case of staff) a change of people, importing those who have the right attitudes. Related key words are 'regeneration', 'sense' or 'sensitivity'. This latter pair are interesting in that, in spite of their obvious relationship, they are used in the text with quite characteristic but different objects. The word 'sense' occurs primarily – but not exclusively – in descriptions of the deprived areas or their populations (often the ambiguity – area or population – is unresolved). Thus, in the list of problems 'associated with the communities themselves' we have 'sense of hopelessness', 'sense of dependence' and 'sense of anonymity and irresponsibility'. 'Sensitivity', on the other hand, is typically to be acquired by officers: thus the Red Book calls for 'a concerted and sensitive effort on the part of all public agencies', identifies as a problem 'insensitivity in service delivery' and advocates services which are 'known by and sensitive to the community'.

The debate which was identified in assessing the possibly critical rationalist character of the documents thus takes on a different light.

The Red Book expects there to be 'efforts to encourage communities to articulate their feelings', and in some situations a 'catalyst' may be necessary 'to reactivate community feeling'. The goal of this sort of discussion seems to be a situation in which the community and the officers associated with it have 'a sense of responsibility for and commitment to the community'. This last phrase occurs in the immediate context of community regeneration as 'an educative exercise in the broadest terms'. Elsewhere the Red Book call for officers, members and community to be involved in an 'educative, regenerative process' which 'cannot be all in one direction'.

The question arises: 'who is being regenerated in community regeneration?' It seems as if the phrase 'community regeneration' implies the regeneration of officers to turn them into people who think in terms of the community and its perception of its needs. The report accordingly calls for, from officers and members, 'a willingness to make themselves available to local groups' – 'themselves', not simply their skills or time, but their whole lives. This might be expected of an elected member who voluntarily commits himself to represent the people of an area, or it might be expected of a minister of religion, but it is being applied here to professional staff. Other occurrences of the word 'commitment' have the same overtones of 'self-offering'.

The question 'who is being regenerated?' and a related question 'what is the process of education involved in this regeneration?' are perhaps most pointed in respect of one particular section of the *AoN* report. This section expands on the process of 'critical review':

> all officials serving a specific area must achieve a unity of approach, an identity of purpose ... This programme, to put over the policy, deepen understanding, heighten awareness, sharpen responsiveness and foster initiative, would be conducted within the community and be offered to staff, councillors and local people.[31]

It seems that everybody is to be regenerated and, more than that, that some social 'thing' is to be created which fuses individuals' understanding, awareness and responsiveness into a single, unitary mind or organism (presumably the unity or 'identity of purpose' is to embrace community and members as well as officers). It is tempting to disregard this passage as an isolated case of the writer's vocabulary having run away with him, but the mystical entities which are necessary to make sense of the passage occur too frequently for this to be a feasible approach to the documents. Perhaps the most striking of these is the idea of 'reactivation of community spirit'. This use of 'spirit', linked as it is with the idea of an educative or learning process rooted in history in the sense that it is located quite unambiguously in people or institutions (rather than in propositions), almost suggests a Hegelian conception of an objective 'community *geist*'.

Two other aspects of the text suggest a sort of idealist critical theory. The first is a methodological essentialism such as that identified by Popper in *The Open Society and its Enemies*.[32] At two key points in the text of the main paper of the Red Book (the introductory identification of deprivation and the concluding paragraph), there are statements which, at least in vocabulary, suggest a broadly Platonic epistemology. The first of these essentialist passages, discussing 'the identification in general terms of the problems found in all multiply deprived areas', claims that this is a straightforward job since 'there already exists a broad intuitive consensus about what causes multiple deprivation'. The second passage begins by pointing out the lack, in local authorities, of any 'expert on deprivation'; there is 'no "Director of Deprivation" with a body of knowledge and experience enshrined in a department to which recourse may be had for technical advice'. The passage immediately goes on to assert that 'it is essentially a human problem'. There is a suggestion that 'technical' advice is thus not really appropriate (given that the report has earlier spoken of the need for officers to 'deal in terms of people as opposed to tasks').

What is needed is the enlightened mind which is theoretically oriented (in the sense in which Habermas identifies it – following *theoria* in contrast with *techné*), which by 'a pure act of intuition unaided by any of the senses' (as Plato puts it) grasps the essential nature of the object, and by a process of *mimesis*, adapts so as to produce an appropriate *praxis* or social behaviour. There is almost a suggestion of the Platonic 'master of dialectic' in the idea of a 'Director of Deprivation', although the 'Director of Deprivation' is a critical rather than an affirmative category.

The other strand which suggests critical theory is the attitude to conflict in criticism. Given the personal conception of the educative process which the policy proposes, it is arguably inevitable that the two categories 'criticism' and 'conflict' should merge. The Red Book speaks of instances in the past where, in consultation of the community by officers, 'conflict' has arisen 'between the standards of the Council and the wishes of the community'. The conflict has generally been resolved in favour of the 'the professional view'. The Red Book poses the questions, 'should the balance be changed?' and (presumably assuming the answer 'yes') 'how should committees and departments 'be encouraged to overcome their natural reluctance to relinquish standards which seem to them to be appropriate?' The personalising of committees and departments is not the relevant point here (legally the Council has a persona, and it is not unreasonable to apply this way of looking at it to its own agents) – the point is that 'opinions' or 'views' are in conflict here rather than people.

The document continues by commenting on the need to manage the sort of 'criticism' which 'will almost inevitably arise' if communities are encouraged 'to articulate their feelings'. The criticism thus arising will be to a 'greater degree than is experienced at present'. 'Members will require to determine what attitude they would take to such criticism', and they, along with officers, may be 'alarmed'.

The report then makes the point that this criticism could be seen as a source of information on 'what is actually happening', but immediately turns to the problem of criticism being 'unjust or ill-informed'. Members are to ensure that criticism is rendered 'constructive and formulated in the light of the fullest possible information available' by 'setting problems in their context'.

As already indicated, this passage could suggest empiricism; bias and incomplete information are connected, and 'setting in context' is a guard against this sort of unfairness. But the CDP documents show, in a different philosophical context, that the idea of setting in context can refer to the identification of the 'basic realities', metaphysical realities which set the deprivation initiatives 'in their proper context'.

What is happening, at any rate, is that criticism of policy is being encouraged, in the knowledge that this will lead to conflicts in which individual officers and members may be 'alarmed', and community 'feelings' will also be aroused or 'activated'. Advice is given (in the immediately following sections) which suggests 'the provision of as full information as possible' and that officers and members 'make themselves accessible to local groups', officials developing a commitment 'to people rather than to tasks' and 'to the community'. That is to say, the advice suggests that factual information and personal qualities be brought to bear on these conflicts (by the people whose 'alarm' and vulnerability to 'unjust' criticism renders the conflict liable to be destructive); in all this it would simply 'fall to members to ensure that any criticism made is constructive'. With information, admirable personal qualities, community feelings and alarmed members and officials all bearing on the question of service delivery, the elected member is given only one piece of advice, namely, 'set the problems in their context'.

The character of this approach to criticism is perhaps most clearly seen in a short passage from the *AoN* report. After outlining the process of 'critical review' of policy by members, staff and community, it states that 'the possibility of conflict is recognised ... it is believed that the positive aspects will be greater than the drawbacks'. This is the most stark statement of the views presented in the documents on criticism and conflict. It must surely represent some sort of 'faith' in the efficacy of criticism virtually regardless of its method or character. These views could depend on a pure naïvety of belief that 'it will all be for the best' – in which case it is tempting to paraphrase the community regeneration theme as 'come on, let's all pull together and think of the other chap, remember the team spirit'. Or else we could see a Hegelian conception of conflict in society producing an historical dialectic which generates a collective mind, the development of which will save or fulfil the human community. What is clear, however, is that, whether the idealism is naïve or Hegelian, it is firmly metaphysical. The word 'belief', in the expression of hope that the conflict will be constructive, and the word 'spirit', both religious words, cannot but colour the word 'regeneration' which is so much at the heart of the two documents. It is important to note that regeneration is a theological term, it is part of Christian belief that a spiritual regeneration or rebirth is a necessary part of human salvation. As with the CDP report we are encountering the language of religious conversion and, in this light, it is not entirely flippant to suggest a convergence between a right-Hegelian tradition and the school of 'muscular Christianity', with its 'cricket match of life' language.

It is difficult to know how much weight to give to the different epistemological identifications. It could be simply concluded that the reports borrow their assumptions from three different and incompatible philosophies. In that the document is written by a committee, this confusion of thought might be expected, particularly since the group is drawn out of an institution which is itself a pluralist society. It could even be seen as the product of one individual to whom the responsibility of drafting the document was delegated, and thus it stands as a testimony to his personal philosophical confusion as much as to the uncritical setting in which he worked. In so far as the document identifies conflicting epistemological positions, and therefore testifies to a basic confusion of thought, it corroborates, in a weak way, the basic thesis that conflicting epistemological positions underlie failures by the Council to proceed effectively with a self-critical analysis.

It is possible, however, to see the documents as having a predominantly critical theorist character. There is arguably more evidence consistent with such an epistemology than with either of the other two; perhaps the evidence of empiricism and of critical rationalism is purely the result of an imprecision over vocabulary (such as one might expect – the members of UDOG are not professional philosophers). Or perhaps there are points where their political awareness leads them to put passages into the language of those other officers (the 'task oriented' perhaps) whose attitudes they are trying to change.

In this regard, the phrase which sets the context for much of the policy development, 'putting our own house in order', although it has critical rationalist overtones, undoubtedly came to have a symbolic function within the authority, and its employment, or the employment of that ethos, may have had more to do with tactically calculated than epistemologically reflective considerations. At any rate, there is certainly scope for epistemological misidentification.

If this is right, that the documents have a broadly critical theorist character, and given the clearly critical theorist character of the CDP report, *Gilding the Ghetto*, then a consistent philosophy can be identified, and the argument on the basis of confusion is weakened. The explanation of failure to conduct criticism then rests on the connected grounds of a weakness internal to critical theory ('too strong') and a conflict between critical theory and its ideological environment. In the language of the policy documents, this would be a conflict between those who call for a self-offering commitment to the community and those who remain task oriented, a conflict between religious and technical conceptions of the officer's work.

To return to the text, there does seem to be evidence of a basic confusion of thought, particularly in the comments in the documents on project evaluation. Thus:

> it is essential that the effectiveness ... be measured through a deliberate programme of ongoing research by those involved in the project ... very serious consideration should be given to the appropriate forms of research as soon as possible.[33]

> Representatives from each scheme will meet to exchange ideas and learn about each other's successes and failures ... The aim is to bring together policy makers, community representatives and officials in a conference, seminar type setting. This would complement the more formalised reporting and monitoring carried out by committees and departments.

> As the approach ... is experimental, it is recommended that an attempt be made to monitor and evaluate whatever takes place. There is a close relationship between the training programme and evaluation, and both may require assistance from outside agencies in the initial stages.[34]

The first of these three passages is from the Red Book, the others are from *AoN*, with a space of roughly six months between the reports. It is only fair to note that there had been the difficult task, in these six months, of identifying the more needy of the forty-five areas, allowing for negotiations with District Councils, and that this had been a major preoccupation for those involved. Nevertheless, it might reasonably be expected that the call for attention to be given to research methods 'as soon as possible' should have borne more fruit in the intervening period. This is not a strong argument on its own, of course, but more careful analysis of the ideas on evaluation suggests that there was, in this period, at least a certain blankness of mind on the issue.

The obvious choice would be that the same sort of indicators which were used in the original identification of deprivation (developed primarily for the Regional Report and expanded for the Red Book) should be reapplied in the initiative areas. The production of the two policy documents took place against the background of similar methods being applied to the assessment of relative degrees of need in deprived areas. The documents themselves suggest a wide range of indicators, many of them quantifiable and many of them not census-dependent. It ought to have been a relatively straightforward procedure to allow a trial period, then compare the analysis for given areas according to a fixed set of variables measured before and after what was explicitly described as an 'experiment', the outcome of which was to be 'measured' or 'monitored'.

A similar striking omission shows in the qualities to be sought in officials to staff the initiatives. The need for 'commitment to the community' or 'sensitivity' is stressed to an extreme degree, yet, in spite of the fact that those involved in the projects are given a key role in their evaluation, there is absolutely no mention of the value of staffing the project with officers who have analytic or communicative skills. Articulate staff characterised by clarity of thought and expression would seem to be valuable people, given the limited description of the monitoring process (using seminars, for example), yet there is no suggestion of the value of such characteristics in either document. Indeed, given that the *AoN* report links evaluation with training, and training seems to be geared primarily to the production of commitment, sensitivity, responsibility and initiative, the suggestion seems to be either that these qualities (commitment etc.) will be of value in helping evaluation to proceed, or that the degree to which staff acquire such qualities (and how could that be assessed?) is the chief measure of the success of the initiatives. If the latter, why bother having the initiatives in deprived areas at all, since success can be achieved without any difference being observed in either the area or its community? The former seems to be the most reasonable meaning; presumably sensitive staff (party to the 'broad intuitive consensus') can sense the degree to which deprivation has been alleviated or the community regenerated.

The only thing which does seem clear on the issue of evaluation is that there is no clear statement either of the object of study or of the criteria by which it is to be evaluated. The closing paragraph of the main paper, dealing with evaluation, points out that both training and evaluation 'may require assistance from outside agencies', and this, understood as a cry for help, may be a reflection of confusion reigning in the documents. Certainly this admission of the Council's inadequacy to the task of evaluation is in marked contrast to the closing paragraph of the CDP report. Taking the Strathclyde texts in comparison with *Gilding the Ghetto*, then, it seems fairer to conclude that there is a basic confusion over evaluation rather than that there is a basically critical theorist position.

Considering the texts overall, however, we need to remember that the categories used in our analysis, the three philosophies of knowledge or conceptions of criticism, are not definitive but are a help for untangling a web of often conflicting assumptions, as with the Coventry CDP typology. We should not expect to find any one document fitting neatly into any one category. Given this qualification, then, the most striking feature of the documents is the language of regeneration, sense and sensitivity, attitude and commitment. It dominates the texts, and the scientific language of carefully monitored experimentation is like a fish out of water.

Thus, what emerges is 'something like' a critical theorist position, but with the qualification that the degree to which the authors themselves are aware of their own assumptions is considerably less than that found with CDP. Given the lack of a thorough knowledge of the literature on the philosophy of knowledge among the officers responsible for the documents (which is perfectly reasonable), this situation seems likely. Even if there were an awareness of epistemology on the part of a number of officers in the group responsible for the documents, the lack of such an awareness on the part of the individual charged with the bulk of the drafting could produce the same result.

At any rate, the important issue for the argument of the book is not the historical detail of the drafting of the documents but the epistemological assumptions they contain. In so far as any conclusion is possible, it seems fairest to say that the documents have a critical theorist character – a religious character – in contrast with the technical character of the task oriented officer's conception of his work. As we will see in the next chapter, the interview texts tell a different story.

CODA: PHYSICAL PLANNING AND POLICY PLANNING

The policy documents are relatively formal and public texts, the interview material is informal, a record of conversations. As a transition we can usefully consider two short texts which have an intermediate position; they are internal memoranda which relate to tensions between the Physical Planning Department and the Department of Policy Planning.

The two documents are dated roughly one month apart, and seven months earlier than the Red Book. Both focus on the work of UDOG, as preparation of the Red Book was getting under way. Neither document, it should be stressed, is addressed directly to the author of the other. Nevertheless, they suggest a struggle to control the work of UDOG.

The differences between Physical Planning and Policy Planning are connected with the ambiguity of the Paterson Report, and with the production of the Regional Report, which was the vehicle for a corporate approach to the analysis of needs and priorities within the Region. The Regional Report, with the provenance of the legislation instituting it in the Physical Planning profession, was produced by the Policy Planning Department. The supplementary volumes were produced in the Physical Planning Department, where much of the analytical groundwork was done. The relationship between the two components of the report was fixed in consultation with the Scottish Office, and in the event only the Regional Report itself (a relatively brief document) was formally submitted to the Secretary of State. Nevertheless, the analysis underlying the two components cannot be easily separated, and the supplementary volume on deprivation was, for internal policy development, as important as, if not more important than, the formal Report itself.

The upshot of this is that much of the overall work on the Regional Report was done within the Physical Planning Department, which therefore carried out a corporate research programme such as Paterson envisaged being undertaken by the Policy Planning unit. When UDOG was instituted, much of its work was done on the basis of this analysis from Physical Planning, but UDOG was chaired and serviced (almost as if it were a committee of elected members) by staff from Policy Planning. When the Red Book and the *AoN* report emerged they bore Policy Planning's imprint. As already noted, the Council's Policy Review Group (PRG) on structures became aware of this ambiguity (and of a corresponding overlap of activity and duplication of effort in other departments) and recommended that Physical Planning's research and intelligence function be absorbed, eventually, by Policy Planning (or that both should be absorbed by the Chief Executive's Department).

In February 1976 a note was prepared by two members of Physical Planning, Paul Scott and Jane Powell, for a meeting of UDOG. Mr Scott was then leading the Regional Report group within Physical Planning and Miss Powell was a member of that group. The note had two main concerns: firstly, to point out the need for UDOG to make suggestions for policy on deprivation, 'as specifically requested ... on several occasions by the Politicians of the region'; secondly, to point out the amount of work done on the analysis of deprivation by staff in Physical Planning. This work was seen as forming a major part of the basis on which recommendations for action should be constructed. There was a fear that Policy Planning (still a new department without a clearly established body of professional experience to draw on, unlike Physical Planning) lacked the ability to handle the analysis. The following two paragraphs are given in full, one being taken from the early part of the document, the other being the final paragraph:

> We are worried ... not because it looks as if there is to be progress, this we hope, but because there are indications that Policy Planning intend to organise future action including the collecting and monitoring of information. Whilst recognising the coordinating role that Policy Planning can play, we are dubious of their ability to pull together the relevant information, to establish the relevant criteria for selecting areas and proposing action, and to undertake further research. If they do, then we feel that there is unnecessary duplication and a failure to recognise the expertise that already exists in our Department, gained through the experience of the study to date.
>
> Finally, we would like to stress that, however serious the Officers' Group may be to engage themselves in developing recommendations, it should not ignore or duplicate the work and knowledge which exists in Physical Planning. There is a commitment to this work which if stilted could seriously undermine the morale and work rate of the whole section.[35]

There is clearly a feeling that Policy Planning are encroaching on to the area in which the professional judgment of physical planners should be exercised. It is possible to understand this as a suggestion that Policy Planning are failing to recognise the restrictions placed on the Chief Executive (as head of a corporate management structure) by Paterson, namely that he should not have authority over officers 'where the professional discretion or judgment of the principal officers is concerned'. This, however, requires the staff responsible for the paper to be seen as speaking for their directorate – which, arguably, they were, in representing their department on UDOG, but at the same time, arguably, they were not, in that another physical planner (and member of the Directorate) was also representing the department on UDOG.

There is at any rate an interesting contrast between the views of these physical planners and those of the Director of Policy Planning as expressed in a note to the Director of Physical Planning. The note is dated 25 March 1976 and is primarily concerned to respond to the support volumes to the Regional Report:

> My principal concern, however, relates to the supporting document on Urban Deprivation and in particular to section V. While there is obviously much valuable statistical material, the document goes much further than I feel requires to be done for the purposes of the Regional Report and completely disregards the role of the Urban Deprivation Officer Group in which you are playing a prime part through Steve [a Depute Director of Physical Planning]. Again, even just glancing through the Report, there are many considerable errors: statements attributed to the sphere of influence of other departments, which are not factual; many opinions and criticisms which I am sure cannot be substantiated; and also expressions of opinion affecting outside agencies which could well be in the same category.
>
> As you know, the role of the Urban Deprivation Officer Group is to look in a corporate way at your Report on Census Indicators, to take on board any further factual information which you have gathered, to consider the views of other departments of the Region and the Management Teams of District Councils, and to present to the council for further consideration a number of areas which are agreed corporately at officer level as requiring attention. I also intend that the officer group on a corporate basis should pose possibilities for supervision and management of coordinated effort in areas which are finally selected. Some of the views expressed in your draft document on matters of management are certainly worthy of consideration but my intention is that the draft produced by the Officer Group would be subject to informal political discussion before any formal report is released.[36]

The final paragraph is this:

> The contents of the report on Urban Deprivation, however, are in my view not relevant to the Regional Report itself and, above all, completely disregard the efforts we are making to fulfil the remit given to us by the Policy and Resources Committee in bringing forward a co-ordinated approach on a corporate basis.[37]

Like the first document, this asserts that the function of one department is being disregarded by another department whose staff are going beyond their remit. Several other points are raised, however. One is that the work of Physical Planning is pre-empting discussion which ought to take place before recommendations go to committee. The discussion on UDOG is being pre-empted, as is the informal political discussion. This is a disagreement over the appropriate forum for the discussion of corporate policy, or even over the importance of the institutional framework itself.

The very character of the two documents demonstrates this. One is a document submitted by two relatively junior staff to an interdepartmental group with a range of staff from Depute Director level down into middle management. These staff are taking a direct lead from political opinions expressed (presumably in Council minutes) by members without concern for the mediating role of the Directorate. The other document is a letter between two individual principal officers defending not only the jurisdiction of the different professions but also the forum, largely informal, provided by the direct contacts between principal officers and senior politicians (committee chairmen and Labour Group leadership). The Physical Planning document gives prior urgency to research and policy development to help tackle deprivation, and is prepared to push against UDOG's remit. The Policy Planning document defines UDOG's remit as it does in order to establish the priority of maintaining the institutional framework (both formal and informal). To pre-empt the interview data very slightly, and to recall issues raised in the chapter dealing with corporate planning and Strathclyde's management structures, these two ways of looking at policy development correspond to two different models of management. These are referred to in the interviews as the 'top down' or 'line management' model, and the 'bottom up' model. The Red Book and *AoN*, with their emphasis on corporate management, both advocate the 'bottom up' approach.

The two memoranda can also be characterised by using language which we have already referred to as common currency among officers within the authority. Senior staff in Policy Planning would be 'dragging their feet', and the relatively junior staff in Physical Planning would be 'mavericks'.

Although both texts carry a number of 'should' statements, their language is otherwise quite divergent. The Policy Planning document is the first so far examined to lay any weight on 'the facts'. It explicitly values 'factual statements' over 'opinions and criticisms which cannot be substantiated'. Apart from this vocabularistic point, it places a high value on statistical data – the only parts of the document being criticised which are explicitly 'valuable'. 'Census indicators' and 'any other factual information' are clearly referred to in a way which indicates the importance to Policy Planning of 'hard' data. The only opinions which are given a comparable value are those of other agencies, which form a sort of data in their own right and are primarily for UDOG to report and to bear in mind as a guide to what is politically feasible for the Council.

The Physical Planning document also gives weight to 'the collection of information' and 'monitoring'. Arguably, however, the thing which is given the highest value is the 'commitment' of staff involved with the development of deprivation policy. Of course, whether this document values information or commitment most highly is not of paramount importance. What is clear is that the vocabulary of the Physical Planning document has a clear relationship with the Red Book and the *AoN* report (these too spoke of 'information' and 'monitoring' rather than 'facts') whereas the Policy Planning document has not.

In comparison with CDP, the Physical Planning document adopts the attitudes of the authors of *Gilding the Ghetto*, while the Policy Planning document adopts the attitude which the CDP workers identify in the Home Office. This comparison with the CDP report (where the closing paragraphs speak of 'struggle for control of our own work') puts the struggle identified in the two memoranda in a different context. It appears not as an 'empire building' battle, an outbreak of tribal warfare in the professional subculture, focusing on the personal interests of the immediate contestants, but rather as a struggle between different ways of looking at the question 'How should the institution conduct its policy of self-criticism?' Beneath these two ways of looking at policy development lie two fundamentally different ways of looking at the world – two different rationalities.

7 Interview texts and exposition

INTRODUCTION

The policy texts which we examined in chapter six had already been introduced in earlier chapters; the interview texts need some introduction of their own. The main background here is the conflict which arose over Stan Hughes' policy proposal, which we referred to in chapter one, and we present a narrative of this incident. As a shorthand, it seemed appropriate to refer to the story as 'Jarndyce'; it involved a lengthy period where the outcome was uncertain, several individuals' futures seemed to be at stake, and the root issue seemed to be the right of a particular profession to make a certain sort of judgment.[1]

Following the Jarndyce narrative we present the interview texts, one after another, without comment, before proceeding to examine them in the light of the theories of knowledge characterised in chapter five. The texts are simple transcripts of interviews conducted with officers and members who were involved, in one way or another, with the work of UDOG, the production of the key policy documents (the Red Book and *AoN*) and Jarndyce. Interviews were informal, although interviewees were given a brief note, in advance of our meetings, of areas to be covered. The particular sections of the text which are presented are simply those which bear most directly on the production of the policy documents, on the Jarndyce incident, and on the unwritten rules governing officers' behaviour. The only important limiting factor was the desire of several of the interviewees for particular sections of the conversations not to be recorded, or for material not to be published. We have honoured those requests.

In fact the interview material forms far and away the largest part of this chapter; the exposition of it is relatively brief. This is important; the interview material is expounded in a way which pays particular attention to the language of the interviewees, but it would be a serious misunderstanding of the chapter to regard the content of the interview texts as unimportant. The interviews represent a straightforward attempt to get at an explanation of events surrounding Stan Hughes' policy proposal. The replies of interviewees are largely couched in general terms, presenting what might be regarded as an ethics of local government practice, and a description of the process of policy development. The exposition which follows the interviews, then, takes these explanations seriously, as accounts worthy of being assessed in their own terms. The interviewees challenge the philosophy from chapter five as much as the philosophy from chapter five challenges the interviewees; anecdote and theory are ultimately inseparable categories.

JARNDYCE

Like the difference of opinion between Physical Planning and Policy Planning, Jarndyce involved a conflict of interpretations of the corporate management process; it involved two departments and the question of the jurisdiction of officers at various levels on matters which involved the staff of both departments. It also arose in the context of a corporate review group assessing the contributions which different departments were making or should make to the deprivation strategy. The group included officers and members. It was chaired by Councillor Young, the Secretary to the Labour Group, and other members present at its meetings included Councillors Worthington and Harley, both senior members of the Labour Group. The officers were at Depute Director level in a range of departments. By the wish of those contacted, and at the express request of Councillor Young, they will not be named. The point of noting the membership of the group is that, even more so than in UDOG (the Urban Deprivation Officer Group), the individuals had considerable experience at senior levels in the management of local government. They had a close awareness of the policy of the Council, of the personal views of the political leadership, and of the views of the Directorate.

The failure of the particular proposal on which Jarndyce centres cannot, therefore, easily be put down to irresponsible behaviour or ignorance. This does not entirely rule out inexperience – experience always has scope for increase, at least until death. However, it seems possible that the reasons for the failure of the proposal may arise primarily from the basic character of the exercise, rather than from the personal qualities or deficiencies of the people involved.

One of the main reasons for looking at the incident in depth is the seriousness of the issues in the eyes of those who were directly involved.

The officer at the centre of events was made to feel that his position in the authority had been put at risk. He spoke of his head being 'on the chopping block' and Councillor Young spoke of him being 'shat upon from a great height'. The initial reaction of them both was that the incident was far too sensitive to allow either of further investigation or of any publication. As Councillor Young commented at one point where further information about the incident was being sought, 'You haven't heard about it.'

Time is a great healer, however, and what follows is a narrative of events in Jarndyce, with most of the names replaced by pseudonyms, and the identities of the departments thinly veiled.

Strathclyde Regional Council's review of its Area Initiatives began early in 1979; the Council's departments were requested to submit reports on their activities in Initiative areas, with a view to establishing the impact of the projects on mainstream departmental policy. These reports formed the basis of the review group's discussion, which also looked at wider aspects of the deprivation strategy. The review group met on a number of occasions during spring and summer of 1979, and Councillor Young's paper to the Labour Group was circulated in autumn 1979. Prior to all this Stan Hughes, one of the officers in the group, had been involved in the Policy Review Group (PRG) on departmental structures. He had been working with a small team on the structure of one particular department, and, along with an elected member (not a member of the Labour Group), had suggested an approach which might improve the effectiveness of work done by staff in that department. That suggestion, in a general form, is contained in the report of PRG, which was widely available, at least within the authority; it was also mentioned in the course of an oral presentation of the PRG conclusions to a meeting where a number of members, including senior members, were present.

In the discussion on deprivation strategy in Councillor Young's group, the general issue came up of the accountability of the staff of various departments. Stan Hughes' suggestion in the PRG report had addressed the same issue and this was pointed out. Councillor Young expressed disappointment that the suggestion had not been taken up before, and Mr Hughes asked if it should be picked up by the current group. Councillor Young agreed to this.

Mr Hughes later felt that, given a general familiarity with each other's ideas, he and Councillor Young may have established in a very brief exchange that Mr Hughes should prepare a paper on accountability for consideration by the group, but that this may have gone unnoticed by some other members of the group. At any rate, following this exchange, which took place in the presence of Mr Robinson (an officer in the department about which the paper was to be written), Mr Hughes did prepare a paper.

By the time the paper was finished the group had stopped meeting and Councillor Young was preparing to report to the Labour Group. Mr Hughes took a copy of the paper to Councillor Young, handing it to him personally. Mr Hughes asked if Councillor Young remembered how it had come about; Councillor Young replied that he did, and that he would read it with interest. Mr Hughes left the matter, understanding that any further action on the issue would be the responsibility of Councillor Young. His only other recollection of even mentioning the paper was in a passing reference to it during an informal conversation with Mr Robinson.

The next that Mr Hughes knew of the matter was when 'All hell was let loose.' Mr Davies, another member of Mr Hughes' department, informed him that writing the paper was ill-advised, Mr Hughes should not have done it. Mr Hughes understood that Mr Davies had been asked to say this by Mr Austin, his Director, after Mr Macleod, Director of Mr Robinson's department, had complained either to Councillor Stewart or to the Chief Executive (hence, presumably, Councillor Young's reference to a great height). In a later conversation with Mr Austin, Mr Hughes was told that there had been discussions with Councillor Stewart about his (Hughes') future in the authority. Mr Hughes understood this as 'a warning shot across my bows ... It's the sort of thing John Austin does when he wants to frighten you.' In fact no subsequent disciplinary action was taken against Mr Hughes. The proposal was completely rejected – any further consideration of it was seen as quite out of the question. Discussing the matter with Mr Hughes and Mr Robinson it was clear that there was no personal animosity between the two, although both felt that there was a lack of trust between senior officers of the two departments. Mr Hughes had assumed that Mr Macleod (Mr Robinson's Director) had heard of the paper from Mr Robinson, and that this had sparked off the conflict. Mr Robinson was concerned that Mr Hughes should have thought this and stressed that he had not told his Director about the paper. The route to Mr Macleod remains a mystery.

Both Mr Hughes and Mr Robinson were confident that Mr Macleod had not seen a copy of the paper, and that the conflict arose not from its contents, but from the fact of it having been written by an officer not from Mr Macleod's department. Mr Hughes felt that he had been seen as breaking the rule that 'you don't criticise another department in front of an elected member or in public'. His breaking the rule, rather than the content of the paper, was also the cause of his own Director's displeasure.

To preserve confidences, text from interviews with Mr Hughes is not presented, other than the brief remarks already given, and the paper is not presented in any detail, although Mr Hughes did provide a copy.

TEXTS

Alan Robinson: April 1981

Robinson [People in local government are] sensitive to criticism, there's no doubt. We're all that way. But I think in local government, despite the corporate management approach – maybe because of the corporate management approach, and because heads of departments are more accountable to senior management teams and the like – there is an even greater sensitivity about criticism. And therefore the one head of department has to be most cautious about what he says about the other. Now, I hope you can see it in this light, this is not a criticism of ... I want to make this clear, that I've heard a lot of criticism of Stan Hughes, but personally I get on well with Stan, and I hope he said that to you too.

Smart Yes, he did.

Robinson I get on well with Stan, ... and I trust Stan, and ...

Smart I'm sure he wouldn't have mentioned your name to me if he ...

Robinson And I'm not particularly sensitive, but I've got a lot of colleagues who are very sensitive. And I know that that incident, together with other wee things has led to, well, ... a less fruitful cooperation between the two departments. There has been a reluctance to take the barriers down really. And the fault's not – well obviously we must be partly to blame – but a lot of that comes from the other department because they tend to have more than their fair share of way out, hard left, outspoken critics. And in the circles in local government which we mix in, that may come to be all right, but certainly isn't at the moment; and if you're prepared to stand up on your two feet at a public meeting and castigate the service which this department provides, or any other service, you've got to be prepared to bear the consequences. You know, it's not ...

Smart What exactly would the consequences be?

Robinson The consequences of this incident you're speaking of ... the consequence is that there is not between the two departments the mutual confidence that there ought to be, and I would say that while we more or less cooperate according to the letter of the policy, it's not as friendly and fruitful as it might be ... there is ...

Smart The thing that puzzles me is ... Stan Hughes is on a fairly formally constituted corporate group, with representatives from a range of departments, under the chairmanship of a fairly senior elected member, which is set up ostensibly to review the deprivation policy ...

Robinson Aha.

Smart ... which must mean to review departmental policy on deprivation ...

Robinson Aha, yes.

Smart ... and then he writes this paper – and it wasn't standing up at a public meeting. If he only passed one copy to the chairman of the group he was far from standing up at a public meeting and making criticisms of the service. He was simply passing a paper to the chairman of the group, which seems to me perfectly reasonable. It seems a bit unfair that when he went about it that way he should be treated as if he had made a public criticism.

Robinson Yes, well, if I had been in Stan's shoes I think I would have gone about it in this way: I think I would have gone to my head of department and said, 'Look, Ron Young has asked me to write a paper on accountability in the ... service'.

Smart So you would have gone to the head of your own department?

Robinson Yes, if I'd been in Stan's shoes, and 'would you clear that with David Macleod, or will you sound David Macleod on what he thinks about it?' And having written the paper – this is standard local government procedure – I would have submitted it to David Macleod for his comments. Are you sure Stan didn't do that? It still escapes me how such a ...

Smart Well, I'd be amazed if Stan hadn't mentioned that, if he'd done it. No, I'm sure he didn't.

Robinson You see, why is it Ron Young was in danger of taking action? As I understand it ...

Smart No, I don't think Ron Young was in danger of taking action. As I understand it ...

Robinson Oh he, ... Oh, he was, because I got ...

Smart Ron Young was more concerned because he would be associated with Stan Hughes and so with the criticism which Stan Hughes got; it would reflect badly on him in the Labour Group, it would not do his reputation any good, or not do any good for the deprivation policy.

Robinson Well, this is always a danger, this is a political danger – this is an aside – in all of these groups. I don't know why this should be, well, I know ... the Tories always tend to line up in favour of one particular approach to the service, and the Labour boys tend to line up with – you

see, there's the other service, B – they always tend to line up with B in
the criticisms of the service ... and I suppose that Ron Young would be
very sensitive about not lining up with one or the other of them.
  Anyway, I'm still at a loss to discover how it surfaced, that document.
But I know it did surface and I do know that Stan Hughes – now I don't
want you to quote this – got into hot.water, and I do know that I phoned
Ron Young. I remember summoning up enough courage to say, 'Well,
look, I think I'll say a word on behalf of Stan Hughes.' And I did, took
him off whatever hook he was on ... I'm not sure.
Smart You had a word with?
Robinson With Ron Young. I phoned Ron Young.
Smart I thought you were saying you had a word with David Macleod.
You didn't have a word with David Macleod about it?
Robinson Well ... I think Stan asked me to speak to David Macleod to
let him know that Stan hadn't been intending to criticise the department
in any way, and I said that to David Macleod. But I'm still at a loss to
discover how it went from Stan to me to Macleod and from there to
Boyle.[2] It may well be that David Macleod took it up and didn't let me
know exactly what was happening. But I'm not sure, he's not usually like
that. All that I'm fairly confident of is that it wasn't just a straightforward
cribbing job; but I honestly can't remember how it came about, and I do
know ...
Smart What I'm trying to establish is what Stan Hughes could have
done that would have got this issue on to the agenda in a legitimate manner without causing all this damage to people's careers, left, right and
centre. Now you talk about him checking on it with his Director, to
check with David Macleod.
Robinson Well, you see, I could give you the answer to that.
Smart Would David Macleod's objection simply be that he hadn't done
that then? Because if ... trying to keep it even more quiet than ... You
see, I got the impression that, my first reaction when I heard of it was
that it was almost the very nature of the suggestion which made it
impossible, given the attitude of David Macleod, and the service, A, in
general, made it impossible for him to legitimately put it on the agenda.
Robinson Well, let me tell you of devices that I would use if I wanted to
do something. You mustn't be ... in dealings in local government with
fellow officials, you mustn't be sleekit; and I'm not using that against
Stan. I've already told you of the possibility that he would go to his
Director and say, 'Look, we're not satisfied with the handling of deprivation, something should be done about it. What about arranging a
meeting with A and we'll have a joint meeting and discuss one or two
things?' If John Austin went to David Macleod and David Macleod said,

'No, you're not doing that ...', then it would be up to John Austin to, if he felt strongly about it, to go to the politicians, to go to his Chairman and say, 'Look, Bill, we feel that we're not, ... that A are not ...'. And you're right into major criticism of another department, you're on very dangerous ground. Now, if you do it that way, you may gain your point and the thing may surface as an official approach, that's if Bill wins through. Since it would involve another department, Bill would probably have to take it to the Labour Group, and he could be defeated there. But immediately you take that step of going to the Chairman, then somehow or another you've broken one of the unwritten laws of local government, that officials are officials and members are members. You see, ... you're aware of this, aren't you?

Smart This is one of the major conclusions I'll be ...

Robinson You see, never, never in Christendom would I go to an elected member about anything that a member of staff senior to myself would say to me, you know, by way of discipline. I would never go and complain to the Chairman and say, 'Look, so and so ...'. That's part of the unwritten, sort of, ethic.

This you'll also find, by the way – I'm not talking about the whole of the profession, but at official level – very very doubtful if you'll find an official in A with an affiliation to a political party, very very doubtful. But you'll find this in B. I mean, I wouldn't be a member of a political party, and neither would David Macleod, no matter which way we were, because that just wouldn't be ... because we were ...

Smart Is that because you're just a generation older, or nearer to the top of the hierarchy?

Robinson Yes, that could be so, yes, that's a possibility. I was brought up to believe that no matter what my own personal political feelings were, that I should be prepared to serve the whole spectrum of politicians, Labour, Tory, Communist or what have you, and to give them all the same service. Now, that's the way we were brought up in local government. If a Commie asked me to do something that's within my power, I would do the same ...

Smart In speaking to folk who are actively involved with political parties, I've been surprised how much that attitude goes along with party membership.

Robinson Yes, well, I've been amazed at B committee meetings. I sometimes have to attend them. I've been amazed by some of the political statements being made by members of staff. You know, I would never make an attack on this government or any other government before a committee. That's not a part of my job. My job is to put up facts and information to members and make recommendations and leave them to it. I would never dream of saying before a committee, 'Margaret Thatcher is this, that or the next thing ... and we ought to be doing this', but B staff would, quite a lot during that period when they were discussing the new Bill. They were making open political statements about the government telling lies, about the government doing this or that.

Smart Back to what Stan Hughes could have done, then. What seems to make his action more reasonable is the fact that it's down in black and white in an earlier report ...

Robinson Yes, aha.

Smart ... that something needs to be done about accountability, and that such and such is a good idea. He simply puts his paper forward to Ron Young and 'all hell is let loose', to quote him. What could he have done, given that concern, that idea ...?

Robinson Well, my simple reply to that would be that he shouldn't have had that ... I was going to say that he shouldn't have that concern. Did he have that concern as an official in the B department or as a member of the public at large, or do you not distinguish between them?

Smart Well, you do distinguish between them, obviously.

Robinson Yes. If he had that concern as a member of the public at large then obviously he can get at the public at large and try and set up some sort of thing there. But if he got his concern, or if he had his concern as an official of the B department then there are ways in which he ought to proceed, and I think I've indicated what they are. Really he should ... I'm trying to think myself what I would do if I were opposed to some practice in another department – as an official, it would need to be as an official. As a member of the public I'm free to speak or to join societies or parties and so on, to move against any policy in the other department. Let me see now what I would think.

You may not agree with this. The B department took a decision to give a grant to some particular society. It's just my personal view, but I wouldn't have done it. How would I have gone about trying to get that overturned? I don't think I would have done anything. I think – maybe you'll regard this as the weak way out – I would have said, 'Well, that's a concern of ...'. I'm speaking now as an official, not as a member of the public. As a member of the public I would have my own means of getting at that sort of policy. As an official I would say, 'Well, that's a matter for B.' If on the other hand it was a matter that impinged on the A department, I would see my course of action quite clearly. Let me see if I can take a simple example.

Let's take something where there's a joint responsibility, centres which don't have any recognition in the A Acts or the B Acts. Youngsters are in a centre, and B decide to appoint certain staff to these centres. We're still responsible for the youngsters in these centres. Now my own feeling – I wouldn't bother about that – but if I did feel keyed up about it I would write a paper for our own senior management team, and I would say, 'B are perhaps encroaching into our line of business, they are providing staff for these centres and we are responsible for the children in these centres. I propose that we should do ...'.

Right, now, having got that far, I'm keyed up about B appointing staff – which I'm not but some of my colleagues are – so I'm worked up about it and I write a paper for our management team, and one of the first recommendations is that we go to the B director.

That's agreed, that we go to the B director, and I'm asked if I would have a word with David Macleod. I say, 'Look, David, you're appointing staff to these centres, that's our line of business, I object.' We'll make this as simple as possible. He says, 'Go to hell, I'm continuing to do it.' And my comeback is, 'Well, if that's your way, I'm putting a paper up to the A committee and from there to the Regional Council.'

Now, that's the procedure, and at the end of the day, the Regional Council will say, 'B will appoint staff to these centres', or 'they won't', and whatever way they decide, that's the policy, and I would accept that. Now these are the procedures. But if you're going to criticise another department, or object to a practise in another department, you've really got to go to that other department first of all and press them to the wall, and only when you don't get any satisfaction do you feel free in conscience to say, 'Well, we're going up to our A committee, or to our Chairman of A.' And if he agrees he would maybe take it up with the Labour Group, or with the chairman of B. That happens not infrequently, and that's the way you deal with matters that are properly for another department.

Smart You wouldn't go for generally cultivating informal contacts with two or three elected members who happened to be interested in that sort of thing, and getting them perhaps to informally contact folk in other departments? Would you consider that to be ...

Robinson No, I would consider that just a wee bit unethical in the present situation.

Smart Or perhaps, through that same sort of informal contact, getting the elected member to raise it, perhaps with the Labour Group, not as having come from you, as if it was his own interest?

Robinson I would regard that as unethical too. Or maybe not 'unethical', not a proper way of proceeding. Having said that, ... no, I don't think I would get someone ...

Smart What about getting folk, maybe two or three levels below you in the hierarchy, and gaining their confidence and then trying to work by them making contacts at their own levels in other departments...?

Robinson Well, that's the way we hope that things would work but, you see, this is again one of the faults with cooperation. We agree on policies at, maybe, the directorate level; it's when you come to put them into effect that very often the troubles begin and, really, there have to be directors ... But getting at elected members, I wouldn't want to appear to you to be holier than thou. I'm just setting out what the ideal ... At times I've often said to a person like Dick Stewart ... I would never say to him, 'Here, look, Dick, you ought to make an enquiry into accountability in, say, teachers.' I would go to my own boss first of all before attempting anything like that. But I wouldn't want you to think that I've never said to an elected member, 'Oh, I don't fancy that', that sort of approach. But I would consider it unethical in the local government official context, for me to go to members and say, 'Oh, look, I don't like what's happening in, say, B.' At the same time, when a member of an officer member group, I would think nothing of attacking a practising member of the staff of B, or I would think nothing of their attacking something in A. But at that you're not being explicit, you're not asking anybody to do it. If they want to take it up, they take it up. Does that help you?

Smart Well, that last thing seems to be more or less what Stan Hughes was doing, that's the trouble. He was just in a corporate group with officers and members there, where he ought to have been able to do that, I would have thought.

Robinson Maybe the mistake was that he ... made by Ron Young in asking him to do it. If you're asking me, and I've told you before I'm a friend of Stan Hughes, if you're asking me, within the present context of local government organisation: one, Ron Young should never have asked Stan Hughes to do that; and two, Stan Hughes shouldn't have done it in the way he did do it. I would be quite definite about that.

If Ron Young had worries about the earlier report not being implemented, or if he had worries about accountability, then he has his procedures, either through the Labour Group or direct to the Chairman, Charlie Kirk: 'Look, Charlie, you're not implementing, what are you going to do about it?' And Charlie Kirk would then come to the Director of A and would have a discussion about it there. Given that Ron Young had made a mistake, and he did make a mistake, and he asked Stan to do it, then Stan should have said, 'Well, look, Ron, I think we should bring the Director of A into this.' I'm certain that's the procedure that would be approved.

So I think that Stan made the fatal mistake of being an outsider and writing a paper about the A department. That's supporting your theory, isn't it? There are ways round these difficulties. What do you feel yourself, personally? What would you feel about Stan going to two or three elected members and saying, 'Here, it's about time these places were wakened up'?

Smart I would say that ... the impression I've got from speaking to quite a few folk is that it wouldn't be unreasonable to go to one or two elected members and sound them out and suggest they take it up. One of the criticisms of the Policy Planning Department, when UDOG was running, was that Policy Planning failed to put pressure on elected members ... failed to take an initiative in saying, 'Such and such an issue has come up and we feel that you ought to make some sort of political decision on it.'

Robinson Yes, and they're still failing. They've got this huge big structure now and it's failing too, or so far, although maybe they're trying to find their feet. You see, the Chief Executive's Department was set up so that services could be coordinated. We're still waiting for that coordination. And again, I doubt if it can succeed, because – and this was said, this was said to Boyle, the man responsible for it – within the local government Acts, the adviser to the Regional Council on Education is the Director of Education, not the Chief Executive; the adviser to the Regional Council on Social Work is the Director of Social Work, not the Chief Executive, the adviser to the Regional ...

Smart And you've got the same for Police and the same for Fire. Yes, I was surprised to see that on reading through the Act, because the Local Government Scotland Act really is, ninety per cent is just laying down responsibility, and yet for those services you get a clause left which says, 'the authority shall appoint an officer to be called the Director of Education, he shall ...'.

Robinson Yes. So there are these big inertias built into the system. But Policy Planning didn't do that, you're right. Far too often decisions are taken in local government, and in national government indeed, by groups of people who are not really fully acquainted with the scene. I think that's in the nature of things.

Smart Right, that sounds quite like an issue that came up in connection with the Priesthill Area Initiative. The problem that arises there is that, the problem that arose, that folk who were working in the area – basic grade Social Workers, folk from Housing Management, which makes it even more complicated in bringing in another organisation – these people had one view of the way matters ought to be dealt with, and felt that the people who took the decisions, at the top of the hierarchy, at headquarters, didn't have an ability with ...

Robinson ... with the scene ...

Smart ... and there seemed to be no way – no mechanism worked out that really bridged the gap, and the only way that it can be bridged, as far as I can see, is to somehow give the folk who have got that experience a legitimate voice in policy decisions, at least in providing information at ...

Robinson ... committee level ...

Smart ... committee level, which means, unfortunately, that you've got to have some sort of mechanism whereby ...

Robinson The argument against that is that you're bringing in too much emotion.

Smart Well, it comes round to that, but you've got to have some sort of mechanism which allows for conflict of opinion to be brought – because that's the problem, the problem is that the people at the lower level will see the failings in the traditional manner of service delivery, and you've got to have some forum which is legitimate for that conflict of opinion to be aired in front of the folk, chairmen of committees, or directors or depute directors, who are making the decisions.

Robinson I would accept that, I would accept that's a legitimate thing to ask for. Because far too many decisions are taken in isolation, away from the scene of what's being discussed.

Smart But the trouble is that you come up, again and again, against the sort of unwritten rule, that people don't criticise in some sort of public forum. And you've almost got to the stage where ... I've said before, that you've got to take account of these unwritten rules, and if you take account of them and are careful of how you go about change then you can achieve change. It worries me that what I'm almost saying when I say you've got to provide this forum is that you've got to somehow change that rule, you've got to try and get an alteration in that unwritten rule.

Robinson Yes, well, I would agree that's one way of going about it.

Dick Stewart: June 1980

Smart One question is about how much influence Directors or senior officials have on policy as it's being decided. Some folk have said that they've almost got more access to the folk who are making the decisions than some of the back bench members – I don't know if you talk about 'back bench' members – but that they've got a sort of privileged access. Citing, for instance, the Policy Review Group on Structures and the Directors of Education and Social Work, refraining from making comment to the working group but then, when the report was finished, coming to yourself and saying, 'We don't like such and such ...'. So that's one question, just how much do the senior officials have access in that sort of way?

Stewart They have access, but not as implied in that, that they've got undue influence on policy. They've got a contribution to make and are brought in on certain aspects for discussion. But no undue influence at all, in fact to the contrary. They're justly entitled to state their point of view, along with everyone else, more so on the practical side of implementation of policies, but ... no undue influence.

The officials, and I think this is one of the things that you'll recognise about Strathclyde, at least the leadership ... they, I think, are quite pleased that they have the type of leadership that's a firm leadership, and have policies, and policies that they're prepared to implement, as distinct from the type of Councillor that they can either manoeuvre, or don't know where the hell they stand with them. And I think this is generally recognised by our officials.

To say they've more access than the back benchers is nonsense; there's nothing to stop any back bench member, if he wants to discuss anything, from coming and discussing it. Again, you have the few that have had that opportunity, don't take the opportunity because it would deprive them of having the chance to say that they don't get the opportunity of coming.

Smart You mentioned the reaction, earlier on, of a lot of members to the Red Book, the deprivation policy, talking about the members' practical concern over against the 'theoretical' sort of material in the deprivation policy. What do you think was the reaction of the Directors of departments to the sort of thing that was coming out of, say, the Urban Deprivation Officers' Group?

Stewart Oh, I think on the whole it was welcomed by the Directors, because I'm fairly certain that the whole lot of them recognised the problems of the deprived areas, and that something had to be done. And I think they've enough sense – I'll be disappointing you – to know that where you can get success in a difficult area, it reflects on them to their credit as well ... And I don't think they're that, shall we say, stupid, not to try and implement policies.

Smart What about an aspect of that group in particular, and also Ron Young's review group more recently, where you've got a corporate group, you've got officials from a range of departments, discussing as a group, so that you get officials from one department, either just in the discussions, or maybe putting a paper to a group like that, you get them making comments, not always entirely complimentary, about other departments, or about the service that other departments are responsible for?

Stewart Well, yes, this again, I think, is perfectly natural, that you can get an official from a department being critical of other departments and it sometimes being resented.

Smart There's one instance I have in mind, I don't know whether I ought to go into it, but ...

Stewart This is where B was critical of A. Is that the one you're particularly referring to?

Smart Yes. To quote Ron Young, the official from B was 'shat upon from a great height' because of it.. Talking to Ron Young I got the impression that it had caused quite a bit of upset. I came across the story speaking to the official concerned, and I'd wanted to follow that up, naturally, although obviously not wanting to do anything that's going to make a scandal or anything like that.

Stewart Well, this is what you tend to get ...

Smart Ron Young's reaction was that I hadn't heard of it, you know, and I ought to keep really quiet about it.

Stewart Well, the position is, and it's not anything that anybody need be frightened of or scared about, when you have joint working groups you're going to naturally get officials ... they're there to express their points of view on other departments. How they do it is sometimes different and they ought to not get carried away with their own judgment as being necessarily the right thing anyway. And when they are making criticisms, of the other departments in particular, they ought to make sure that what they are putting forward as a criticism is a factual criticism.

Smart So that it wouldn't be right for them to make judgments?

Stewart No. I think if you're criticising another department, or in anything, when you're doing that at the top level, you've got to be careful of what you're criticising, and that you're doing it based on fact, and being able to stand up to the accusations or statements you're making. And in this case I think the person who was making the criticism – and no doubt believing it – wasn't aware of all the facts concerning it.

Smart In spite of having worked, in another context, with that department, or on that department, for a year.

Stewart Yes, in spite of working on that. I think there is an element, probably, in what he was doing ... there was an element of truth and an element of lack of knowledge, a combination of both.

Smart Lack of knowledge about how to go about getting a fair criticism across?

Stewart His presentation, that's right, yes, and the method of doing it. And I think he was, shall I say, misdirected as well, in doing it the way he did it. I think it was an inexperienced person, without mentioning any names, that asked him to do it, when he ought not to have been asked to do it. If you're wanting an inquiry made into a department you don't go to somebody from another department to do your dirty work to try to prove a thing. And I think that's what was there. I don't think it basically had anything to do with a free discussion between officials and members at all, I think this was a separate axe being ground.

Smart I don't know whether it's right or not, but I'm just wanting to be sure whether we are both talking about the same case. Would it be possible to mention the name to check, on the understanding that it doesn't go any further?

Stewart Aye, as far as I'm concerned, aye.

Smart It's Stan Hughes' paper to Ron Young's group.

Stewart Yes, that's right.

Smart I got the impression, actually, that Stan Hughes had more offered to Ron Young to write it, but that may be wrong.

Stewart Yes, well, I think it was a combination of ... autosuggestion and inexperience, that if he voluntarily offered it, then it was inexperience on his part to have offered to do that type of thing.

Smart Let me explain why we were getting on to the other question which I had, which is, that there seems to be a number of what you might call 'unwritten rules' about how you go about different things in local government, that have got to be followed or else. And the one that you were saying there, you know, that if you want to say something critical about another department you don't get somebody from outside the department to do it, that's the sort of thing that I'm thinking of. Another would be, a couple of folk have said that, certainly at directorate level, it is just not ever done for one Director to make critical comments about another department in front of other folk ...

Stewart Aye, publicly ...

Smart Aye, now, as a complete outsider, you can guess at what sort of unwritten rules exist, from common sense, but you can never be sure. Now the other question was, what would you say are the main rules, what to do, what not to do maybe, in situations like that or just generally?

Stewart I don't know if I'd put it in the terms 'unwritten rules'.

Smart Well, that's actually taking somebody else's words.

Stewart Aye, but I wouldn't put it in those terms, that they're unwritten rules. I think it's a question of common sense prevailing.

Smart It is just common sense, is it?

Stewart Yes. You don't, I mean, a Director, or it might be anybody, you don't bull-headed rush into being a critic, or condemning. It's the sheer common sense of doing the thing, and where and when you do it. Nobody takes kindly to being criticised on a particular point that's their profession, because if you start that – say the Director of Education and the Director of Social Work, they've common fields, but once you depart from that common field, again, each is entitled to their own opinion, but one has got to carry it out.

And it depends on what the field is. If you're discussing common problems, each are equally entitled to their say, and to criticise each other for what they're doing or not doing in that particular joint venture. But if it goes into whether the curriculum of the second year is the proper curriculum, and it's the Director of Social Work that's doing it, then the Director of Social Work has no more right than anyone else to make his contribution. As I say, it's purely a matter of common sense. And, rightly, the professional resents being accused of unprofessionalism, if it comes to that, by someone who's not in the profession.

You've got to take a specific issue really to deal with it, rather than say in general. If it's a joint policy – say on the under-fives, you see, where up to three it's the Social Work, from three to five it's the Education – I'm sure that both can be equally critical of the way that others are doing it. And it can be discussed and thrashed out in that way. Once it goes beyond the fives, the age of five, then there's a natural resentment if the Director of Social Work is telling how he's going to run his education for over-fives.

In the same way there would be natural resentment from Social Work if the Director of Education was telling him how to run old people's homes, or his mentally handicapped places. So it's in the context of the thing that you've got to look at it. In the same way, you could get a technical ... without it even being in the realms of anything else ... between, say your Sewage, Water and Roads, on the way to tackle the technical problems of the thing. I don't know if that's dealt with it, Harry?

Smart Well, it has to a point. It raises a question of how much different areas of the work of local government – the Education service, Social Work, Police and so on – ought to be professionalised at all. Maybe there's one question.

Stewart Yes, well, it comes to that. This is what we're hoping to have a much wider forum on, now, with the creation of the Chief Executive's Department, and the Chief Executive responsible for his departments. You now have the machinery where a proper corporate approach can be made, and can be carried out.

Smart So what should Stan Hughes have done, then? Should he have waited for a machinery like that to come into being?

Stewart In the first place, when he was dealing with this, he ought to have, I would think, have gone to the A Department and said that he'd been asked, or had volunteered, to do a paper on an aspect of A. At least that was the first common courtesy, you see.

Smart Right.

Stewart And once he had done that, and he was reaching conclusions, he ought to have had the courtesy to put his paper to them.

Smart Before letting the group see ...?

Stewart Before letting the group see it, in order that at least they had a sight of the paper and were then prepared to face the criticisms that would come. These, as I say, are common sense, common courtesies, that ought to be done. In the same way as Stan Hughes would equally – you see, and I like Stan, I think he's an able fellow. I think he's maybe more experienced to get at the higher level. And when you approach it and do it that way ... he'd have the resentment from A that he had been asked or was writing a paper on their Department that they knew nothing about. And it's not as if it was the type of paper that needed to be done on largely factual stuff, that ought to have come from the A Department.

Smart I'm stuck because I don't know exactly what the paper was about because from both Stan Hughes and Ron Young, as soon as I came across it, I got this sort of scared reaction from both of them. In fact the most scared reaction that I've come across about anything so far, and so I more or less let it go.

Stewart Yes, well, as I say ...

Smart But if I could just add, it did look, from the outside, bearing in mind both their criticisms of the department concerned, and bearing in mind what folk had said about the indecisiveness or the lack of total commitment from the Labour Group to some of the aspects of the deprivation policy ...

Stewart No, I don't think that had anything to do with it, Harry.

Smart Aye, but it did look plausible that you'd got, that what you had there was a very strong entrenched professional interest which was capable of ...

Stewart No.

Smart ... of swinging an issue its own way.

Stewart No, that wasn't it at all. It was the method by which it was done, not by the results, but ...

Smart Yes, I can see that, but ...

Stewart ... and that's why both of them shied off.

Smart It did look pretty plausible from the outside.

Stewart Yes, yes. No, it was not because of what was said, or anything at all, it was because of the method by which it was done, and that's why, I should imagine, both shied off, because they knew that both had had the wrong type of approach to doing that type of thing. I think there was more of that than anything else, Harry.

James Ford: April 1980

Ford I remember, as a much younger man in the Clerk's office, wondering why it was that certain things were done or certain things weren't done. I can well remember the frustrations at times: 'Why has this happened or why has that happened?' But normally it's a fairly close knit, very good set of personal relations within the one office. You got the story or you ... To be honest, I've always been in a situation where I was involved with committee work, and I worked with members, albeit in a junior capacity in those days, and one got to learn the ropes and the realities of the decision-making process.

People in other departments tend to work away a wee bit and then suddenly find themselves, when they get into their late thirties, perhaps, thrown into the committee melting pot; and they find dealing with members a bit difficult. And it really is the realities of the game. It's a very very difficult situation at times, to be almost a kind of bridge on the one hand between views coming forward on corporate exercises and, you know, politicians, whom one has a considerable respect for, but they're all kind of different in their approach to things. And that's what's been decided and that's got to be implemented and conveyed.

And, you know, that's just life, and it's a very difficult thing to explain and I'm sure that people who haven't been involved in that perhaps see it differently. And maybe there's a problem ... I often say that the biggest problem Strathclyde has is communications, that maybe we don't do enough of it. As I've said, I think the obligation to communicate really lies with the department. In some cases it may be fair to say that the communications are good but that people don't really want to listen, or won't accept the explanations. However, you carry on.

Smart In answer to your comment on how I seem to have taken up junior officers' grievances or frustrations: I take your point, but for me to accept your explanation, that these frustrations arise because people aren't aware of the realities of the decision-making process, it means I've got to be able to believe in quite a – not division of opinion, perhaps – but a lack of any clear cohesion of opinion within the Labour Group. Because, certainly, a number of the folk I've spoken to have got fairly close contacts with, as far as I can see, quite a number of the Labour members, and they feel that, they say, that they definitely do believe in elected members having the final decision. They would themselves be worried about any short-circuit of that. But they feel that by having an informal contact with elected members, that they're being virtuous, or correct or proper. That means you've got to be able to say to them, 'Well, in fact ...', and fair enough, it's just what you would say you don't go and talk about. But I have no direct evidence to support this split – split is too strong a word. Do you see what I mean?

Ford Yes, I do, I do.

Smart The other thing is that – the other reply is that the frustrations are not so much that their own ideas haven't been taken up, as that the Red Book – and more importantly the spirit of the Red Book, this is where it gets awkward – the spirit of the Red Book isn't accepted amongst the officials of the authority. They feel that the majority of the officials of the authority, at all levels, have a view of deprivation which is fairly close to what the Red Book actually rejects – they're blaming the victim. And I think that's probably the biggest frustration; and their grievance, then, is that whoever is responsible, whether it's the central coordinating body or the individual departments, whoever is responsible hasn't pushed the Red Book and the *Areas of Need* report firmly and far enough to the whole of the authority's staff.

That's what they would want to see done, and the sort of things that they're recommending, I think, are not so much that the policy documents be changed, or the nature of the policy altered, as that a more aggressive attitude be taken to ensuring that officials don't have the freedom ...

Ford Is that their role? Irrespective of whether they're right or wrong, is that their role as junior members of staff?

Smart Well, not all too junior.

Ford But is that their role?

Smart Well, I don't know; that is the central question that's coming up. What exactly should an officer's role be? That's where I would like us to spend more time in discussion.

Ford Well, I think the hard answer – it's a very difficult area – the hard answer to that situation is that we have had ... first of all the coordination arrangements have had to be set up. There have been two seminars, one of P&R last year, one of P&R this year, apart from the Labour Group seminar, that have looked at the pace, speed and direction of the deprivation policy, raising all these questions about, perhaps, unresponsiveness or slow response from middle management and all the various other things, that people are really reluctant to do it, that they're not diverting mainstream budgets to the extent that they should. These are discussed in full, on the Sub on Deprivation, in seminar form, with the nominated deputes as we call them from other departments, in one or two cases with the directors of departments, with the coordinators and with the local members, and representatives of area teams; and the issues are brought firmly and fully to the surface. And the decisions on the extent to which things need speeded up, or how do we overcome blocks and otherwise, are very much political decisions.

Now I might feel that there are other aspects of the Council's policy that aren't proceeding quickly enough, others might feel that there are other things. That depends on the things one's interested in. But I would have thought it's kind of difficult for people who aren't involved – don't see the whole spectrum, don't see the whole pressures, that aren't party to these review discussions – to make that kind of remark, which they can't justify.

We all know of examples where certain things happen – and 'My God, do they not know there's a deprivation policy?' – and efforts are made to sort it out. But in big local authorities, by and large, things have to be done on a gradualist basis. You can't publish a book and say, 'That's our policy' on something like deprivation, and automatically expect everybody overnight to implement it. I personally feel that one of the ideas the late Convener had at one time was to take the public halls in the region and have all the staffs in, hundreds of staff in, and to spell out the political message.

Smart Yes, that's the sort of thing ...

Ford That, in fact, didn't happen. We got a training budget, money for training. Training has happened in the coordination arrangements. The reason more hasn't happened is that there haven't been the staff resources to do it. All these things come into it and it's bloody easy for people to criticise without realising conflicting pressures.

Smart Right, that is, in terms of specific recommendations, that's one of the more common, that there should be a much greater training emphasis.

Ford Aha, well, the whole question of training, again, is being raised at these seminars. Now, if it so happens that members last year heard all the stories, heard all the warts and said, 'Look, we'll try and improve that and the next thing', that's it, and it may well be that individual members, individual elected members or members of staff, felt that the decision was the wrong one or that they should have tried to do more, but ... that's life. So ... I don't know what the answer to that one is. If that's what people think, that's what people think.

If they choose to have – something I've never personally favoured – but if they choose to get particularly friendly with individual members and to hear of their grouses and grievances and try to feed that back into the system – I personally don't ... sort of acknowledge that. Having said that, it's fairly easy for me to say that, having for many years had contact with elected members. For those that don't have it, they seek the alternative outlet of a personal relationship with somebody who is a member and through that they get their – small 'p' – political satisfaction, if I could put it that way.

Smart Talking about Paterson, and ambiguities in Paterson, that strikes me as a fairly glaring problem with it, because it comes out fairly strongly in favour of a break away from the traditional model of an officer's position in relation to members generally. It seems to want to steer a middle course between emphasising, on the one hand, that all decision making is in the hands of the whole Council and, on the other hand, saying that officials have got to be in on policy making at all stages and that officials do get involved anyway and therefore we ought to face up to the realities and accept it. I find it impossible to see a really coherent view developed, and I wonder if that ambiguity is one of the problems that is causing these frustrations.

Ford Well, that is an ambiguity. I don't think that it was ever envisaged by Paterson, or anybody else, that people other than heads of departments or deputes should be in a position to give policy advice on important issues. Paterson never said anything ... what Paterson said was the system of not having a Chief Executive, and authorities where members took decisions without the benefit of political advice, tended to be an overstatement of the situation, at least with reference to some of the previous authorities. What Paterson said was, 'Look, there needs to be a focal point for decision making, namely the Policy and Resources Committee linked to the political process, and a focal point, not for policy decision making but for policy advice, through the Chief Executive', and that there should be facilities for the two meeting up more in a proper considered forum, which is the Policy and Resources Committee.

Smart Well, maybe it's a weakness in the way it's written.

Ford It certainly never suggested for one minute that the moment you become a local government employee that you're going to have a say in policy formulation.

Smart OK, but the sections that deal with it don't introduce any differentiation between directors and depute directors on the one hand, and junior staff on the other.

Ford Oh, I don't see that. Well, quite frankly, because nobody ...

Smart Presumably everybody would be so ...

Ford Presumably the people on Paterson never thought otherwise, it was so self-evident. Having said that, I am not a person who subscribes to the view that people outside that band, the select band if you like, don't have a contribution to make. And personally, I think it's a very good idea ... I think that any head of department who doesn't sound out the opinions of staff and people who are expert on a thing, 'How should we tackle this?' ... but at the end of the day I think it's up to the Director of Physical Planning or the Director of Roads, the Director of Social

Work or whoever it is to say, 'That's my view as Director of Social Work.'

Now, that is not to be confused with the kind of development aspects where you have officer member groups and you involve back benchers and middle management staff to look at a problem and come up with recommendations. But at the end of the day, it's the chairman of committee, and he'll say, 'Well, I've listened to it all, and my view as chairman of such and such is ...', and the rest of the committee decide whether or not they'll follow that. In the same way it would be quite wrong if the Director of Education, say, didn't have the opportunity to say, 'Well, that might be what my staff have said, or people down the line have said about a particular issue, that's been the subject of this corporate consideration, but my view is that certain matters have been overlooked, and I'm paid as Director of Education, so my advice is *a*, *b*, and *c* ...', and if the committee doesn't take it that's up to them.

So it's this kind of dilemma between closed government and open government, very open government. We're somewhere in between in Strathclyde. But certainly I've never heard of any suggestion that Paterson talked about every official having the right to give policy advice, because, in that event ... why have heads of departments at all? You'd just have a staff meeting of the forty people in the finance or accountancy section and they'd give their advice on some financial matter. You don't need a hierarchy.

I mean, I could give you countless examples – which I won't give you because they're confidential, many of them – of situations where either I or John Fuller have taken up with a head of department or a depute something which has concerned us in relation to the initiative areas, and said, 'Look, that is not good enough. Priority has not been given as it should be and something is going to have to be done about it.' I could give you countless examples of that.

Smart There's no way you could anonymise one, is there?

Ford Well, not really, no, because I think that would be ... You'll just have to take my word for it, that there are numerous examples where we've done that. If somebody in a department – and I think possibly the problem is that some of these people you're talking about are people who lead a maverick existence – but if somebody in the Social Work Department, say, in a coordinated area, feels that another department aren't responding properly, say, then the machinery is there for that to be dealt with, either through the coordinating machinery, or, in the end of the day, by the thing being passed up the line and the Director of Social Work phoning me or the Chief Executive or somebody and saying, 'Look, I can't get anywhere with this because of the fact that there's non-cooperation.'

In fact he wouldn't do that, he would go and see the head of the department that was alleged to be not cooperating. And these would be sorted out on a daily basis. The problem is those that haven't got service responsibility and are perhaps taking a bird's eye view of it and hearing things and tittle-tattle and so on, that don't have a vehicle for pushing the thing through.

Smart Resource departments generally ...

Ford Yes, and I don't know what the answer to that is because (a) it's not really their job ...

If I could put it this way: I would never, even for purposes of confidential academic research, never criticise or cast aspersions about a fellow official in the Regional Council without that fellow official knowing that I was going to do that. What does concern me ... it's clear to me that certain people, fairly senior, and I know who they are, have said things, unjustified things about me without ever having the courage to say them to my face. But that's an individual's make-up that get's me ... but I wouldn't do that.

Smart Would it be fair to say that the position that you're describing there is a fairly common practice amongst local authority officers who've been in the service over a longer period?

Ford That they wouldn't criticise?

Smart Yes.

Ford Yes. I would say that. Certainly, if you spoke to the Director of Finance, or the Senior Depute Director of Administration – because we don't have a Director of Administration at the moment – but they would say exactly the same thing that I'm saying to you.

Smart This is another instance where you're picking up a convention which is probably ... people would take it for granted who've got the experience ...

Ford Yes, yes.

Smart ... but if you come in completely green, without knowing ...

Ford Yes, that's a severe ... that's a major question really. Because, as I say, it's difficult for you to do meaningful research without knowing the kind of ins and outs of things. On the other hand, those that do observe the conventions know that the reason, perhaps, and it's purely hypothetical ... Say we'll take the Regional Chemist, because that will never happen in his case. Maybe people in Physical Planning and others are criticising him terribly, 'Oh, he's not doing that, and Policy Planning ought to be pushing him more and more.' And the Director of Policy Planning knows that the reason this fellow's not doing that in accordance with the spirit of the Red Book is because, perhaps, his chairman doesn't want him to and has told him not to. However, you know, he would never say that kind of thing to people, because it's none of their business why the chap ... They ignore ... they're kind of seeking a perfect world, seeking a perfect world.

The great problem about the deprivation document is this: that it poses the dilemma of the top down and the bottom up approaches; and advocates a bottom up approach, but doesn't face up to the realities of what happens on a day to day basis when the top down and the bottom up meet each other.

Smart Right.

Ford Now, the Director of Policy Planning can see that, the Director of Education, the Director of Social Work, all these guys can see that. The chap who's by and large interested in the bottom up approach – and I may say I'm interested in the bottom up approach – but the chap who's solely interested in that, it's very easy then to turn round and say ... that things are being thwarted and the spirit is not being observed. But the problem is posed.

The political answer to that is not given in the deprivation documents, and that is probably the theme that Stewart in particular could help you on. I mean, that is the reality of the situation. We have done tremendously efficient and effective things with our financial planning approach and other things which probably some of the people you've talked to didn't think mattered: 'What difference does that make?' These have made a substantial difference to deprivation and everything else. But the bottom up approach at times meets these, and these are really just kind of dealt with on an *ad hoc* basis, because they're possibly insoluble.

Bill Collins: June 1980

Collins I think that most people in the Regional Council have a view that they're earning a living, like anybody else earning a living, and come to it with no greater or less commitment than you'd expect from people doing any other occupation. It does run through the service, and particularly at a senior level, of all kinds, a strong feeling for public service. Now, how one interprets public service varies enormously. Some people would interpret it as bringing their expertise and knowledge to be employed in the public good, and would see themselves as the best arbiters of public good, and do become frustrated and so on at political interference, as they would feel it, in sound professional decision-making – objective thinking. But it is done, nevertheless, out of a strong feeling of public service.

I would also say that most of them work hard; and almost all the people in my own experience, with a few exceptions, who are at senior level in any of the organisations, and a lot of people down the line, work very hard too – are committed. I think it would also be true to say that more people in Social Work would feel that way. I could introduce you to a lot of people in Social Work who in their own words would say something not dissimilar to what I'm saying, in terms of the way they see their job. I think that's something to do with the nature of the Social Work job.

Smart What interests me is ... if you accept that a lot of folk are in employment with the Regional Council simply because they're wanting to earn a living – which is a perfectly respectable thing ...

Collins Sure.

Smart ... what is the position of somebody who comes into the Council with some concern to do something for the public, or for the poor, but who comes in at a fairly junior position with – a lot of folk would say, quite rightly – no voice in policy, and maybe to some extent forced to go along with policy which he would prefer not to be part of? What do you do then? How would you ...? There's a problem in that you could also come to the opinion that, unless you are prepared to accept the sort of view that the directorate – the senior officials and the traditional system, as it was when you came into it – unless you're prepared to accept that sort of view, you're never going to get to a position where you can influence it and change it.

Collins Yes, I think there's a problem there.

Smart Those folk who stay inside thinking, 'Well, in ten years' time I might be able to do something about it' – in ten years' time will be in a position to do something about it but will have accepted the values that go along with it and they won't want to do anything about it.

Collins I think that you need hierarchy, just simply to get things done, in order simply to have decisions made, because the complexity of views ... that people hold, if they were all given free rein and equal weight, would result in paralysis in almost everything. I mean, it would not be possible to go forward because there would never be sufficient consensus on many issues to do so. So, I think you need hierarchy for some sense of direction. You certainly need hierarchy for some lines of accountability, because if there aren't people who can be made accountable then you're going to end up saying the whole organisation is, for everything. And that, for somebody who was looking for redress, would be an impossible situation; it would be nobody's responsibility. So that, I think, you do need the system for that.

At the same time, it's very important for management – and the councillors, both have the responsibility – to recognise that the public purse pays for a whole range of skills. Because people are at the top of the tree, if you like, or in the senior positions, they don't necessarily have the ultimate superior wisdom on all topics and issues. I think the Council should equip itself to listen to others. That's where I think the kind of start that's been made in Strathclyde with officer member groups is important. That in policy making and key client areas councillors get alongside field workers and people actually running establishments and dealing with the problems. Both in determining the policy and in helping to support the implementation of the policy, I think that kind of development should be taken up by other departments of the Council. It shouldn't really lie as a Social Work initiative as it is at the present.

It also ... a lot's got to do with how you manage things internally anyway. If I've got a problem to look at I tend to get a mixed group of people together, so that I've got a Social Worker and an Area Officer, and a residential worker and a senior manager and so on, and I'll ask them to get into a huddle and think about it – wherever possible – it depends on the nature of the topics. Where it is appropriate, and where it's possible to try to consult, you simply take the product of their work and send it round the system and give people the opportunities for comment and observation.

We also have standing groups in Glasgow on development of services, and a standing invitation to anybody, absolutely anybody who's got any idea, be it a big one or a small one, that they want to put into the system, then it can be, it will be taken in and listened to. But people don't use that kind of opportunity very widely. A few people do but generally that one's not taken up. But it is an attempt to get round the difficulty, I think, the constraining difficulty that hierarchy creates.

So that's my view. I would also say this, though, maybe in a kind of purer sense, and maybe just to put the balance of the thing: there are people who work in local government who, unconsciously perhaps and out of a real concern for their job but, nevertheless, who do assert a kind of right, as they feel it, to be heard and to influence things. That, I feel, is inappropriate.

Certainly that happens in some of the most political Social Workers, and you say to them: 'Look, mate, you're only a citizen out earning your living, and ... it's not appropriate for you to claim that because you're a Social Worker earning your living from the public purse that somehow or other it's appropriate for you to exert a kind of direct influence on a whole range of broader political issues. If you want to do that become an elected member, get into parliament, join your local Labour Party, kick up hell through your trade union, by all means do it through channels.' But as an individual, other than the various channels that are open, there's a limit to how far that kind of thing can be asserted. That is a relatively rare thing, but there are some people who would assert that. And I suppose we've got, in the Social Work Department, a significant percentage of people in political groupings of various kinds. I think they run the danger, really, of using their job to indulge themselves a bit.

Smart How much do you think an individual can achieve on his own?

Collins What I think individuals can do on their own is – if they're really determined – they can set up small alternative models, that people can look at and try and learn from. That's the best way, if you really want ... I mean, it may be the hardest, but it's also the best way if you want to influence. If you don't like the way things are being done, try to show a better way and show that it works in the measures that people use.

Smart And would you say that's what you were doing, for example, in Greenock and Port Glasgow?

Collins Yes, and I think there are plenty of opportunities within our own service to do that. You do it on a relatively small area, but show a better way of doing things, on an area basis or for a client group. Nothing succeeds like acknowledged success, I mean, there's no doubt about that. Nothing fails like failure, and that's not often understood.

There is a view, and one that I've got constantly to counter, that somehow or other failure, disaster, breakdown, will persuade people to invest resources or money in your efforts. That somehow or other if the Social Work service was to fail hopelessly tomorrow, if we said we hadn't enough Social Workers to do any reports for the courts, or something of that kind, that's an example, that would win us an immediate rush of a million pounds from the Council to do something about it; would it hell. It would have exactly the opposite effect, and it makes it very difficult to get any kind of understanding for the service. Whereas things that are done and done well and are recognised by people in local neighbourhoods to have made some kind of impact, that creates the climate, the kind of constituency if you like, for pumping more into the Social Services.

So demonstration models I would certainly say are one way of using your individual power. Another is local persuasion. That certainly helps, and that can be done, certainly in a department like Social Work. I think it can happen in schools, although there are difficulties with the headmaster's role there in many schools. But people who are, if you like, at the basic level in an organisation, if they've got good enough arguments and agreed that they need to be equipped with good capacities of articulation and so on, if they've got that they can often have a very considerable influence on people. I think they often underestimate their power in that.

Smart Sounds a wee bit too good to be true, almost.

Collins Well, perhaps – I think that's the way a lot of things feel, you see, from people who feel themselves in the organisation lower down and so on. I think what they don't realise is that if they were Dick Stewart tomorrow their frustrations would be bloody enormous. You see, they fall into the other model of saying, 'Christ, they're all bureaucrats and they're all politicians lining their own pockets', and so on, which I think is the saddest kind of thing we've got in our society, that kind of cynical view. Then they start to sour themselves, and their own position ... and the minute they do that they don't understand the power they themselves have got, which is very considerable indeed.

Smart To maybe make it more concrete, a story has come my way in the past year or so, of a Depute Director of one particular department, which I would have thought was a fairly senior post ...

Collins Yes.

Smart ... in, as far as I can see, a perfectly proper capacity as a member of an interdisciplinary group involved with one of the elected members – making comments on one particular aspect of the service which another department, a different department, is responsible for; a department which he has some knowledge of but which he's not a member of; writing a paper on it, and being, to quote Ron Young, 'shat upon from a great height'; the matter frozen and the paper not circulated and everybody up in arms about it and the person concerned being, as far as I could see, quite worried that the situation had arisen, and Ron Young certainly being quite concerned that it shouldn't be made more public. That does tend to suggest a fairly ... that while an individual can maybe do quite a bit, that his scope is really only for dealing with fairly superficial things. It suggests that there may be quite an entrenched interest in favour of the status quo which, when the crunch comes, can probably stop ...

Collins There's always an entrenched interest in favour of the status quo, always, I mean you can just take that as read at any time. And therefore it does need a bit of skill, certainly, of thinking about it, as to how you go about changing the status quo. At your peril do you ignore the human dimension.

I mean, it's not an intellectual exercise, changing the status quo – so you don't write a paper that's so sensible that nobody can fault your argument, because that won't take you very far if you haven't taken some of the key human beings with you. Or it depends on the issue. Sometimes you need the key human beings. Well, it's always something worth trying – sometimes you'll never get them – but what you can then do is create a climate around them where they'll move anyway. In other words, you

make sure that you've got the union or the staff or the media, or
something ...

Smart Well, I would have thought that ...

Collins ... that's impinging ... So there's a variety of other ways of going
about trying to get that.

Smart Given that the fellow was part of a group which was being led by
Ron Young, who as Secretary of the Labour Group presumably has
some clout in the Labour Group ...

Collins That's right, yes.

Smart ... it looks as if there's a professional vested interest which is
capable of stopping a particular enquiry which has got elected member
approval, superficially. Maybe that's me reading the situation wrongly.

Collins Yes, I don't know anything about the particular case.

Smart I should have thought that it should have been possible for Ron
Young to call the bluff of the offended party and ...

Collins Yes, but he's maybe been sat on by his own political leadership.
Presumably that's supported the ...

Smart Right, but that doesn't ... that's not anything to undermine the
existence of that vested interest. That's really just saying that's how the
vested interest has managed to actually stop ...

Collins It's true; all I'm saying is that it is a business ... if you want
change then think about all of these things, I mean, it's not a naïve business of kind of ... sticking up a critical paper or something. You've really
got to try to look at where resistance is going to come, and soften it up.
That is part of the business. Some people might call that 'tactical' or
'machinating', 'scheming', all kinds of words for it ...

Smart 'Machiavellian' has been ...

Collins 'Machiavellian' has been used as a description. I don't think it
is particularly helpful. The thing, the truth is that we live in a human
world, and a human organisation. We don't live in an intellectual or pure
world, and human beings are frightened and human beings have got
vested interests, and human beings have got fixed views and prejudices
... and if you want to change anything you're going to have to move these,
somehow. That's how change is effected.

And there are many ways of doing it. Of course, for some things the
intellectual thing is right, a good argument, and cost things – that often
is the case – and if you can really demonstrate clearly that you can make
things better, or even not make them worse, and save money, then that's
a very good argument. Where you're into things that are deeper than
that ... who does what, and where the boundaries of people's jobs and
responsibilities are, then you're taking on ... and power, where power
lies ... you've got to do a lot of softening up on that kind of issue, other-

wise you're going to run into, sooner rather than later, you're going to hit the brick wall. And it's a real brick wall. I mean, it's not really one or two people being awkward in the system. It usually is a very real brick wall, where the individual who may be the person who's, kind of, doing the clamp, probably represents a massive, an absolutely massive block interest that you've done bugger all about trying to take with you.

Smart How much can you use ...

Collins I mean, I could write eloquent papers slamming other departments ... I don't know that that would take me, would take us anywhere. So what I do is, take Education for example, I work with Education, I meet them regularly, I have a number of members on my staff who work on an ongoing basis with Education officers on a variety of projects, and what we're doing is in various ways, through engaging Education staff at lower levels in thinking about change in, say, the way service for the under-fives is delivered, and their community work set up.

We're in a process, then. I think it will take about four or five years to come to fruition, to work through. I'm fairly confident that within Glasgow we'll have made a really big stride forward in the way Education does things in about five years' time. But it takes that, it takes that investment, and it takes the investment of a lot of people down the line and up the line and through the system.

Smart Do you think there is a place for the sort of line that Tony Benn argues for the Civil Service, where the only way that you can actually effect any change is to blow the whistle and try to get some sort of public outcry against abuses?

Collins There are times when that is the only answer, sure.

Smart Do you think that ever applies in local government?

Collins Hmm, there are times in local government when that would be ... the right answer is to blow the whistle.

Smart How would you decide?

Collins I would never blow the whistle.

Smart You'd get an elected member to do it?

Collins I would never blow the whistle ... yes, an elected member may well blow the whistle.

Smart Would there ever be a time, though, when you might say, you might be concerned about something to the point where you would actually go out of your way to get hold of an elected member and say to him ...

Collins ... to blow the whistle ... Never done it, never done it, but I don't ... I've never actually had to do that ... What you find is, you know the elected members who might be concerned on a particular topic and they might blow the whistle. But blowing the whistle is a really last resort thing, very very much a last resort thing, for ... Could I be clear about this. It's a last resort thing for me, so I wouldn't, I don't really use it. But for people down the line in the system it's much more legitimate and for elected members it's absolutely legitimate, that they ...

Smart Lower down the line within the official system?

Collins Oh yes. You see, where I would feel it's not appropriate for me to do it is that I become, through my position, I become privy, really, to information on that kind of confidential basis where you are in a relationship with others. I reckon that one of the privileges of the job in a way is that you've got that information which you wouldn't ... and you've got the opportunity to make your points about what it is that you think is so deplorable that it needs to be changed. And certainly I would always confine my activity to trying to do that. I would certainly see members to get them going on the issue and try to bring my weight to bear. I see that as a necessary part of my job.

Smart Outside of speaking at committee meetings?

Collins Oh aye, it needn't be at committee meetings, it could be over cups of coffee and pints of beer and telephone calls and all that, yes, sure. But that would be done on the basis of saying that these members themselves have got legitimate responsibility or legitimate interests and right to know, yes. What I wouldn't do ... to say to them ... is to go to the *Evening Times* about it.[3] I wouldn't suggest that as a tactic. Once they've got the information you might get the odd one that would do that, but that wouldn't be my objective.

Smart There was quite a bit of that going on when they were announcing the restructuring of the PTE.[4] Did you see that, about a month ago?

Collins Yes, that's right.

Smart Big things in the *Evening Times*: 'I am going to fight to the last ...'

Collins ... straw'. That's right, and there's this, it's amazing how people get screwed up on restructuring issues, and these are always issues of people defending interests, and they come to the media to defend a particular interest, and that's, I suppose, legitimate enough. It's just not ... it's something I wouldn't do because ... I'll put it this way: if you blow the whistle, even once, in a ... then you undermine yourself for the future. That's a fair point; it's a fair point to say that if you're in the business, in the magic circle, if you like – I suppose there'd be the wider magic circle and the inner magic circle, I'd be in the wider circle – then one of the rules of the game is that you don't blow the whistle. And if you did blow the whistle then you'd have to be prepared to find yourself outside the circle, or outside the game altogether, which I think is maybe how the thing works. And that's a fair enough rule, as long as within the circle you're able to get, to use tactics within it, and to try to fight for your point of view and persuade and so on.

Ian Beaton: April 1981

Beaton Now, what you have said is partly true, and what Dick Stewart has said is partly true, and what Alan Robinson has said is partly true. There is a procedure for going about getting change. I would say that the sensitivity of one department about criticism is a factor, but should you get over that factor by going about it in the proper manner which Dick Stewart and Alan Robinson have suggested that someone should go about it ... he didn't tell you why he didn't institute some sort of exercise. If Dick Stewart believes – and I'm quite friendly with Dick Stewart and I can talk bluntly to him – if he is so critical of the A Department, one immediately asks the question, 'Why do Ron Young and Dick Stewart, who are two very powerful politicians in Strathclyde, why do they not go to the Labour Group and say, "Hey, we could do with a bit of accountability"?'

Smart Right, that question has raised itself in my mind quite often over Ron Young, but ...

Beaton Will I give you part of the answer?

Smart Go on.

Beaton Part of the answer is this, that once you get over the sensitivities of the A Department – suppose I was sensitive and I didn't want Stan Hughes saying anything about the A Department – assuming that you get over that, you're then faced with what the Marxists would perhaps point to, you're then faced with this huge big professional body known as the A profession, who will make damn sure that you'll never ... because that's where the real vested interest lies, not ... not with me or my boss, that's where it lies.

And we can be as sensitive as we like; we can also be confident because we know that, first of all, it would be difficult to get such an exercise started. And I'm not talking about the A profession. I'm talking about the whole Scottish Office, the whole system of ... So that what the Marxists say – and I'm not a Marxist – but there is an element of ... there's this huge big resistance to change due to the fact that people are quite happy, those who count are quite happy – count in this context – are quite happy with what they're doing. Now you'll have a job to refute that.

Smart But the fact that that huge resistance is there doesn't ...

Beaton Dick Stewart recognises as a politician that it's there, maybe not explicitly, but ...

EXPOSITION: INTERVIEW TEXTS

The first thing to be said is that the interviewees present a remarkably consistent account of why Stan Hughes' proposal failed, and they produce a consistent account of the procedures which he *should* have followed. If a consistent position emerges from the interview texts on the way criticism should proceed throughout the local authority, including junior staff, it is (unsurprisingly) firmly 'top down', in contrast with the 'bottom up' approach advocated in the policy documents. This is the view from the top; the institutional framework is defended by insistence on the informal rules or 'unwritten ethics' governing behaviour within the authority. Stan Hughes is criticised for writing a paper on another department; the content of the paper is not the main reason for the criticism, 'it was the method by which it was done'. Similarly, officers who urged a particular course of action on the Policy Planning Department are criticised; regardless of the content of their suggestion, they are transgressing: 'Irrespective of whether they're right or wrong, is that their role?' The unwritten rules are either explicitly identified as rules or ethics, or appear in generalised statements about what should or should not be done, such as 'when they are making criticisms ... they ought to make sure that what they are putting forward ... is a factual criticism'.[5]

Apart from the prominence of rules or procedures, however, there is a firmly anti-idealist theme in several of the texts. In a number of places the word 'real' or 'reality' occurs in a way which is quite similar to its occurrence in the CDP document. Thus James Ford speaks of 'the realities of the game' or 'the reality of the situation' or 'the realities of what happens on a day to day basis', referring to the behaviour of identifiable groups of officers or members (although refraining from giving names). Bill Collins speaks of hitting 'a real brick wall ... a very real brick wall' which is made up of human beings with vested interests, fixed views and prejudices. Ian Beaton refers to 'this huge big professional body known as the A profession ... where the real vested interest lies', and where people 'are quite happy with what they're doing'. These realities are to be faced up to, and anyone who wants to achieve change must come to terms with them. People who fail to do so are acting in a naïve or idealistic manner: 'they're kind of seeking a perfect world, seeking a perfect world' or failing to recognise that 'it's not an intellectual exercise, changing the status quo ... it's not a naïve business of ... sticking up a critical paper ... the truth is that we live in a human world, and a human organisation. We don't live in an intellectual or pure world.'

These two characteristics of the interview data are not unrelated. The rules protect officers of one department from criticism by outsiders: 'so I think that Stan made the fatal mistake of being an outsider', or they protect senior officers from criticism by junior officers: 'is that their role, as junior members of staff?' To keep the rules is 'common sense', where criticism of a group of people by others brings 'natural resentment' and this resentment can be allayed by the critic's observation of 'common sense, common courtesies that ought to be done'. This idea of common sense is important, as we will see below, for understanding the interview texts as a whole.

Interview texts and empiricism

The rules insist on criticism which is factual or which can be substantiated, and in this way they defend people against unfair or unjustifiable criticism. This is particularly clear in the interviews with Dick Stewart and James Ford.

Dick Stewart outlines the rules governing criticism, laying emphasis on the role of 'facts'. 'Right' criticism here is criticism which starts with facts. His view clearly incorporates the empiricist idea of theory 'growing' from or being 'built' or 'based' on facts. The facts have priority:

> they ought to make sure that what they're putting forward as a criticism is a factual criticism ... if you're criticising another department, or in anything, when you're doing that at the top level, you've got to be careful of what you're criticising, and that you're doing it based on fact, and being able to stand up to the accusations or statements you're making. And in this case I think the person who was making the criticism – and no doubt believing it – wasn't aware of all the facts concerning it.

As we noted in chapter five, this is an indicator of empiricism. In James Ford's interview, 'facts' are not prominent, but two related ideas, both present in Dick Stewart's remarks above, are evident. These are the importance of the whole picture ('all the facts') and the importance of remarks being justifiable ('being able to stand up to the ... statements you're making'). Thus, 'I would have thought it's kind of difficult for people who aren't involved – don't see the whole spectrum, don't see the whole pressures, that aren't party to these review discussions – to make that kind of remark, which they can't justify.' Similarly, he comments unfavourably on people who 'have said things, unjustified things about me'.

Both these accounts also use the ideas of criticising a policy and attacking a senior official's character virtually interchangeably. James Ford's comment above illustrates this but it is clearest in Dick Stewart's remarks, as in the passage already quoted; a criticism has to be based on fact, and this seems to be a parallel idea to that of 'being able to stand up to the accusations or statements you're making', where accusation and statement (of criticism) seem to be the same thing.

Later Dick Stewart talks of the danger of 'bull-headed' rushing 'into being a critic, or condemning', criticism and condemnation standing as equivalents again, with the observations that 'Nobody takes kindly to being criticised on a particular point that's their profession', and 'rightly, the professional resents being accused of unprofessionalism ... by someone who's not in the profession'. To make critical comment on a policy, or a point of view expressed by an officer, where the subject is a matter dealt with by one profession and the critic is not a member of that profession, is to accuse of unprofessionalism. To criticise a policy or a theory (point of view) is to attack a person.

Given this, it is not surprising that Stan Hughes' action (albeit prompted by Ron Young) is interpreted as not having 'anything to do with a free discussion between officials and members at all ... this was a separate axe being ground'.

Two important qualifications need to be made here. Firstly, that the grinding of axes is often significant. No one seriously believes that it never happens. The rules thus defend people from accusations which might be made in such a way as to limit the victim's effective right of reply – they defend the right to a defence, and thus uphold traditional liberal individualist values. So James Ford comments, 'I would never ... criticise or cast aspersions about a fellow official without that fellow official knowing I was going to do that.' Secondly, the link between a policy and a person differs from the link between a theory and a person, in that a policy has more direct implications for people besides the policy maker than does a theory. This does not deny Habermas' point about the reality of the link between knowledge-growing and the pursuit of interests. It suggests, for example, that the naïve nuclear physicist whose theoretical work is given a weapons application is not as directly implicated in the slaughter which may ensue as is the person who makes the application. Intention is important, as well as action. A policy is more like an application than a 'pure' theory, and so, for accountability to be meaningful, some link is necessary between policy and the person responsible. Bill Collins makes this point when he says:

> if there aren't people who can be made accountable then you're going to end up saying the whole organisation is [accountable] for everything. And that, for somebody who was looking for redress, would be an impossible situation.

The purpose of these qualifying statements is to guard the idea of fairness or justice from being thrown out with the bathwater of a theory of criticism which sees an inevitable link between person and policy or between person and theory. It is, in effect, to reassert that the theory of knowledge cannot be invoked in a reductionist manner. It cannot resolve injustices on its own, nor make the conflict of interests disappear as if by magic.

Given these qualifications, then, the position which is emerging is of a conception of criticism which is basically empiricist in character. The anti-idealism of the documents suggests either a critical rationalist or an empiricist view of the theory of knowledge; the close link between person and point of view indicates empiricism. There is a further characteristic of the documents, however, which coincides quite strikingly with Horkheimer's identification of empiricist 'traditional thinkers':

> The scholarly specialist 'as' scientist regards social reality and its products as extrinsic to him, and 'as' citizen exercises his interest in them through political articles, membership in political parties or social service organisations, and participation in elections. But he does not unify these two activities, and his other activities as well, except, at best, by psychological interpretation.[6]

The pattern which Horkheimer points out here, the 'as' and 'as', occurs repeatedly in the texts. The following exchange, for example, sets up the polarity three times in the space of a few sentences:

> **Robinson** Did he have that concern as an official in the B department or as a member of the public at large, or do you not distinguish between them?
> **Smart** Well, you do distinguish between them, obviously.
> **Robinson** Yes. If he had that concern as a member of the public at large then obviously he can get at the public at large and try and set up some sort of thing there. But if he ... had his concern as an official of the B department then there are ways in which he ought to proceed ... I'm trying to think myself what I would do if I were opposed to some practice in another department – as an official, it would need to be as an official. As a member of the public I'm free to speak or to join societies or parties and so on, to move against any policy in the other department.

A similar point is made by Bill Collins, although here the precise 'as' and 'as' formula does not appear:

> There are people who work in local government who, unconsciously

perhaps and out of a real concern for their job ... assert a kind of right, as they feel it, to be heard and to influence things. That, I feel, is inappropriate ... and you say to them: 'Look, mate, you're only a citizen out earning your living, and ... it's not appropriate for you to claim that because you're a Social Worker earning your living from the public purse that somehow or other it's appropriate for you to exert a kind of direct influence on a whole range of broader political issues. If you want to do that become an elected member, get into Parliament, join your local Labour party, kick up hell through your trade union, by all means do it through channels.' But as an individual ... there's a limit to how far that kind of thing can be asserted.

Apart from these two passages, however, where the parallel with the Horkheimer essay is particularly striking, the same attitude underlies much of the interview text. Alan Robinson comments critically on officers who 'were making open political statements about the government', in contrast with his own position and that which he feels characterises his department or people of his seniority, 'I wouldn't be a member of a political party'. Bill Collins speaks of people 'in political groupings' who, in asserting their right to influence policy, 'run the danger, really, of using their job to indulge themselves a bit'. James Ford disapproves of officers who:

> choose to get particularly friendly with individual members and to hear of their grouses and grievances and try to feed that back into the system – I personally don't ... sort of acknowledge that. ... they seek the alternative outlet of a personal relationship with somebody who is a member and through that they get their – small 'p' – political satisfaction.

It is something about the people which is being criticised, they 'indulge themselves', or, to quote James Ford again, they 'lead a maverick existence' or 'that's an individual's make-up that gets me'. Given that Horkheimer is describing two different conceptions of theory (traditional and critical) which become eventually two different ways of being, and given Habermas' misgivings over statements which are 'too strong', it is not surprising that representatives of traditional theory (senior officers in the interview texts) should see representatives of critical theory as mavericks (driven from the herd by gadflies).

One group objects to a distortion of their selves produced by the distinction ('as' official, 'as' citizen) and its members insist on being themselves; the other group insists on the distinction ('as' distinguished from 'as') and on a corresponding readiness to divorce personal feelings or ideas from activity as an official: 'I was brought up to believe that no matter what my own personal political feelings were, that I should be prepared to serve ...'. The 'facts' which it is an official's job to provide thus become, to use Horkheimer's language, extrinsic to the official 'as' a person with his own feelings or concerns: 'My job is to put up facts and information to members and make recommendations and leave them to it.'

The struggle which the CDP workers believe to be necessary, a struggle which resists the institutional framework (of problem definition, job remit, and rules of procedure) in order to be faithful to a personal insight, is therefore ruled out: 'I would never make an attack on this government or any other government before a committee. That's not part of my job.'

This attitude to an officer's role, however, does not rule out changing the status quo. The interviews certainly provide a contrast on this point with the two policy documents, but the contrast is in the conception of the process of change. In the policy documents the process requires the regeneration of human beings. It is emphatically a human process in that human attitudes are seen as the key things to be changed, and human attitudes are required in order to achieve change. Change requires officials who are committed to producing sensitivity: 'it is essentially a human problem' and the officers who can tackle it will be characterised by 'a commitment to people rather than to tasks'. In contrast, and to borrow the language of the Red Book, the conception of the process which underlies the interview texts is that it is a task, a technical exercise. Bill Collins makes this explicit:

> it is a business ... if you want change then think about all of these things ... You've really got to try to look at where resistance is going to come, and soften it up. That is part of the business. Some people might call that 'tactical' or 'machinating', 'scheming'.

What it requires is skill and the investment of time and effort. Alan Robinson similarly uses language which suggests that it is a technical exercise: 'let me tell you of devices that I would use if I wanted to do something.' Yet this is closely bound up, in Bill Collins' interview particularly, with a sort of humanism. Almost immediately after the last quoted comment he says:

> the truth is that we live in a human world, and a human organisation. We don't live in an intellectual or pure world, and human beings are frightened and human beings have got vested interests, and human beings have got fixed views and prejudices.

As in the Red Book, human attitudes or sensitivities are the primary things to be recognised. The key difference is in the clear objectivity of these attitudes in the interview texts – objects to be recognised, steered around or manipulated by a detached change-agent – while in the Red Book they are to be the focus of critical reflection, as much to be changed *in* the change-agent as *by* him.

On this issue the interview language sounds more appropriate to Popper's 'piecemeal social engineering'. Certainly the suggested methods for pursuing change are not clearly empiricist. The framework is firmly realist rather than idealist, and unambiguously analytic rather than dialectic, but, as noted earlier, realism is as much a characteristic of critical rationalism as it is of empiricism. In Bill Collins' comments in particular there are other remarks which suggest a critical rationalist position; the following two remarks are perhaps the most clear. Firstly:

> What I think individuals can do on their own is ... set up small alternative models, that people can look at and try and learn from. That's the best way ... it may be the hardest, but it's also the best ... If you don't like the way things are being done, try to show a better way and show that it works in the measures that people use.

There is a parallel with Popper's conception of knowledge as something that grows when the scientific community chooses the best of a range of competing hypotheses. 'In the measures that people use' suggests an idea similar to that of the philosophical chapter, where dogmatism over the criteria for evaluation of theories is avoided for the sake of debate. It does not preclude there being absolute criteria (of truth or goodness) but concedes that the levels of certainty or agreement which would be necessary to apply such criteria are not likely to be achieved, and that some decision has to be taken. Secondly:

> Of course, for some things the intellectual thing is right, a good argument, and cost things ... if you can really demonstrate clearly that you can make things better, or even not make them worse, and save money, then that's a very good argument.

Again, the emphasis is on a proposal which is better rather than a proposal which is the right one, and a proposal which is better in the eyes of the people who are being persuaded ('in the measures that people use'). Another point which is being made here is that clarity of communication is important; as indicated earlier, the two policy documents were quite free of any suggestion that the ability to think and speak clearly would be important for officials involved in the deprivation strategy. Bill Collins comments:

people who are ... at the basic level in an organisation, if they've got good enough arguments and agreed that they need to be equipped with good capacities of articulation and so on, if they've got that they can often have a very considerable influence on people.

Along with these indicators of critical rationalism there is a view that knowledge is not absolute, and that the growth of knowledge depends on a community, and on a certain scepticism towards knowledge claims. Thus senior officers 'don't necessarily have the ultimate superior wisdom on all topics and issues' or 'they ought not to get carried away with their own judgment as being necessarily the right thing'. For an idea to promote learning within the community, the source is irrelevant – a frequent Popperian theme – what matters is the content. This 'suggestion box' approach surfaces in Bill Collins' reference to 'a standing invitation to anybody, absolutely anybody who's got an idea, be it a big one or a small one, that they want to put into the system'.

The tension which this evidence of critical rationalism produces within the interview data – which is predominantly empiricist – is best approached by looking at the idea of 'common sense'. Dick Stewart described the approach of 'those that observe the conventions' as simply common sense. It is a basic human characteristic, it might be applied to describe the way a 'sensible' person thinks about a whole range of issues which professional philosophy conventionally itemises as epistemology, ontology, ethics and anthropology. It goes further than this, however, and is aware of the typical reactions of ordinary human beings in a wide range of situations, so that it recognises, for instance, that 'nobody takes kindly to being criticised on a particular point that's their profession'; it is the product of experience of the 'human world' or of a 'human organisation'.

However down to earth it may be, whether it be seen as 'intellectual' or 'practical', as 'anthropology' or 'experience', it is philosophically ambiguous. Its ambiguity exactly parallels the ambiguity of common sense in Popper's philosophy.

On the one hand, in Popper's attack on empiricism, he labels the 'wrong' theory of knowledge 'the common-sense theory of knowledge' ('the bucket theory of mind').[7] On the other hand, he is often concerned to assert the basic correctness of the common sense approach to thinking, learning and the solving of problems. At times he is even prepared to state that this 'reinstatement' of common sense, following the impact of mystifying (Hegelian) philosophies, is one of the main aims of his whole work. One of the clearest of his defences of common sense is the defence of the realist outlook on the world – the same outlook which characterises Dick Stewart's common sense. In so far as common sense is both empiricist and realist in character it is identical in Popper's identification and in the interview data.

In the light of a critical rationalist philosophy, then, the crucial question for a defender of the rules would be: 'Are you prepared to ditch the empiricism of your common sense outlook?' and the critical theorist will answer for the defender: 'No, because the empiricism of it is inseparable from the realism, which recognises that the empiricist character of the common sense rules is a powerful means to the preservation of the status quo.' The question can be translated, for practical purposes, into: 'Are you prepared to concede that facts are actually dependent on theories, that is, that your "information" is filtered through experience? If you are, then you must concede that policy suggestions can reasonably be made which are critical of the status quo, which may turn out to be useful but which, at the time of their making, cannot be "justified" or demonstrated to be "based on fact".' This question is neither clearly articulated nor clearly answered in the texts, but lies beneath the two-sided position which emerges.

Dick Stewart's insistence that criticism should be 'based on fact' reflects a theory of knowledge which sees facts as 'clean' of theory, and the starting point or 'base' from which theory or policy or policy criticism should grow. The idea is that the fair theorist or critic looks impartially at 'all the facts', and constructs a theory which, as far as possible, does justice to all of them.

By contrast, Bill Collins suggests that people set up 'alternative models', that 'the council should equip itself to listen to others', and that there should be a suggestion box for anyone within the organisation. This concedes the basic point that ideas come first and that they should be given the chance to demonstrate their value rather than being immediately ruled out of court on the grounds that they are not 'factual'.

In fact the tension over this issue has a more central position in the deprivation strategy, since the Council, by allowing a policy to go ahead which is explicitly 'experimental' (the Area Initiatives – set up to provide alternative models of practice), regardless of its character as idealist or 'anti-task' or whatever, has actually conceded the same point which underlies Bill Collins' remarks. It has thereby reconciled itself to one of the basic objections to such experiments – they cost money. Local government had faced, even before 1979, a reduction of budget in real terms.

It is perhaps significant that the phrases which suggest critical rationalism come predominantly from Bill Collins, and the phrases which suggest empiricism come mainly from Dick Stewart, but this is not pursued here. For the commentary they have been taken as a range of articulations of a broadly agreed position: a firmly 'magic circle' and 'top down' position on matters of management, upholding the unwritten ethics of local government. This view maintains the distinction between political members and politically neutral officials, although it is more directly articulated in terms which seem to suggest an analytic philosophy ('as' and 'as', for example) than in terms which suggest a specifically local government tradition. Thus, the interviews are taken as broadly empiricist in outlook, adopting a realist position, opposing idealism, seeing an inevitable link between a person and his point of view.

What is clear is that the dialectical or Hegelian character of the two policy documents is absent. There is none of the 'religious' vocabulary of regeneration, commitment or spirit. The humanism of the interviews is pragmatic and individualistic, in contrast with the 'community' preoccupation of the documents and their blurring of subject/object boundaries. The interviewees seek arguments buttressed by facts, the policy documents seek staff with a sensitivity to intuitions. For the overall argument of the book, if an empiricist position exists in the interview texts, even if it is leavened by critical rationalism, and if the interview texts are free of the broadly Hegelian character of the policy documents, then the central hypothesis is corroborated.

It may be possible to demonstrate differences within the interview texts but in the last analysis these would only be significant in contributing to an explanation of events in Strathclyde which sought to establish the actions or beliefs of particular individuals as significant aspects of a unique set of circumstances. Such an analysis might be attempted as a piece of historical accountancy, but it is not the aim of this book to undertake such an analysis – the aim, as outlined in the first chapter, is to seek general solutions to a general problem.

8 Conclusions: the breakdown of criticism

THE TEXTS COMPARED

In chapter one we suggested that the local authority had incorporated conflicting theories of knowledge, and that these conflicting theories of knowledge might be found in policy documents and in the views of officers and members. We suggested that this might shed some light on cases where the authority's policy of self-criticism, part of its approach to urban deprivation, had broken down. We suggested that different theories of knowledge held by individuals within the authority might underlie conflicting moral and practical positions, and that these conflicts might hinder the constructive criticism of policies.

In fact both sets of texts, the policy documents examined in chapter six and the interview transcripts examined in chapter seven, show some confusion, certainly enough for organised chaos to develop and to frustrate hopes of 'a learning local government'.[1] Much stronger corroboration for our hypothesis, however, appears when we look at the contrast between the two sets of documents. On the whole, the policy documents correlate with the critical theory of the Frankfurt School, where change is an imperative, challenging institutions, ideas and individuals. The interview texts show, above all, a wariness towards criticism, and an empiricist concern very like that which Adorno describes – 'where are the facts?'.[2]

The policy documents have little time for facts (although some of the officers responsible for the documents had shown a tremendous commitment to gathering facts which would demonstrate the character and effects of deprivation), seeing instead the personal attitudes of officers as paramount; the interviewees see the factual character of criticism as vital. The policy documents present criticism as a good thing regardless of the danger of conflict: 'it is believed that the positive aspects will be greater than the drawbacks';[3] the interviewees see criticism as inherently dangerous: 'you're right into major criticism of another department, you're on very dangerous ground.'[4]

The conflicts which develop flow from differences over the nature of the objects for which the authority's deprivation policy is being developed. There are even differences over the real object of the policy, and over the separability of subject and object of policy. There is a disagreement, it seems, over whether a separation is possible between the local authority as the learning subject and areas of deprivation (or local government services in areas of deprivation) as the object. Behind these differences, as Dahrendorf comments on the Positivist Dispute, lie the names of Kant and Hegel.[5]

However, both sets of Strathclyde texts acknowledge ideas and policies as inherently personal; if ideas are wrong, people are wrong, and are to be changed. 'Be transformed or be transferred' was the message which the policy documents delivered to staff in the deprived areas, and the same message was delivered by his Director to Stan Hughes. The policy documents blame the attitudes of local authority staff for the problems of the deprived areas, and the interviewees focus on the personal failings of people involved in criticism and conflict within the local authority; they are irresponsible, immature, inexperienced or naïve.

Given these contrasts it seems inevitable that one group (the officers responsible for the drafting of the policy documents) will, in following their convictions, break the rules of the other group and so be seen as improperly motivated, as 'mavericks'. In reacting by invoking the rules, attempting to abort discussion and to discipline junior staff, the senior officers will inevitably reinforce the convictions of the junior staff that a personal struggle is going on. As the struggle intensifies, the motives of the two sides become the focus of attention – the content of proposals takes second place to 'the way it was done'.

It may even be that the language of the two groups is too unrelated to allow mutual comprehension, so widely do the texts diverge. The 'essentially human problems' of the policy documents may well lead to proposals which could only appear revolutionary from the 'top down' and pragmatic viewpoint of the interviewees. It would be impossible to see such proposals as making adjustments to policy within the existing framework; by their language alone they would inevitably (if unintentionally) threaten the whole framework.

On the other hand, the closed character of the senior officers' position towards criticism which is not 'factual', and the limits on expenditure which preclude the offering to critics of chances to let their proposals 'become factual' through some sort of experimentation, is such as to preclude learning other than as a minor modification of existing policy. This sort of minor adjustment or 'modification learning' may be possible when the data which would allow a modification to be suggested as a factual criticism already exists (because collected in the course of existing service delivery, for instance).

This suggests an application of Kuhn's description of a scientific revolution in the policy sphere, taking Kuhn's model as a model of 'corporate rationality'.[6] Both the critical theory of Strathclyde's policy documents and the empiricism of senior officers and members limit learning to these two alternatives, relatively trivial 'modification learning', or a 'paradigm shift', a fundamental change of understanding. This latter would be achieved by the traditional process of promotion and retirement whereby yesterday's mavericks become tomorrow's directorate. Both models of criticism, the critical theorist and the empiricist, provide a logical buttress to the psychological or personal factors which in Kuhn's model of theory-change ensure close ties between a theory and the personalities proposing it.

So we have an element of corroboration for our hypothesis of chapter one; conflicting epistemologies have been established, and their character has been identified as inimical to learning. That identification can be made at a philosophical level, and a correlating identification has been made in the world of practical politics. Both critical theory and empiricism carry the risk that corporate learning will be aborted if they are held by any significant group of actors involved with policy development or implementation.

Although there is corroboration, however, there is also a degree of refutation, since one component of the initial hypothesis does not really stand up in the light of the empirical data. That is the irrelevance of interests to the epistemological conflict, which was posited at the beginning of the book when we discussed the problem of non-learning.

The difficulty comes from the fact that the rules governing officers' behaviour have a dual character. They are derivations of a theory of knowledge which is empiricist in character, but they are also part of the machinery of the defence of interests. They act, quite openly, to protect senior officers – and whole professions – from 'unfair' criticism, but they also limit fair criticism. In so far as professional people owe their livelihoods to the exclusive nature of professional qualifications, and the rules defend them from criticism by anyone outside the profession, the rules act to defend livelihood. This is clearly not accidental, it is a characteristic of the rules which senior staff are quite conscious of. It is interesting to see that, in Hume's philosophical project, it was equally consciously an aim of the empiricist system to limit controversy and the free-for-all criticism of ideas, and to inhibit in particular any criticism of society or of ideas which came from a religious perspective.

So, from Strathclyde, we have Ian Beaton's comment about 'this huge big resistance to change due to the fact that people ..., those who count ... in this context – are quite happy with what they're doing'. We also have Bill Collins' comment on human beings with fears and fixed views and prejudices, and the way, in particular, that 'it's amazing how people get screwed up on restructuring issues, and these are always issues of people defending interests', and we have Dick Stewart's comments about the 'natural' resentment of professionals criticised by people outside their own profession.

These interests, and particularly the inevitability of the human reaction of defence of personal interest, are the 'realities' which dictate an anti-idealist outlook to the senior officers and members. They represent an accommodation to a world that simply *is*, in contrast to the critical theorists' incorrigibly metaphysical notion of a human nature which (more or less inevitably or essentially) is altruistic or eirenic.

The coincidence of rules as theory of knowledge and rules as an interest-defensive mechanism raises the question of their being amenable to analysis as discrete objects. The rules seem to represent the imposition of a conservative theory of knowledge on a supposedly rational institution by a group (the professions) whose interests are served by the institution being 'crippled' in its ability to uncover the exploitive character of élitism (professionalism) in society.

This is to identify Ian Beaton's 'huge big resistance to change' with the Frankfurt School's 'societal totality', and to identify the empiricist 'conventions' governing local government officers' behaviour with the 'rules of exclusion codified in a political system' which Habermas, following Offe, makes use of in his work on legitimation, pointing to such rules as 'empirical indicators of suppressed interests'.[7]

It is still possible, however, to see a set of complementary true answers to our question from the opening chapter – 'Why was Stan Hughes' proposal rejected?' So, a theory which sees criticism breaking down because of conflicting theories of knowledge might be set alongside theories of the operation of interests within the local authority – an analysis of the sort of empire building which many actors identified as a significant factor in explaining events such as Jarndyce.

EXPLAINING JARNDYCE

To conclude the analysis then, we propose a series of generalised 'explanations' of the Jarndyce incident. The basic thesis can be presented in several forms: 'All non-factual criticism of local government policy is considered by senior managers to be improper; Stan Hughes offered a non-factual criticism of local government policy, therefore Stan Hughes' criticism was judged to be improper.' Alternatively, 'The substance of any policy proposal made in a manner which breaks the unwritten rules of local government behaviour will not be discussed; Stan Hughes' proposal was presented in a manner which broke the unwritten rules, therefore the substance of Stan Hughes' proposal was not discussed.' Or, 'In an institution whose rules are constructed on empiricist lines, individuals holding a non-empiricist theory of knowledge will inevitably break the rules', and so on.

All these presentations, and others, are corroborated; to some degree they translate each other, but they also offer complementary explanations. Part of the problem here lies with the veiled metaphysics of popular ideas of 'explanation' or 'cause' as something which penetrates to the *real* reasons, the *real* story.

Of explanations such as we have suggested for Jarndyce, the components which deal particularly with Stan Hughes are the most difficult to demonstrate. Such demonstration would rest primarily on the identification of Stan Hughes with the opinions expressed in the Red Book and the *AoN* report. In interview he accepted this – he was a member of UDOG, and one of the group on UDOG whose views the documents most directly incorporate – but it is not prudent, despite time's healing hand, to present direct evidence for this.

It is possible, however, to present a short extract from the paper at the centre of Jarndyce, and a comparison of it with the policy documents and their exposition can be made. The extract is presented below; the phrases in brackets are edited to preserve the sense as exactly as possible while removing references which would make the specific objects of the paper's proposals clearly identifiable. The extract is from the paper's concluding paragraph:

> It must be acknowledged that the introduction of [this new management process] will meet with considerable opposition and initial bafflement, on the part of various groups in various areas. [This process] is itself [one which will lead] to changes in attitudes, relationships and responsibilities. Such changes may be resisted. Comprehension and commitment will only follow from the clear demonstration of the scheme's success in practice, from which the advantages to all parties may be manifest. Initially, therefore, [this process] should be introduced only in certain parts of the region, as a pilot project. The [particular sites] and the teams of regional councillors [to monitor the scheme] should be selected with care.[8]

There are phrases in the text which suggest an approach similar to Bill

Collins' – small alternative models being spoken of here as 'pilot projects' whose success will have to be acknowledged 'in the measures' used by the people who are likely to react in opposition. There is also a realistic appraisal of the inevitability of opposition to change: 'such changes may be resisted' or 'will meet with considerable opposition'. It is not sufficient to point to this sort of language, however, given the example from the *AoN* report where such apparent realism was followed immediately by one of the most naïve statements to be made in any of the documents examined ('the possibility of conflict is recognised. It is believed the positive aspects will be greater than the drawbacks').

Certainly some phrases are parallel with the phrases in the policy documents which were taken as indicators of a critical theorist position. Following the recognition of the likelihood of conflict, the next sentence speaks of the process of implementation as likely to lead to 'changes in attitudes, relationships and responsibilities'. The paper expresses a hope that there will be eventual 'comprehension and commitment', and to further that (by giving the pilot projects a healthy start) there is a suggestion that the right sites and personnel 'should be selected with care' – just as with the proposal of the Area Initiatives it was acknowledged that, to get them off to a good start, staff with the right attitudes might need to be brought in from other areas.

At any rate, the language is not at all empiricist, which is the important point for the question of its fit with the statements contained in the syllogisms. The proposal is not 'factual'; the rest of the document outlines an idea which might work (so Dick Stewart's assessment of it as not factual is fair) and suggests a course of action which would give the proposal a chance to prove itself. Rather like the proposal from Strathclyde's Policy Review Group on departmental structures (reviewed in chapter two), the most striking feature of the paper is its implied attack on the traditionally privileged professional judgment of the staff of one particular service.

PUBLIC RATIONALITY

The question asked in the introductory chapter looks for an answer in the form of positive theory ('Why does criticism break down?': 'Because ...'). The book as a whole, however, is really more concerned with the normative question – 'How *should* criticism of society proceed within a pluralist society?'

The simple answer, of course, is 'not according to procedures which guarantee that the debate will be aborted' – a reply which presupposes a minimum of ethical theory and is clearly reasonable, but which contributes very little, as it stands, in the way of practical advice. A further answer would be 'not according to empiricist principles', since they are not really compatible with debate and have traditionally been associated, in the history of ideas, with attempts to curtail debate.

That is, the evidence from Strathclyde supports the contention made in chapter four that empiricism is inseparable from a wilful narrowing of debate in pluralist society. In chapter four we observed that 'social function mirrors the logical content and explicit motive of empiricist philosophy'. That observation was prompted simply by a refusal to ignore empiricist intentions to put foundational issues 'beyond question', and a refusal to ignore the empiricist attitude to metaphysics. The same observation now stands supported by the character of the unwritten rules in Strathclyde – by their empiricist character and their social function as defensive of the interests of professional staff.

In making this point, of course, we are also asserting that there is an important difference between critical theory and empiricism on the question of their tendency to abort debate. Both theories of knowledge *do* endanger debate; in this we have suggested that the empirical evidence from Strathclyde supports the more narrowly philosophical analysis of chapters four and five. In the case of empiricism, however, the problem is rooted in an opposition to the very idea of truly open debate, while in critical theory there is a commitment to debate which is wide open (a commitment equally apparent in the philosophical critical theory of chapter five, and in the practical critical theory of the policy documents). To put it differently, critical theory has a problem with its tendency to dogmatism, and is struggling (particularly in the work of Habermas) to overcome that problem without losing its distinctive character as dialectical and emancipatory. In the case of empiricism, on the other hand, it is difficult to see how it could lose its opposition to open debate and still be recognisable as empiricism.

In that case, rather than pursue a purely normative question, with the inevitable danger of the pursuit of ever more rarified abstractions, the point is to ask whereabouts empiricism is to be found in public life, with a view to challenging it there, particularly in the concrete forms it takes, and particularly where it can be found in the company of 'codified rules of exclusion'.

A corporatist perspective (as in Simmie's work in Oxford) would seem to offer most help in identifying entities for analysis within the broad cultural landscape within which political and administrative decision-making takes place.[9] Simmie's work is also valuable in highlighting rule-setting at a national level as a key device used by powerful organisations in their attempts to shape the outcome of local decision-making processes. This is an appropriate way to view what this book has highlighted about rule-setting, both informal and formal (the placing of firm safeguards for 'professional judgment' in social legislation, for example).

As a first step, the recruitment (selection) processes which govern access to public institutions (the professions, Whitehall, the local government service, the judiciary, for example) are clearly of great importance as hiding places for rules of exclusion, quite apart from the administrative cultures and the 'unwritten rules' to be found within these institutions.

Fundamental to any exploration of Whitehall or the professions, however, is an exploration of the role of the formal education system in feeding decision-making institutions and in propagating philosophical ideas. Such an exploration would need to be wide ranging, both historically and socially.

However, this is both a theoretical and a practical issue; it is as much an agenda for investigative journalism as for academic research, and it is also a practical policy suggestion. The first requirement is to publish and examine the unwritten rules, both within and outside of the institutions whose staff they govern. Both public and professionals have a stake in the way these rules operate, and both need to be involved in their examination. The examination should, of course, be carried out in public terms, it should not be dominated by a vocabulary drawn from the professions (including professional philosophy).

In fact we have to ask whether academic philosophy or social theory is capable of pursuing an analysis of unwritten rules of exclusion, particularly when there are such close links between the formal education system and the operation of selection processes which apply those rules, and when the world of academic philosophy and social theory is itself so firmly professionalised. We also have to ask whether an institution-centred method is appropriate for the exposure of these rules and of empiricism. It may be that a biographical focus would more clearly expose the ways in which a professional culture, or a series of ideas about the growth of knowledge, is absorbed. To use jargon, we are concerned with a process of socialisation.

Perhaps most importantly, however, we need translations between the language of professional culture and the language of non-professionals. This is partly a matter of translating between a language which is emotion-laden and languages which have been stripped of emotion or 'sensitivity', or between language which is personal and language which is technical. It may be that this calls not for a theoretical mode of thought or discourse, but for something both more oblique and more direct – in the way that creative writing, for example, demands both realism and empathy. In 1982 Strathclyde Regional Council published a booklet outlining their social strategy for the eighties.[10] They quoted the following lines from Eliot's *Four Quartets*, which make an appropriate conclusion to this book:

> And so each venture
> Is a new beginning, a raid on the inarticulate
> With shabby equipment always deteriorating
> In the general mess of imprecision of feeling,
> Undisciplined squads of emotion. And what there is to conquer
> By strength and submission, has already been discovered
> Once or twice, or several times, by men whom one cannot hope
> To emulate – but there is no competition –
> There is only the fight to recover what has been lost
> And found and lost again and again; and now, under conditions
> That seem unpropitious. But perhaps neither gain nor loss.
> For us, there is only the trying. The rest is not our business.

Coda

Councillor R.G. Young, Strathclyde Regional Council

So ist die Welt und musst nicht so sein.

Brecht

THE IMPORTANCE OF LANGUAGE AND PROCESS

It is good of Harry to give me this opportunity to reflect on the events of almost ten years ago. The T.S. Eliot quote which ends the previous chapter is a significant one. The 'venture' in which some of us have been engaged since the beginning of the 1970s – trying to create, in J.D. Stewart's language, 'the responsive authority'[1] – has been difficult not least because we have lacked a clear and common language in which to conduct it.

'Generating understanding and commitment'[2] in local government about urban conditions and regeneration is organisationally complex in three respects. First, a number of very different *groups* are involved. These include professionals – highly trained specialists each with their own language and boundaries, often reflecting academic specialisms. There are also generalists, not just administrators but a growing breed of civic entrepreneurs, and then there are politicians, business people, and finally, citizens, whether organised or not.

The individuals who make up these groups are, secondly, situated in different sorts of *agencies*. At least five types can be distinguished: national/local, elected/non-elected, statutory/voluntary, permanent/temporary, and profit-making/non-profit-making. Each of these agencies has its own cultures, procedures, constraints, loyalties and language. Each agency has its own role, although not necessarily the dominant one some imagine or would like to have.

Thirdly, of course, many different *tasks* are involved in urban development; these tasks are economic and social, and relate to housing and to the wider environment.

Given all this complexity, and its fragmentation of vocabularies, it is amazing that any progress is made.

The importance of the book's theme

Harry Smart's own venture is to offer a different explanation of decision processes from that which focuses on the conflicts of individuals or of groups with political, professional or class loyalties. He looks rather at the 'black box', the subtle interplay of exchanges between senior people in an organisation, the unspoken rules and assumptions which govern their behaviour. The tension he suggests between propositions, people and 'process' is not new – remember, for example, Warren's fascinating piece on 'Truth, Love and Social Change' as far back as 1967, and also Graham Allison's three perspectives on the Cuban Missile Crisis.[3]

The contrast, however, which he draws between the rhetoric of innovation and critical analysis on the one hand and the apparent reality of inertia, collusion and downright repression is one which has long awaited proper treatment in the literature of British public administration.

In this coda I shall try to do two basic things; I shall put the story in a wider and longer context, and I shall comment on the issue of 'learning organisations' which is so dear to my own heart.

WHAT WAS THE REGION TRYING TO DO?

Strathclyde Region's 1976 deprivation strategy has been and still is an almost unique venture in the UK in trying to use public services and structures to equalise life chances. What has been particularly unusual is the combination of managerial and political approaches, based on a recognition of the limits of political change. Look at one section of *Social Strategy for the Eighties*, the review we published in 1982:

> Behind this lay a fairly coherent critique of local authority management which it is important to spell out: it came very much from the experience of councillors and officials struggling in the early 1970s with rehabilitation schemes and has found expression – in a rather bland and diluted way – in such different national documents as the Seebohm and Paterson Reports, viz:
> - the boundaries between local authority departments are too strongly defended;
> - the professionals who inhabit them are too blinkered in their perceptions of problems; and too casework oriented;

- the departments are too hierarchical (and therefore oppressive of initiatives);
- it is the better off who make most use of our services and are quickest to articulate demands for more.[4]

In other words, the machine was suspect. It was indeed part of the problem – alienating, unequal in its resource allocations, repressive of initiatives, complacent, and so on. These features had to be changed if the access, opportunities, resources and self-image of those who lived in stigmatised council estates were to be improved. But the limits of internal change (given the features of the machine at our disposal) were obvious. Hence the reliance in our early years on a combination of management changes *and* encouragement of community initiatives and action – what I have subsequently called 'the pincer movement'.

At one stage in the interviews Harry asks why a more direct approach was not attempted. This assumes that politicians all share the same values, if not the same priorities. The harsh reality (if I am allowed to use that word!) is that Labour Councillors (even senior ones) are not homogeneous. More to the point, even if they did share the same aims and priorities, concerted action on their part through the local authority machine is very often counter-productive. That is a basic community development lesson we took very much to heart in the 1970s. Our business was creating the conditions of change.

The Jarndyce incident

The Jarndyce incident was caused, quite simply, by the suggestion that each school should draw up (on a democratic basis) a statement of its aims and of the programmes which fitted these aims. This statement was to be used as a framework of accountability. This obviously was the suggestion made in the earlier PRG Report. More to the point, it was part of a much wider local accountability process which was being suggested by Stan Hughes. Ironically that wider review process is, even as I write, being introduced as part of the reorganised Social Work planning process within the Region.

Much of the value of *Criticism and Public Rationality* depends on how typical the Jarndyce incident was of experiences in the development of deprivation policy. How often, in other words, did proposals run into the brick wall of vested interests? The answer is very often. Much of the early experience of the member/officer group was of reports running into the complacency and vested interests of the Departments. This accounts for the analysis we offered in *Social Strategy for the Eighties*.

The impact of Strathclyde's deprivation policy

The public agencies in Strathclyde have achieved much in the last fifteen years; the transformation in the heart of Glasgow – and in its morale – is one of the clear successes of European urban regeneration. For that, Strathclyde Regional Council, the Scottish Development Agency, Glasgow District Council and the Labour Government of 1974–9 can take much credit.

But in a sense the environmental, commercial and housing improvements have been the easy bit. For those of us who were in on the battles of the mid-1970s there is still much to be done, particularly for the marginalised groups.

Sure, we have established Strathclyde Community Business Ltd, which has helped more than fifty local collectives into existence in areas of high and long-term unemployment.[5] Sure, we have moved to integrate Pre-Five services in an effort to deal with the scandalous neglect of children from working class families at that critical stage in their life development.[6] And a range of ambitious economic and social initiatives have been established now in most of our worst housing schemes.[7]

Yet initiatives are still made to jump through hoops; groups go on re-inventing the wheel. Change occurs not because of local government processes and cultures but despite them, and owes much to obstinate, idealistic individuals who refuse to take no for an answer. The crucial questions are, why should this be so, and can it be changed?

In *Social Strategy for the Eighties* we attempted to supply some answers, and to start a debate. It is relevant to quote from the document at length, and the passages below begin with a quotation from Robin Hambleton which Harry might well have used himself:

> Approaches like the American Model Cities Programme and the current British Inner City Initiative, by attempting to build positive discrimination in favour of specific areas into existing services, by insisting on a more co-ordinated approach to the problems of these areas and by attempting to open up the processes of decision making, challenge fundamental organisational principles of urban government – uniformity of service provision, functional service management, and formal political and departmental hierarchies of control.
>
> In these circumstances it is inevitable that new initiatives will be faced with formidable opposition from entrenched interests. Whilst some opposition may take the form of hostile resistance, a more subtle and probably widespread response is to absorb the threat – to defuse, dilute and redirect the energies originally directed towards change.[8]

And again –

> The existing inequities in service allocation did not happen by accident; they are mediated through the administrative machine by generally well-intentioned professionals and administrators practising apparently fair and neutral principles. To tackle these inequalities therefore requires more than a general expression of intent handed over, in traditional style, for implementation. It demands the alteration of the structures and the working relationships within the Council and a rethinking of traditional assumptions.[9]

What we were asking our staff to do in 1976 was to accept that fairly simple things were needed from them in the first instance; not massive spending but just a commitment, firstly to those who lived in these areas, secondly to attempting new relationships both with their colleagues in other departments and with residents. We were also asking for imagination and courage; in encouraging staff to bring forward proposals for better practice despite the discouragement we knew they would encounter from the rules, traditions and prejudices which seemed deeply engrained in certain departments.

Even then, we had examples of good practice developing in some localities by dint of individual officers or politicians being prepared to try something different. In some places it had been police initiatives, in others adult education, and in yet others health initiatives. In many cases these were accompanied by rapid improvements in the indices of social malaise. The tragedy, however, is how isolated such simple initiatives were – and how many obstacles seemed to be placed in their way.[10]

Many people also think that the emphasis we have placed on community development and inter-departmental or inter-agency work in these areas is either a gimmick or something to do with procedures. It is neither. It is a fundamental point we were concerned to make about the contribution which can come from people not normally classified as experts, if only their skills are recognised and used.

The majority of staff are discouraged from joint work with councillors, other professionals and residents in these areas by the way the traditional departmental system of local government works. Career advance depends on one's work as a professional or manager in a particular department and not on the collaborative ventures emphasised in this document and the earlier one of 1976. That is the crucial issue that must now be faced and resolved. Exhortation and good intentions are no longer enough.[11]

Some six years later the same frustrations were obvious. In a major review of the Council's priorities and structures in the summer of 1988 the Labour Executive had occasion to say the following about the deprivation strategy:

And from this has come some very creative work; but it has had to fight all the way against departmental rigidities. It is, after all, there that the perceived administrative and political power is seen to rest.

The trappings of corporate power – the Policy Committees and Chief Executive's Department – have not, arguably, fundamentally affected the agendas of these departments. The power of these corporate structures is negative rather than positive although we should not underestimate the way the Chief Executive's Department has been able to encourage more entrepreneurial behaviour particularly amongst younger staff.

The question must be posed: how well served are we by our traditional departmental structure which reflects one particular set of professional perceptions, is organised hierarchically, controls the committee agenda, and makes joint work at a local level fairly difficult?

It was these considerations which led us, ten years ago, to embark on such things as the Member-Officer groups, the Area Initiatives, the Chief Executive's Department, and the Community Development Committees.[12]

CAN LOCAL GOVERNMENT EVER DELIVER?

The last few years have seen a renewed interest, in local government, in good management practice. The 'public service orientation' of the Swedes,[13] let alone the privatisation agenda of the Conservative government, has had a dramatic effect on thinking. The talk now is of the need for goals, and of the need for better performance review and accountability.[14] The question, however, is whether the cultures and values embodied in British local government can change fast enough.

We need to consider the following factors in particular. Firstly, there is the problem of the *segmentalist* culture (the phrase is from Kanter's fascinating book on innovation – and lack of it – in American private companies[15]) and the cultural and other constraints on excellence. It refers to phenomena more normally covered by terms such as 'departmentalism' or 'bureaucracy', which have become such powerful clichés as almost to sustain the inertia.

Secondly, we need to consider the political values embodied in British local democracy. We are so parochial that we fail to appreciate that we are, in European or Western terms, somewhat unusual in certain aspects of local politics. For example, the spread of local authority responsibilities is unusual, and arguably so wide as to reduce politicians to a managerial role. In many other countries local politicians operate as the catalysts of change locally in a *pluralistic* rather than a monopolistic institutional setting.

We are also unusual by virtue of our confused leadership. Because of the English mistrust of politics, the line between 'administrative' and 'political' is still drawn, and is embodied in our dual leadership roles – Leader and Chief Executive (for the local authority as a whole), Chairmen and Directors (in departments). This is a recipe for irresponsibility and confusion; little wonder that local government was once called 'The Unaccountable State',[16] or that people like Michael Heseltine are calling for the American or German pattern of leadership.[17]

We are also unusual, in British local government, in facing the attack which has come in the last decade from central government. This has not only distracted the time and energies of key people in local government, but has made them defensive and hesitant about giving hostages to fortune by themselves being critical of organisational performance.

The present state of local government can only be changed by a determined effort to bring the feudal empires that are local authority departments under proper control. Having clear targets, priorities and annual reports from the Directors on performance would be a useful start, and might well also make it easier for the sort of questions which *Criticism and Public Rationality* raises to be pursued.

At stake now, however, is not just whether local authorities can do more, but whether local government wants to survive. And survival will involve a redefinition of the *role* of local government and of its councillors and officials. British local government is moving to more of an enabling role, and that is no bad thing. The corollary is that the role of councillors should become less managerial and more concerned with the dynamics of change and influence. It also means that officers should be placed in more action-oriented than bureaucratic roles, probably in a local development agency or matrix rather than in large hierarchical structures. The debate this requires needs fresh concepts and perspectives which take as their starting point not current vested interests or the tired clichés of party ideologists, but the need to empower and develop the organisational capacity of the significant number of disadvantaged groups in a rapidly changing society.

Notes and references

The following abbreviations are used in the text and in the notes below:

AoN	*Areas of Need – The Next Step*
CDP	Community Development Project
CIUD	Census Indicators of Urban Dep.̄ivation
DoE	Department of the Environment
EPA	Educational Priority Areas
GEAR	Glasgow Eastern Area Renewal (Project)
IAS	Inner Area Studies
INLOGOV	The Institute for Local Government Studies
KHI	*Knowledge and Human Interests* (by J. Habermas)
LGSA	*The Local Government (Scotland) Act, 1973*
OSE	*The Open Society and its Enemies* (by K. Popper)
P&R	Policy and Resources (Committee)
PRG	Policy Review Group
SRC	Strathclyde Regional Council
UDOG	The Urban Deprivation Officer Group
UDU	The Urban Deprivation Unit
WCSP	The West Central Scotland Plan

Introduction: rationality and power

1 The interview was recorded with Councillor Young in September 1979.
2 Simmie, J. *Power, Property and Corporatism: The Political Sociology of Planning*, London, Macmillan, 1981.
3 Davies, J.G. *The Evangelistic Bureaucrat: A Study of a Planning Exercise in Newcastle upon Tyne*, London, Tavistock, 1972, p. 227.
4 A useful review of early managerialism in a relevant context is provided by Peter Saunders in *Social Theory and the Urban Question*, London, Hutchinson, 1981. The key work is in Ray Pahl's *Whose City?* (London, Penguin, 1975) where the idea is floated of managers as relatively independent variables (independent, that is, of broader socio-structural

constraints) – as Saunders identifies it, a broadly Weberian view of politics (see Saunders, *Social Theory*, pp. 122–5). In this approach, and in Pahl's subsequent work where the role of the state becomes more prominently problematic, there is a clear underlying assumption that power is the primary category.

5 The literature on professionalism is remarkably diverse and fragmented, but the wide reach of the fragments says something on its own about the penetration of the idea of professionalism into intellectual culture. See, for example, Alexander Murray's *Reason and Society in the Middle Ages* (Oxford, University Press, 1978) or the less radical *Profession, Vocation and Culture in Later Medieval England* (edited by C.H. Clough, Liverpool, University Press, 1982) for a relatively broad historical perspective. Paul Halmos (ed.) has a useful introductory essay to *Professionalisation and Social Change*, Sociological Review Monograph, 1973, but unfortunately he rather caricatures the Frankfurt School (much less of their work was available in English, of course, when he wrote). See also Jackson (ed.) *Professions and Professionalisation* (Cambridge, University Press, 1970) for a sociological perspective; see also material examining either the technical or the ethical dimensions of professionalism in respect of, for example, Education or Social Work (e.g. Bligh [ed.] *Professionalism and Flexibility in Learning*, Society for Research into Higher Education, 1982, or, Lubove *The Professional Altruist: The Emergence of Social Work as a Career 1880–1930*, Cambridge Mass., Harvard University Press, 1965). Perhaps the foundational work here ought to be Durkheim's easily overlooked *Professional Ethics and Civic Morals* (London, Routledge, 1957). Already, though, the range of the literature points to the need for the broad cultural context to be set in a wide-ranging political and historical review.

6 DoE, *Census Indicators of Urban Deprivation*. As far as Strathclyde is concerned, the relevant reports are Working Notes No. 6, 'Great Britain', and No. 10, 'The Conurbations of Great Britain'. Number 6 (February 1975) says, for instance: 'This pattern is repeated for every combination of indication tested, reinforcing the conclusion that when deprivation is measured at small area level, Scotland and Clydeside have more of it than anywhere else; it is more severe there, and there is more of it in the same places' (p. 12). Similarly, in Note 10 (June 1975): 'Overall, Clydeside, Tyneside and Merseyside emerge as the conurbations with the highest levels of deprivation' (p. 5) and '[Clydeside] emerges as being considerably worse than the other conurbations' (p. 13).

1 A rational response to deprivation

1 DoE White Paper *Policy for the Inner Cities*, 1977, paras 59–61.

2 Parliamentary Debates, 19 July 1977.

3 INLOGOV *Tackling Urban Deprivation: the Contribution of Area-based Management*, December 1977, p. 92.

4 Idem, p. 92.

5 INLOGOV/Home Office UDU *Local Government: Approaches to Urban Deprivation*, UDU Occasional Paper No. 1, October 1976, p. 38. The report published in 1976 was 'in essence' the report submitted to the Home Office in 1974, based on research carried out between December 1973 and April 1974.

6 Idem, pp. 38–9.
7 Hambleton, R. *Policy Planning and Local Government*, London, Hutchinson, 1978, p. 67.
8 Idem, p. 68.
9 Idem, p. 68. Hambleton quotes Schon, D.A. *Beyond the Stable State*, London, Temple Smith, 1971, p. 30.
10 Edwards, J. 'Social indicators, urban deprivation and positive discrimination', *Journal of Social Policy*, 1975, vol. 4, p. 280.
11 Higgins, J. *The Poverty Business*, Oxford, Blackwell, 1978, p. 135; quoting Edwards, J. 'Social indicators'.
12 Idem, p. 135.
13 Idem, p. 138; quoting Mays, J. 'The Research Smokescreen', *Guardian*, 1 January 1969.
14 Dearlove, J. *The Reorganisation of British Local Government: Old Orthodoxies and a Political Perspective*, Cambridge, University Press, 1979, p. 258.
15 Idem, p. 259.
16 Idem, pp. 11–12.
17 The Programming, Planning, Budgeting System was the project planning system introduced by the Defence Department in the United States in order to improve central control. PPBS became a primary source of ideas and models for the corporate planning movement in general, in both business and government, in the United States and in Britain. Robin Hambleton gives a broad review of the origins of corporate planning in PPBS; see *Policy Planning and Local Government.*, London, Hutchinson, 1978.
18 Habermas, J. *Legitimation Crisis*, London, Heinemann, 1976.
19 See particularly DoE *Census Indicators of Urban Deprivation* (CIUD), Working Note No. 6, 'Great Britain', February 1975, tables 2–8. See also note 6 to the Introduction of this book.
20 The phrase can be found, for example, in *Multiple Deprivation*, the report from UDOG of October 1976, Glasgow, SRC, p. 9. The report is also known, colloquially, as the 'Red Book'.
21 Young, R.G. 'Strathclyde Region's Deprivation Policy 1976/79', paper presented to the Labour Group of SRC, 1979, p. 1.
22 Idem, p. 5.
23 SRC/Glasgow District Council *Priesthill/Nitshill Initiative, First Annual Report*, 1979, p. 2, paras 1.13–1.14.
24 Idem, p. 13, para. 2.9.
25 Coventry CDP Team *CDP Final Report, Part 1: Coventry and Hillfields: Prosperity and the Persistence of Inequality*, 1975, p. 10.
26 CDP, Inter Project Reports *Gilding the Ghetto: The State and the Poverty Experiments*. The section setting out the conclusions of the report begins: 'The state's fight against urban deprivation has been exposed, like the "emperor's new clothes", as empty rhetoric.', 1977, p. 63.
27 Coventry CDP *Final Report*, p. 63.
28 Hamnett, C. *Multiple Deprivation and the Inner City*, Open University, 1976, pp. 22, 55.
29 Young, R.G. 'The All-Embracing Problem of Multiple Deprivation', *Social Work Today*, 1976, vol. 8. no. 9, p. 9.
30 Coventry CDP *Final Report*, p. 11.

31 See Adorno, T. *et al. The Positivist Dispute in German Sociology*, London, Heinemann, 1976. The book contains a series of papers; we refer in particular to contributions by Popper, Adorno and Habermas. All the contributors have published widely elsewhere, and we refer to several key works beyond those immediately addressed to the Positivist Dispute. Unfortunately it has not been possible to respond to the appearance in English of *Theory of Communicative Action* by Habermas, nor to the appearance in translation of work by Claus Offe.

32 See, for example, *Marx and Engels: Selected Works in One Volume*, London, Lawrence and Wishart, 1968, p. 30.

33 The phrase forms the title of a paper by Jürgen Habermas, in Adorno *et al. Positivist Dispute*, pp. 198–225.

34 Idem, p. 129.

35 Dahrendorf seems to attribute to Adorno the view traditionally attributed, with some carelessness, to Hegel, that the individual mind forms the objective material world, or that 'Reason' reified forms the objective world; it is hard to take 'reproduce reality itself in the cognitive process' (p. 125) otherwise (unless it is an infelicity of translation). It is not certain that even Hegel really asserted this, deeply embedded as the myth has become in the cognitive landscape. At best, Dahrendorf's phrase is misleading.

36 Idem, p. 129.

37 Idem, p. 125.

38 Idem, p. 125.

39 It may be useful to bear in mind a rather Gadamerian idea, 'the universality of the epistemological problem'. This is an adaptation of the title of an essay by Gadamer, 'The universality of the hermeneutical problem' – see Bleicher, J. *Contemporary Hermeneutics*, London, Routledge, 1980.

2   Strathclyde: management structures

1 Hambleton, R. *Policy Planning and Local Government*, London, Hutchinson, 1978, p. 45.

2 Idem, p. 57.

3 HMSO *The Local Government (Scotland) Act 1973*, section 123.

4 HMSO *The Social Work (Scotland) Act 1968*, section 2(1).

5 Idem, section 124 (1).

6 *LGSA* 1973, sections 56 (1); 62; 64 (1).

7 Scottish Local Authorities Association *The New Scottish Local Authorities: Organisation and Management Structures*, 1973. In keeping with established local government convention we refer to the report simply as 'Paterson', or the Paterson Report.

8 Paterson Report, pp. 14–15.

9 Idem, p. 16.

10 Idem, p. 27.

11 Idem, p. 27.

12 Strathclyde Regional Council, Council Minutes, 4 November 1975, p. 1007.

13 Paterson Report, Appendix 10.

14 Idem, Appendix 11.

15 Idem, pp. 23–4.

16 Idem, pp. 68–70.

17 Idem, pp. 23–5.
18 Idem, p. 70.
19 SRC *Report of the Policy Review Group on Departmental Structures*, p. 1. The main report (from which the quotation is taken) is undated. There is a supplementary paper dated September 1978. Both are purely internal documents.
20 *The Report of the Royal Commission on Local Government in Scotland*, Edinburgh, HMSO, 1969 (the Wheatley Report). The Wheatley Report corresponds to the Redcliffe-Maud Report for local government in England and Wales and is often referred to simply as 'Wheatley'.
21 Paterson Report, pp. 31–2.
22 Idem, p. 33.
23 Idem, p. 17.
24 Idem, p. 18.
25 Idem, p. 20. The Strathclyde Joint Advisory Committee was an *ad hoc* body with representatives from the pre-reorganisation authorities. Its purpose was to coordinate the transfer of service operations from the old to the new authorities, and to establish unified management of services which had previously been managed by several different authorities but which were to be taken over by the Regional Council. Effectively this is the body which produced the interim management structures for the Regional Council.
26 Paterson Report, p. 20.
27 Idem, p. 21.
28 Idem, p. 22.
29 Wheatley Report, p. 230.
30 Dearlove, J. *The Reorganisation of British Local Government: Old Orthodoxies and a Political Perspective*, Cambridge, University Press, 1979, pp. 114–16.
31 SRC *PRG Report on Structures*, p. 1.
32 Idem, p. 6.
33 Idem, p. 6.
34 Idem, p. 7.
35 Idem, p. 7.
36 Idem, p. 8.
37 Idem, p. 9.
38 Idem, p. 9.
39 All from idem, p. 10.
40 Idem, pp. 16–17.

3 Strathclyde: deprivation policy development

1 Central Advisory Council for Education (England) *Children and their Primary Schools*, generally known as the Plowden Report, 1967.
2 Home Office, Ministry of Health, Department of Education and Science, *Urban Programme Circular*, 4 October 1968, p. 1.
3 Home Office *Community Development Project: Objectives and Strategy*, 1970, para. 3. This is a duplicated pamphlet which runs to 8 sides of A4 paper; 1970 is the date of a revised edition.
4 Idem, para. 4.
5 Idem, para. 5.

6 Idem, para. 6.
7 Idem, para. 9.
8 Idem, para. 12.
9 Idem, Annex A.
10 CDP *Inter-Project Report*, 1974, p. 23.
11 Idem, pp. 52–3.
12 DoE *Change or Decay: Final Report of the Liverpool Inner Area Study*, 1977, p. 1.
13 Idem, pp. 203–4.
14 Scottish Development Agency *The Future for GEAR: Key Issues and Possible Courses of Action*, 1978, p. 2. Hugh Brown was a Minister of State for Scotland, and Chairman of the GEAR Governing Committee. His comments are in the foreword to what is basically a public relations promotional booklet. As a consequence of inter-agency disagreements, this was for some years virtually the only policy document on GEAR that anyone could wring from the SDA (the coordinating agency).
15 Lawless, P. *Urban Deprivation and Government Initiative*, London, Faber, 1979, pp. 128–30; Lawless quotes Weightman, G. 'The CDP File', in *New Society*, vol. 35, no. 702, 16 March 1976, p. 608.
16 Higgins, J. *The Poverty Business*, Oxford, Blackwell, 1978, p. 98.
17 Joseph, K. Comments from a widely quoted speech to the Pre-School Playgroups Association on 29 June 1972. The quotation is taken from Hamnett, C. *Multiple Deprivation and the Inner City*, Milton Keynes, Open University, 1976, p. 20.
18 Rutter, M. and Madge, N. *Cycles of Disadvantage: A Review of Research*, London, Heinemann, 1976.
19 DoE 'CIUD Working Note No. 1, 1971 Census: Extraction of Indicators of Deprivation', June 1974, p. 1.
20 DoE 'CIUD Working Note No. 3, The North West Planning Region', 1974, p. 1.
21 DoE 'CIUD Working Note No. 6, Great Britain', 1975, p. 1.
22 Corporation of Glasgow *Areas of Need in Glasgow*, 1972. This document embodies research carried out by the Scottish Development Department (that part of the Scottish Office roughly equivalent to the DoE), using 1966 sample census data 'to identify those basic factors which are indicative of serious deficiencies in the social and environmental well-being of the city' (p. 1).
23 Wedge, P. and Prosser, H. *Born to Fail?*, National Children's Bureau, 1973; as the cover puts it, 'The National Children's Bureau reports on striking differences in the lives of British Children', – using a statistical survey of all the children born in Britain in the week 3–9 March 1958, and with generous use of black and white photographs of children living in poverty. Condemned by some as sensationalised and unhelpfully stigmatising. It included a brief section on the distribution of 'disadvantage': 'the most disturbing proportion was found in Scotland, where one in every 10 children was disadvantaged' (p. 17).
24 DoE *Census Indicators of Urban Deprivation*, Working Note Nos 6 and 10, 1975. See also note 6 to the Introduction (of this book) above and notes 19–21 of this chapter.
25 *West Central Scotland Plan* 'Supplementary Report 4: Social Issues', 1974.

The study began in 1971, and by 1974 was consciously aiming its material at the emerging local authorities.
26 Graham, S., Winter, R. and Young, R. 'An experiment in Social Policy Formulation in Greenock and Port Glasgow', Working Paper III, Local Government Research Unit, Paisley College of Technology, 1973, p. 3.
27 Taken from Ferguson, R. *Geoff: The Life of Geoffrey M. Shaw*, Gartocharn (Glasgow), Famedram, 1979, pp. 53–4.
28 SRC Minutes, 1975, p. 267.
29 Idem, p. 267.
30 Idem, p. 359.
31 SRC *The Context of the Regional Report*, 1975, p. 77.
32 Idem, p. 11.
33 Idem, pp. 11–12.
34 Idem, p. 13.
35 SRC Policy and Resources Committee, Minutes, 1975, p. 1068.
36 SRC *Strathclyde Regional Report 76*, Supplementary volume on 'Urban Deprivation', 1976, p. 57.
37 Idem, p. 69.
38 Idem, p. 72.
39 Idem, p. 75.
40 Idem, p. 74.
41 Idem, p. 75.
42 SRC *Multiple Deprivation*, the report from UDOG, October 1976, p. 1. The report is often referred to as the 'Red Book', on account of the red manilla cover with which copies of the report were distributed. Confusingly, officers and members also referred, at around the same time, to the Red Book on staffing, which gave target staffing levels for service departments of the authority.
43 Idem, pp. 1–2.
44 Idem, p. 2.
45 Idem, p. 7.
46 Idem, pp. 7–8.
47 Idem, p. 8.
48 Idem, p. 9.
49 Idem, p. 16.
50 Idem, p. 15.
51 Idem, pp. 17–18.
52 Idem, p. 18.
53 Idem, p. 18.
54 Idem, p. 20.
55 SRC *Areas of Need – The Next Step (AoN)*, April 1977, p. 5.
56 Idem, p. 6.
57 Idem, p. 6.
58 Idem, p. 7.
59 Idem, p. 8.
60 Idem, p. 8.
61 Idem, p. 9.

4 Traditions of rationality

1 References are to Cornford, F.M. (trans., ed.) *The Republic of Plato*, Oxford,

University Press, 1945. The account of the Cave is on pages 227–35.

2 Idem, pp. 221–6.

3 Idem, p. 229.

4 Idem, pp. 230–1.

5 Taken from Connerton, P. (ed.) *Critical Sociology*, Harmondsworth, Penguin, 1976, p. 220. The comment as quoted reverses the order of the two sentences.

6 References are to the Everyman edition of the *Metaphysics*, 1971. This passage, p. 115.

7 Idem, p. 119.

8 Aquinas, *Commentary on Aristotle's Physics*, Oxford, Blackwell, 1963, p. 592. 'The Philosopher' in Aquinas is Aristotle.

9 Aristotle, *Metaphysics*, p. 51. The comment introduces a discussion of 'wisdom as the knowledge of causes'. Nevertheless the introduction goes on to affirm that 'Wisdom, again, is not to be identified with sense perception which, though it is our primary source of knowledge of particulars, can never tell us why anything is so (e.g. why fire is hot)', p. 52.

10 Idem, p. 123.

11 Idem, pp. 123–4.

12 Idem, p. 132.

13 Idem, p. 141.

14 The paper is collected in Popper, K.R. *Conjectures and Refutations*, London, Routledge,1972, pp. 312–35.

15 Lukasiewicz, 'Aristotle on the Law of Contradiction', p. 57. The paper is in Barnes, Schofield and Sorabji (eds) *Articles on Aristotle, vol. 3: Metaphysics*, 1979. The paper was first published in German in 1919, first in English translation in 1970.

16 It is also important to point out that the logical demonstration which Popper attempts (of the impossibility of denying the principle of non-contradiction without destroying rational discourse) must involve a circular argument, and this circularity is clear in Popper's article.

17 Aristotle, *Metaphysics*, p. 137.

18 This is apparent in the Philosophical Lexicon which opens the *Metaphysics*, particularly in the chapter on 'mutilated', where Aristotle asserts that 'a whole is not mutilated by the loss of any part taken at random: the parts removed must be (a) such as are not proper to its essence, or (b) extremities or projections. A cup, for instance, is not mutilated if a hole is made in it, but only if the handle or some projecting part is removed. Nor can a man be said to be mutilated if he loses flesh or his spleen, but only if he loses an extremity; and not *any* extremity, but only such as, when removed, cannot grow again.' Idem, p. 42. Apart from raising the question of the essential, this really does approach absurdity.

19 1 Kings 4: 29–34. The quotation is given in the New International version, New York, International Bible Society, 1978.

20 Lewy, H., Altmann, A. and Heinemann, I. (eds) *Three Jewish Philosophers*, New York, Athenaeum, 1969. The quotation is from the section on Philo, edited by Hans Lewy, p. 27.

21 Idem, pp. 29–30.

22 Hume, D. *Enquiries concerning Human Understanding and concerning the Principles of Morals*, Oxford, Clarendon Press, 1974, pp. 5–6. This is the

Selby-Bigge edition, as revised and annotated by P.H. Nidditch, and is based on the posthumous edition of 1777.

23 Idem, p. 6.
24 Idem, p. 16. In his notes to the text Nidditch identifes the 'superstition', as standing for Christianity (p. 357).
25 Idem, p. 165. 'When we run over libraries, persuaded of these principles, what havoc must we make? If we take in our hand any volume; of divinity or school metaphysics, for instance; let us ask, *Does it contain any abstract reasoning concerning quantity or number?* No. *Does it contain any experimental reasoning concerning matter of fact and existence?* No. Commit it then to the flames: for it can contain nothing but sophistry and illusion.'
26 Ayer, A.J. *Language, Truth and Logic*, first published 1936, using the Penguin edition of 1971, pp. 45, 46. It is worth noting Ayer's warm approbation of Hume's philosophy in general, and his view that the 'Commit it to the flames' passage sums up Hume's 'general outlook'. See, for example, Ayer, A.J. *Hume* (Oxford Past Masters), Oxford, University Press, 1980.
27 Kant, I. (trans. Kemp Smith, N.) *Critique of Pure Reason*, London, Macmillan, 1933, p. 667. First published in 1781 as *Kritik der reinen Vernunft*.
28 Idem, p. 17.
29 Idem, p. 189.
30 Idem, p. 190.
31 Idem, p. 190.
32 Idem, p. 76.
33 Genesis 6: 11–13 (NIV).
34 Idem, 6: 5.
35 Idem, 9: 6.
36 Hegel, G.W.F. (trans. Nisbet, H.B.) *Lectures on the Philosophy of World History: Introduction; Reason in History*, Cambridge, University Press, 1975, p. 25. First published in German 1828–30.
37 Idem, p. 31.
38 Idem, p. 32.
39 Idem, p. 33.
40 Idem, p. 35.
41 Idem, p. 43.

5 The Positivist Dispute

1 Taken from Connerton, P. (ed.) *Critical Sociology*, Harmondsworth, Penguin, 1976, p. 222.
2 Idem, p. 222.
3 Idem, p. 224.
4 Idem, p. 220.
5 In Adorno, T. *et al. The Positivist Dispute in German Sociology*, London, Heinemann, 1976, p. 198.
6 Idem, p. 14.
7 Idem, p. 11.
8 Idem, p. 37.
9 Idem, p. 76.
10 Habermas, J. *Legitimation Crisis*, London, Heinemann, 1976, p. 139.
11 Plato, *Seventh Letter*; references are to Hamilton, W. (trans.) *Plato: Phaedrus*

and the Seventh and Eighth Letters, Harmondsworth, Penguin, 1973. This extract from p. 139.

12 Idem, p. 138.

13 Adorno, T. and Horkheimer, M. *Dialectic of Enlightenment*, London, Verso, 1979, pp. xii–xiii. First published as *Dialektik der Aufklärung*, New York, Social Studies Association Inc., 1944.

14 Habermas, *Legitimation Crisis*, p. 116. Habermas quotes Offe, C. *Klassenherrschaft und politisches System*, p. 88.

15 From Connerton, *Critical Sociology*, p. 218.

16 Habermas, J. *Knowledge and Human Interests*, London, Heinemann, 1978. First published in Germany in 1968. This extract from p. 301.

17 Idem, p. 314.

18 Idem, p. 314.

19 Idem, pp. 314–15.

20 Idem, p. 317.

21 Idem, p. 354.

22 Idem, p. 355.

23 Popper, K.R. *Objective Knowledge*, Cambridge, University Press, 1979, p. 93.

24 Idem, p. 24.

25 Idem, p. 147.

26 Idem, p. 148.

27 Popper, K.R. *Conjectures and Refutations*, London, Routledge, 1972, pp. 193–200.

28 Idem, p. 199.

29 In Adorno, T. *et al. Positivist Dispute*, p. 292.

30 Habermas, *Knowledge and Human Interests*, pp. 314–15.

31 Popper, K.R. *The Open Society and Its Enemies*, London, Routledge, 1966, vol. 1, pp. 129–32. First published in 1945.

32 Popper, *Objective Knowledge*, p. 259.

33 Hegel, G.W.F. (trans. Miller, A.V.) *The Phenomenology of Spirit*, Oxford, University Press, 1977, p. 58. First published in 1807 as *Phänomenologie des Geistes*.

34 In Adorno, T. *et al. Positivist Dispute*, p. 58.

6   Strathclyde policy documents: texts and exposition

1 We are not claiming that the specific report, *Gilding the Ghetto*, was itself a direct influence on the policy documents; that would have been virtually impossible, since the Red Book was written in 1976, and the *AoN* report in early 1977. *Gilding the Ghetto* appeared only in 1977. The point is that *Gilding the Ghetto* appeared when the individual Community Development Projects had run their course; it is itself a history of the project and an apologia for the positions adopted by the project teams in the face of opposition from the Home Office and the local authorities in whose areas the projects were sited. By the time *Gilding the Ghetto* appeared, a large selection of individual project reports were available, as were a number of inter-project reports. Many of these reports were extremely widely known. Among individual project reports was the Coventry Final Report (March 1975) which Councillor Young quotes in his article of 1976. Among important inter-project reports was, for example, John Benington's *Local Government*

Becomes Big Business, first published in Spring of 1973, and issued in a second edition in February 1976. Many of these reports were initially circulated among contacts and colleagues in a cheaply duplicated format, only later being more formally 'published'. The process of more formal publication was progressive (although the 1976 edition of *Local Government Becomes Big Business* already shows signs of professionally designed and centralised publication) and continued for some time after *Gilding the Ghetto*.

2 Community Development Project, Inter-Project Reports *Gilding the Ghetto: The State and the Poverty Experiments*, 1977, p. 42.

3 Idem, pp. 52–3.

4 Idem, pp. 63–4.

5 From Connerton, P. (ed.) *Critical Sociology*, Harmondsworth, Penguin, 1976, pp. 218–19.

6 Habermas, J. *Legitimation Crisis*, London, Heinemann, 1976, pp. 118–19.

7 Habermas, J. *Knowledge and Human Interests*, London, Heinemann, 1978. First published in Germany in 1968. The passage referred to, on p. 355, is discussed in chapter five (above).

8 Home Office *Community Development Project: Objectives and Strategy*, 1970, para. 3. This is a duplicated pamphlet which runs to 8 sides of A4 paper; 1970 is the date of a revised edition. The text is also discussed in chapter three (above).

9 Idem, p. 2.

10 CDP *Gilding the Ghetto*, pp. 52–3, 63–4.

11 Idem, pp. 5, 3.

12 SRC *Multiple Deprivation*, 1976. See note 42 to chapter three (above).

13 SRC *Areas of Need – The Next Step (AoN)*, April 1977.

14 SRC *Multiple Deprivation*, p. 1.

15 Idem, p. 5.

16 Idem, pp. 6–7.

17 Idem, pp. 7–8.

18 Idem, p. 8.

19 Idem, p. 6.

20 Idem, pp. 9–10.

21 Idem, p. 10.

22 Idem, pp. 14–15.

23 Idem, p. 16.

24 Idem, p. 16.

25 Idem, pp. 18–19.

26 Idem, p. 20.

27 SRC *AoN*, p. 5.

28 Idem, pp. 6–7.

29 Idem, pp. 8–9.

30 Adorno, T. *et al. The Positivist Dispute in German Sociology*, London, Heinemann, 1976, p. 58.

31 SRC *AoN*, pp. 6–7.

32 Popper, K.R. *The Open Society and Its Enemies*, London, Routledge, 1966, vol. 2, pp. 9–21. First published in 1945.

33 SRC *Multiple Deprivation*, p. 16.

34 SRC *AoN*, pp. 8–9.

35 SRC 'Memo to UDOG', 1976. The document, covering two sides of A4

paper, is a simple internal memo, with the two names at the bottom.
36 SRC 'Planning Director's Letter', pp. 1–2. The document is purely internal,
   a letter from the Director of Policy Planning to the Director of Physical
   Planning, dated 25 March 1976. As with the Memo to UDOG noted above,
   it covers two sides of A4. This extract begins on page 1.
37 Idem, p. 2.

7   Interview texts and exposition

1 See *Bleak House*, by Charles Dickens. A 'narrative' is, of course, a deeply
prejudicial thing, and Jarndyce would require a book of comparable length
to *Bleak House* if we were to pursue all the circumstances and motivations
which surrounded 'the incident' (itself a prejudicial reification, as several
officers pointed out). It is worth reflecting on two texts refreshingly unrelated
either to the positivist dispute or to local government. The first is Lawrence
Durrell's 'Alexandria Quartet', the second is *Exercises in Style* by Raymond
Queneau. References are as follows: Durrell, L. 'The Alexandria Quartet',
London, Faber, 1968, the four novels (with original publication dates) being
Justine (1957), *Balthazar* (1958), *Mountolive* (1958) and *Clea* (1960);
Queneau, R. *Exercises in Style*, London, John Calder, 1979, first published in
Britain in 1958, originally published in France in 1947. I am indebted to Iain
Stuart, then Depute Director of Policy Planning in Strathclyde, who
suggested the relevance of the 'Alexandria Quartet', in which Durrell
presents four separate novels, each having a different view of the same set of
characters and events. In the character of Balthazar, Durrell explains a way
to understand events by looking at the accounts of a large range of people.
An understanding of the events grows by comparing these 'selected fictions',
each unique, as they combine to form one complex story. Clearly the story
can never be regarded as final, as Durrell himself states in his introduction:
'if the axis of the work has been properly laid down it should be possible to
radiate from it in any direction without losing the strictness and congruity of
its relation to a continuum' (p. 305 of the one-volume edition – *Balthazar*).
It is not an original idea, but Durrell works it well and he is, of course, writing
fiction. In Queneau's book a simple set of events is described 99 times, each
description different in style to the others. It is arguably possible to construct
a single image of the event by reading the different descriptions, but
Queneau's point seems to be that it is impossible to provide any single 'true',
account. One either produces account number 100, yet another unique
version, or one replicates and thereby to some degree authorises one of the
99 accounts, but one is then unable to provide any grounds for authorising
that account rather than one of the other 98.
    The one question we have to avoid, it seems, is 'just what did *really*
happen?', as if any account could be regarded as final. This comes
dangerously close to conceding that conflicting accounts are equally valid in
their treatment of single facts, however, and we would not want to concede
that; character 'X' either did or did not wear a hat as he entered the bus, for
example. The danger in the question 'just what did really happen?' lies in the
ambiguity of 'really' – which we have discussed in the text of chapter five when
considering the ways in which ordinary speech can be philosophically loaded.

2 Lawrence Boyle, formerly City Chamberlain of Glasgow and a member of the Advisory Group which drew up the Paterson Report. He became the first Chief Executive of Strathclyde Regional Council.
3 The Glasgow *Evening Times* is the main evening newspaper in the West of Scotland.
4 Passenger Transport Executive; a statutory body with responsibility for public transport planning within Strathclyde.
5 This section of the chapter depends heavily on cross-references to the interview transcripts. References to other sources are given below in the usual way, otherwise we have not cluttered the text with reference numbers; it is generally clear from the context which of the interviewees is being quoted.
6 Horkheimer, M. 'Traditional and Critical Theory', in Connerton, P. (ed.) *Critical Sociology*, Harmondsworth, Penguin, 1976, p. 220.
7 Popper, K.R. *Objective Knowledge*, Cambridge, University Press, 1979, pp. 32–105.

8 Conclusions: the breakdown of criticism

1 See chapter one, 'A rational response to deprivation', p. 12
2 See chapter five, 'The Positivist Dispute', p. 113
3 See chapter six, 'Strathclyde policy document', pp. 130, 136–7
4 See Alan Robinson's interview in chapter seven, p. 153
5 See chapter one, 'A rational response to deprivation', p. 26.
6 Kuhn, T.S. *The Structure of Scientific Revolutions*, Chicago, University Press, 1970.
7 Habermas, J. *Legitimation Crisis*, London, Heinemann, 1976, p. 116. See also note 14 to chapter five (above).
8 'Hughes, S.' for SRC, 1979. It is not possible to give the title of the paper, a copy of which was provided by Mr Hughes as a personal favour.
9 Simmie, J. *Power, Property and Corporatism: The Political Sociology of Planning*, London, Macmillan, 1981.
10 SRC *Social Strategy for the Eighties*, 1982. The extract from T.S. Eliot's *Four Quartets* is from 'East Coker', ll. 178–89, London, Faber, 1959, pp. 30, 31.

Coda by R.G. Young

1 See his book of that title, published by Charles Knight, 1972. Stewart is still trying – see for example his *New Management and Local Government*, London, Allen & Unwin, 1986.
2 The phrase is taken from INLOGOV's important 1974 review of the preconditions for successful local and deprivation strategies. The report was presented to the Home Office in 1974 and finally published by INLOGOV, as *Local Government: Approaches to Urban Deprivation*, in 1976.
3 Allison, G.T. *Essence of Decision: explaining the Cuban Missile Crisis*, Boston, Little & Brown, 1971.
4 SRC *Social Strategy for the Eighties*, 1982, para. 3.9.
5 See the Annual Reports, available from 6 Harmony Row, Glasgow. Also *The First Ten Years – A Decade of Community Enterprise in Scotland*, Glasgow, Community Business Scotland, 1987.

6 See the Regional Council's member/officer group report of 1985, *Services for the Under-Fives*.

7 Detailed in the Council's *Contribution to the Evolution of Effective Inner City Policies*, Summer 1987, and in *Generating Change*, 1988.

8 SRC *Social Strategy for the Eighties*, para. 5.8.

9 Idem, para. 1.7.

10 Idem, paras 3.5, 3.6.

11 Idem, paras 5.6, 5.7.

12 *Council Priorities and Structures*, report to the Executive Committee of the Labour Group, Strathclyde Regional Council, September 1988.

13 See articles by J. Stewart and M. Clarke in *Local Government Studies*, May/June 1986 and in *Public Administration*, Summer 1987.

14 See for example the New Local Government Training Board Series, *Understanding the Management of Local Government* and *Organising for Local Government*.

15 Kanter, R.M. *The Change Masters*, London, Allen & Unwin, 1983.

16 By D.W. Regan in his pamphlet of that title.

17 In an interview in *Marxism Today*, February 1988.

Index